ECONOMIC DEVELOPMENT

ECONOMIC DEVELOPMENT

S.D. Singh

CENTRUM PRESS
NEW DELHI-110002 (INDIA)

CENTRUM PRESS
H.O.: 4360/4, Ansari Road, Daryaganj,
New Delhi-110002 (India)
Tel: 23278000, 23261597, 23255577, 23286875
B.O.: No. 1015, Ist Main Road, BSK IIIrd Stage,
IIIrd Phase, IIIrd Block, Bangalore-560085 (INDIA)
Tel: 080-41723429
Email: centrumpress@gmail.com
Visit us at: www.centrumpress.com

Economic Development

First Edition, 2010

ISBN 978-93-80540-50-4

PRINTED IN INDIA

Printed at Balaji Offset, Delhi.

Contents

Preface vii

1. Introduction 1
2. Sustainable Economic Development 25
3. Transition Economy 79
4. Policy for Transition to Market Economy 123
5. Economic Transition in the Czech Republic 143
6. Economic Development and Loss of Biodiversity 171
7. Economic Growth in Asia 191

Bibliography 289

Index 293

Preface

Economic development is the increase in the standard of living of a nation's population with sustained growth from a simple, low-income economy to a modern, high-income economy. Its scope includes the process and policies by which a nation improves the economic, political, and social wellbeing of its people. Gonçalo L Fonseca at the New School for Social Research defines economic development as "the analysis of the economic development of nations.

The study of economic development by social scientists encompasses theories of the causes of industrial-economic modernization, plus organizational and related aspects of enterprise development in modern societies. It embraces sociological research on business organization and enterprise development from a historical and comparative perspective; specific processes of the evolution (growth, modernization) of markets and management-employee relations; and culturally related cross-national similarities and differences in patterns of industrial organization in contemporary Western societies. On the subject of the nature and causes of the considerable variations that exist in levels of industrial-economic growth and performance internationally, it seeks answers to such questions as: "Why are levels of direct foreign investment and labour productivity significantly higher in some countries than in others?

Mansell and Wehn state that development has been understood since the second World War to involve economic growth, increases in per capita income, and attainment of a standard of living equivalent to that of industrialized countries.

Economy Development can also be considered as a static theory that documents the state of economy at a certain time. According to Schumpeter (2003) the changes in this equilibrium state to document in economic theory can only be caused by intervening factors coming from the outside.

This extremely lucid and comprehensive book will be of interest to students of economics, political science, sociology, policy studies and social and economic development.

— *S.D. Singh*

1

Introduction

Economic Growth Versus Economic Development

Economic development refers to social and technological progress. It implies a change in the *way* goods and services are produced, not merely an increase in production achieved using the old methods of production on a wider scale. Economic growth implies only an increase in quantitative output; it may or may not involve development. Economic growth is often measured by rate of change of gross domestic product (eg., percent GDP increase per year.) Gross domestic product is the aggregate value-added by the economic activity within a country's borders.

Economic development typically involves improvements in a variety of indicators such as literacy rates, life expectancy, and poverty rates. GDP does not take into account important aspects such as leisure time, environmental quality, freedom, or social justice; alternative measures of economic wellbeing have been proposed. A country's economic development is related to its human development, which encompasses, among other things, health and education.

Intensive Versus Extensive Growth

A closely related idea is the difference between extensive and intensive economic growth. Extensive growth is growth achieved by using more resources (land, labour and capital). Intensive growth is growth achieved by using a given amount of resources more efficiently (productively). Intensive growth requires development.

Does Growth Create Development?

Dependency theorists argue that poor countries have sometimes experienced economic growth with little or no economic development; for instance, in cases where they have functioned mainly as resource-providers to wealthy industrialised countries. There is an opposing argument, however, that growth causes development because some of the increase in income gets spent on human development such as education and health.

According to Ranis (2000), we view economic growth to human development as a two-way relationship. Moreover, Ranis suggested that the first chain consist of economic growth benefiting human development with GNP. Namely, GNP increases human development by expenditure from families, government and organizations such as NGOs. With the increase in economic growth, families and individuals will likely increase expenditures with the increased in incomes, which leads to increase in human development. Further, with the increased in expenditures, health, education tend to increases in the country and later will contribute to economic growth.

In addition to increasing private incomes, economic growth also generate additional resources that can be used to improve social services (such as healthcare, safe drinking water etc...). By generating additional resources for social services, unequal income distribution will be limited as such social services are distributed equally across each community; benefiting each individual. Thus, increasing living standards for the public.

To summarize, as noted in Anand's article (1993), we can view the relationship between human development and economic development in three different explanations. First, increase in average income leading to improved in health and nutrition (known as Capability Expansion through Economic Growth). Second, it is believed that social outcomes can only be improved by reducing income poverty (known as Capability Expansion through Poverty Reduction). Thirdly, (known as Capability Expansion through Social Services), defines the improvement of social outcomes with essential services such as education, health care, and clean drinking water.

Models of Economic Development

The 3 building blocks of most growth models are: (1) the production function, (2) the saving function, and (3) the labour supply function (related to population growth). Together with a saving function, growth rate equals s/a (s is the saving rate, and a is the capital-output ratio). Assuming that the capital-output ratio is fixed by technology and does not change in the short run, growth rate is solely determined by the saving rate on the basis of whatever is saved will be invested.

Harrod–Domar Model

The Harrod–Domar model delineates a functional economic relationship in which the growth rate of gross domestic product (g) depends positively on the national saving ratio (s) and inversely on the national capital/output ratio (k) so that it is written as $g = s / k$. The equation takes its name from a synthesis of analysis of growth by the British economist Sir Roy F. Harrod and the Polish-American economist Evsey Domar. The Harrod–Domar model in the early postwar times was commonly used by developing countries in economic planning. With a target growth rate, and information on the capital output ratio, the required saving rate can be calculated. It was the best system.

Exogenous Growth Model

The exogenous growth model (or neoclassical growth model) of Robert Solow and others places emphasis on the role of technological change. Unlike the Harrod-Domar model, the saving rate will only determine the level of income but not the rate of growth. The sources-of-growth measurement obtained from this model highlights the relative importance of capital accumulation (as in the Harrod–Domar model) and technological change (as in the Neoclassical model) in economic growth. The original Solow (1957) study showed that technological change accounted for almost 90 percent of U.S. economic growth in the late 19th and early 20th centuries. Empirical studies on developing countries have shown different results.

Even so, in our post-industrial economy, economic development, including in emerging countries is now more and more based on innovation and knowledge. Creating business clusters is one of the strategies used. One well known example is Bangalore in India, where the software industry has been encouraged by government support including Software Technology Parks.

However, when looking at the growth rate put forward from the neoclassical growth model, it seems to suggest that countries with same characteristics and technology will eventually converge to the same rate of growth. However, one should know that the knowledge presented in countries that promotes technological advancement is not stationary. Meaning that knowledge are linked to individual and not to the country.

According to Lucas Jr (1988) to compensate the movement of knowledge, we should implement factors such as labour factor to predict immigration flow. With labour movement coming into factor, we can then predict the flow of knowledge which can then successfully lead to increase in technology.

Information-led Development

Information-led development (ILD) most commonly refers to a development strategy whereby a developing country makes as a primary economic policy focus the creation and development of a national information technology (IT) sector with the express aim of relying on this sector as an engine of growth. Notable examples of such countries are India and the Philippines.

More recently, a new formulation of ILD has emerged. With origins in community economic development in the United States, the new ILD model describes the use of data to generate actionable information or information solutions to development challenges. Examples of this include the inclusion of non-financial payment obligations in consumer credit files, also known as alternative data, and the use of this information in underwriting, as a means to reduce financial exclusion in the United States, where an estimated 54 million Americans are shut out of mainstream credit access as there is insufficient information about them in their credit files to be scored by a credit scoring model. This variant of ILD was pioneered by PERC, a non-profit policy research organization and development intermediary headquartered in Chapel Hill, North Carolina. Other US-based organizations, including Social Compact and the Local Initiatives Support Corporation, employ variants of ILD, but none has applied this internationally except for PERC.

This development model is gaining traction in emerging markets such as Colombia and South Africa, where the data is being used to reduce financial exclusion and facilitate credit access as a means to build wealth and form assets. It is also attracting increasing attention from development agencies, including USAID, the International Finance Corporation, the World Bank Group, and the Consultative Group to Assist the Poor.

Measuring Economic Development

GDP

North America, even though one of the slowest growing continents, has stable growth. Most of the faster growing economies are in the Caribbean. South America has a Boom and Bust growth with high followed by recession growth, most notable in Brazil, however growth has been stabilizing and the whole continent is growing.

Africa has seen the fastest growing but also the slowest growing/ declining. From the oil fields which made Angola the 3rd fastest growing country in the world, to Zimbabwe the slowest growing and declining country in the world. Oil in Africa has created 'wealth spots' were a few countries have exceeded their neighbours in wealth. Out of the 10 fastest growing countries in the world, 3 were African. Some countries have in the past been the fastest growing in the world. Equatorial Guinea reached 75% growth in 2004 because of oil reserves.

Europe has one of the most stable growth rates. After the fall of the Soviet Union, there was a period of economic decline in Eastern Europe over the 1990s, followed by recovery in the 2000s. The region is now experiencing growth, particularly in those countries that have recently joined the European Union. If the Caucasus were included, Europe would be one of the fastest growing continents in the world. Most countries are growing at a medium speed; however, many smaller countries exceed 7% and grow exceptionally faster than their neighbours. Out of the 10 fastest growing countries in the world, only 1 is in Europe.

Overall in the 20th century Asia was seen as the area with most growth; however, in the 21st century, most of this has been dominated by China. Some spots of growth are starting to appear in East and even South Asia. Most nations with high populations have seen high growth especially. Out of the 10 fastest growing countries 3 were directly in Asia, and 3 indirectly or partially.

Meanwhile Oceania has seen moderate growth. The only exceptional growth in Oceania has been on Vanuatu. Some countries have negative growth, most often due to ongoing wars or hyperinflation. These countries include Palestinean territories, Zimbabwe, Fiji and Chad.

Regional Policy

In its broadest sense, policies of economic development encompass three major areas:

- Governments undertaking to meet broad economic objectives such as price stability, high employment, and sustainable growth. Such efforts include monetary and fiscal policies, regulation of financial institutions, trade, and tax policies.
- Programs that provide infrastructure and services such as highways, parks, affordable housing, crime prevention, and K–12 education.
- Job creation and retention through specific efforts in business finance, marketing, neighbourhood development, small business development, business retention and expansion, technology transfer, and real estate development. This third category is a primary focus of economic development professionals.

Economic Developers

Economic development, which is thus essentially economics on a social level, has evolved into a professional industry of highly specialized practitioners. The practitioners have two key roles: one is to provide leadership in policy-making, and the other is to administer policy, programs, and projects. Economic development practitioners generally work in public offices on the state, regional, or municipal level, or in public-private partnerships organizations that may be partially funded by local, regional, state, or federal tax money. These economic development organizations (EDOs) function as individual entities and in some cases as departments of local governments. Their role is to seek out new economic opportunities and retain their existing business wealth.

There are numerous other organizations whose primary function is not economic development work in partnership with economic developers. They include the news media, foundations, utilities, schools, health care providers, faith-based organizations, and colleges, universities, and other education or research institutions.

With more than 20,000 professional economic developers employed world wide in this highly specialized industry, the International Economic Development Council [IEDC] headquartered in Washington, D.C. is a non-profit organization dedicated to helping economic developers do their job more effectively and raising the profile of the profession. With over 4,500 members across the US and internationally, serving exclusively the economic development community. Membership represents the entire range of the profession ranging from regional, state, local, rural, urban, and international economic development organizations, as well as chambers of commerce, technology development agencies, utility companies, educational institutions, consultants and redevelopment authorities. Many individual states also have associations comprising economic development professionals and they work closely with IEDC.

There is intense competition between communities, states, and nations for new economic development projects in today's globalized world, and the struggle to attract and retain business is further intensified by the use of many variations of economic incentives to the potential business such as; tax incentives, help with investment capital, donated land and many others. IEDC places significant attention on the various activities undertaken by economic development organizations to help them compete and sustain vibrant communities.

Additionally, the use of community profiling tools and database templates to measure community assets versus other communities is also an important aspect of economic development. Job creation, economic output, and increase in taxable basis are the most common measurement tools. When considering measurement, too much emphasis has been placed on economic developers for "not creating jobs." However, the reality is that economic developers do not typically create jobs, but facilitate the process for existing businesses and start-ups to do so. Therefore, the economic developer must make sure that there are sufficient economic development programs in place to assist the businesses achieve their goals. Those types of programs are usually policy-created and can be local, regional, statewide and national in nature.

Development Theory

Development theory is a conglomeration of theories about how desirable change in society is best to be achieved. Such theories draw on a variety of social scientific disciplines and approaches.

Historical Development Theories

Modernization Theory

Modernization Theory is a theory of development which states that the development can be achieved through following the processes of development that were used by the currently developed countries. Scholars such as Walt Rostow and A.F.K. Organski developed stages of development through which every country develops. Samuel Huntington determined development to be a linear process which every country must go through. Modernization Theory, in contrast to Classical Liberalism, viewed the state as a central actor in modernizing "backward" or "underdeveloped" societies. Talcott Parsons' functional sociology defined the qualities that distinguished "modern" and "traditional" societies. Education was viewed as key to creating modern individuals. Technology played a key role in this development theory because it was believed that as technology was developed and introduced to lesser developed countries it would spur economic growth. One key factor in Modernization Theory is the belief that development requires the assistance of developed countries to aid developing countries to learn from their development. In addition, it was believed that the lesser developed countries would develop and grow faster than developed countries. Thus, this theory is built upon the theory that it is possible for equal development to be reached between the developed and lesser developed countries.

Dependency Theory

While Modernization Theory understood development and underdevelopment as a result from internal conditions that differ between economies, dependency theory understood development and underdevelopment as relational. It saw the world's nations as divided into a *core* of wealthy nations which dominate a *periphery* of poor nations whose main function in the system is to provide cheap labour and raw materials to the core. It held that the benefits of this system accrue almost entirely to the rich nations, which become progressively richer and more developed, while the poor nations, which continually have their surplusses drained away to the core, do not advance. Developed in the 1950s, dependency theory shared many points with Rosa Luxembourg's and V.I. Lenin's earlier, Marxist, theories of imperialism; and dependency theory was embraced by many Marxists and neo-

Marxists. Dependency theorists held that for underdeveloped nations to develop, they must break their ties with developed nations and pursue internal growth. One type of policy crafted from this insight was Import substitution industrialization.

World Systems Theory

In response to some of the criticisms of Dependency Theory came World Systems Theory, which the division of periphery and centre was further divided into a trimodal system consisting of the core, semi-periphery and periphery. In this system, the semi-periphery lies between the core and periphery and is exploited by the core and exploits the periphery. This division aims to explain the industrialization within lesser developed countries. World Systems Theory was initiated by Immanuel Wallerstein in, among other writings, *World Systems Analysis*, and focuses on inequality as a separate entity from growth in development and examines change in the global capitalist system. One distinguishing feature of this theory is a distrust for the state and a view in which the state is seen as a group of elites and that industrialization cannot be equated with development. Out of this theory stem anti-systemic movements which attempt to reverse the terms of the system's inequality through social democratic and labour movements.

State Theory

In response to the distrust of the state in World Systems Theory, is state theory. State Theory is based upon the view that the economy is intertwined with politics and therefore the take-off period in development is unique to each country. State Theory emphasized the effects of class relations and the strength and autonomy of the state on historical outcomes. Thus, development involves interactions between the state and social relations because class relations and the nature of the state impact the ability of the state to function. Development is dependent upon state stability and influence externally as well as internally. State Theorists believe that a developmentalist state is required for development by taking control of the development process within one state.

Development Economics Theories

A number of theories are concerned with how economies develop over time. Some of these theories include:

- Comparative advantage: Predicts all countries gain if they specialise and trade the goods in which they have a comparative advantage. This is true even if one nation has an absolute advantage over another country.
- Rostovian take-off model: A linear theory of development that argues that economic modernization occurs in five basic stages of varying length-traditional society, preconditions for take-off, take-off, drive to maturity, and high mass consumption.
- Harrod–Domar model: Explains an economy's growth rate in terms of the level of saving and productivity of capital.
- Dual Sector model: Explains the growth of a developing economy in terms of a labour transition between two sectors, a traditional agricultural sector and a modern industrial sector.

Theories and Models linked to Development

This tutor 2u revision note introduces some of the main theories and models linked to the subject of economic development. Links are provided to further revision notes that explain each theory or model in greater detail.

What do Theories and Models try to do?

Economic development theories and models seek to explain and predict how:

- Economies develop (or not) over time.
- Barriers to growth can be identified and overcome.
- Government can induce (start), sustain and accelerate growth with appropriate development policies.

Theories are generalisations. While LDC's share similarities, every country's unique economic, social, cultural, and historical experience means the implications of a given theory vary widely from country to country.

There is no one agreed 'model of development'. Each theory, like Rostow, gives an insight into one or two dimensions of the complex process of development. Eg Rostow helps us to think about the stages of development LDC's might take and Harrod Domar model explains the importance of adequate savings in that process.

The Main Models:

Comparative advantage	Economic theory predicts all countries gain if they specialise and trade the goods in which they have a comparative advantage. This is true even if one nation has an absolute advantage over another country.
Rostow	This is a linear theory of development. Economies can be divided into primary secondary and tertiary sectors. The history of developed countries suggests a common pattern of structural change:
Harrod-Domar	The Harrod-Domar model developed in the 1930s suggests savings provide the funds which are borrowed for investment purposes.
Lewis	The Lewis model is structural change model that explains how labour transfers in a dual economy. For Lewis growth of the industrial sector drives economic growth.
Dependency Theory	Dependency refers to over reliance on another nation. Dependency theory uses political and economic theory to explain how the process of international trade and domestic development makes some LDC's ever more economically dependent on developed countries.
Balanced Growth Theory	Balanced growth (or the big push) theory. argues that as a large number of industries develop simultaneously, each generates a market for one another.
Unbalanced Growth Theory	Unbalanced growth theorists argue that. sufficient resources cannot be mobilised by government to promote widespread, coordinated investments in all industries.

Open Directory Project

ODP uses a hierarchical ontology scheme for organizing site listings.

Listings on a similar topic are grouped into categories, which can then include smaller categories.

Project Information

ODP was founded as Gnuhoo by Rich Skrenta and Bob Truel in 1998 while they were both working as engineers for Sun Microsystems. Chris Tolles, who worked at Sun Microsystems as the head of marketing for network security products, also signed on in 1998 as a co-founder of Gnuhoo along with co-founders Bryn Dole and Jeremy Wenokur. Skrenta was already well known for his role in developing TASS, an ancestor of tin, the popular threaded Usenet newsreader for Unix systems. Coincidentally, the original category structure of the Gnuhoo directory was based loosely on the structure of Usenet news groups then in existence.

The Gnuhoo directory went live on June 5, 1998. After a Slashdot article suggested that Gnuhoo had nothing in common with the spirit of free software, for which the GNU project was known, Richard Stallman and the Free Software Foundation objected to the use of Gnu. So Gnuhoo was changed to New Hoo. Yahoo! then objected to the use of "Hoo" in the name, prompting them to switch the name again. ZURL was the likely choice. However, before the switch to ZURL, New Hoo was acquired by Netscape Communications Corporation in October 1998 and became the Open Directory Project. Netscape released the ODP data under the Open Directory License. Netscape was acquired by AOL shortly thereafter, and ODP was one of the assets included in the acquisition. AOL later merged with Time-Warner.

By the time Netscape assumed stewardship, the Open Directory Project had about 100,000 URLs indexed with contributions from about 4500 editors. On October 5, 1999, the number of URLs indexed by ODP reached one million. According to an unofficial estimate, the URLs in the Open Directory numbered 1.6 million in April 2000, surpassing those in the Yahoo! Directory. ODP achieved the milestones of indexing two million URLs on August 14, 2000, three million listings on November 18, 2001 and four million on December 3, 2003.

From January 2006 the Open Directory published online reports to inform the public about the development of the project. The first report covered the year 2005. Monthly reports were issued subsequently until September 2006. These reports gave greater insight into the functioning of the directory than the simplified statistics given on the front page of the directory. The number of listings and categories cited on the front page include "Test" and "Bookmarks" categories, but these are not included in the RDF dump offered to users. The total number of editors who have contributed to the directory as of March 31, 2007 was 75,151. There were about 7330 active editors during August 2006.

System Failure and Editing Outage, October to December 2006

On October 20, 2006, the ODP's main server suffered a catastrophic system failure that prevented editors from working on the directory until December 18, 2006. During that period, an older build of the directory was visible to the public. On January 13, 2007, the Site Suggestion and Update Listings forms were again made available. On January 26, 2007, weekly publication of RDF dumps resumed. To avoid future outages, the system now resides on a redundant configuration of two Intel-based servers.

Competing and Spinoff Projects

As the ODP became more widely known, two other major web directories edited by volunteers and sponsored by Go.com and Zeal emerged, both now defunct. These directories did not license their content for open content distribution.

The concept of using a large-scale community of editors to compile online content has been successfully applied to other types of projects. ODP's editing model directly inspired three other open content volunteer projects: an open content restaurant directory known as ChefMoz, an open content music directory known as MusicMoz, and an encyclopedia known as Open Site.

Gnuhoo borrowed the basic outline for its initial ontology from Usenet. In 1998, Rich Skrenta said, "I took a long list of groups and hand-edited them into a hierarchy." For example, the topic covered by the comp.ai.alife news group was represented by the category Computers/AI/Artificial_Life. The original divisions were for *Adult*, *Arts*, *Business*, *Computers*, *Games*, *Health*, *Home*, *News*, *Recreation*, *Reference*, *Regional*, *Science*, *Shopping*, *Society*, and *Sports*. While these fifteen *top-level* categories have remained intact, the ontology of second-and lower-level categories has undergone a gradual evolution; significant changes are initiated by discussion among editors, and then implemented when consensus has been reached.

In July 1998, the directory became multilingual with the addition of the *World* top-level category. The remainder of the directory lists only English language sites. By May 2005, seventy-five languages were represented.

The growth rate of the non-English components of the directory has been greater than the English component since 2002. While the English component of the directory held almost 75% of the sites in 2003, the *World* level grew to over 1.5 million sites as of May 2005, forming roughly one-third of the directory. The ontology in non-English categories generally mirrors that of the English directory, although exceptions which reflect language differences are quite common.

Several of the top-level categories have unique characteristics. The *Adult* category is not present on the directory homepage, but it is fully available in the RDF dump that ODP provides. While the bulk of the directory is categorized primarily by topic, the Regional category is categorized primarily by region. This has led many to view ODP as two parallel directories: *Regional* and *Topical*.

On November 14, 2000, a special directory within the Open Directory was created for people under 18 years of age. Key factors distinguishing this "Kids and Teens" area from the main directory are:

- stricter guidelines which limit the listing of sites to those which are targeted or "appropriate" for people under 18 years of age;
- category names as well as site descriptions use vocabulary which is "age appropriate";
- *age tags* on each listing distinguish content appropriate for kids (age 12 and under), teens (13 to 15 years old) and mature teens (16 to 18 years old);
- Kids and Teens content is available as a separate RDF dump;
- editing permissions are such that the community is parallel to that of the Open Directory.

By May 2005, this portion of the Open Directory included over 32,000 site listings.

Since early 2004, the whole site has been in UTF-8 encoding. Prior to this, the encoding used to be ISO 8859-1 for English language categories, and a language-dependent character set for other languages. The RDF dumps have been encoded in UTF-8 since early 2000.

Maintenance

Directory listings are maintained by editors. While some editors focus on the addition of new listings, others focus on maintaining the existing listings. This includes tasks such as the editing of individual listings to correct spelling and/or grammatical errors, as well as monitoring the status of linked sites. Still others go through site submissions to remove spam and duplicate submissions.

Robozilla is a Web crawler written to check the status of all sites listed in ODP. Periodically, Robozilla will flag sites which appear to have moved or disappeared, and editors follow up to check the sites and take action. This process is critical for the directory in striving to achieve one of its founding goals: to reduce the link rot in web directories. Shortly after each run, the sites marked with errors are automatically moved to the unreviewed queue where editors may investigate them when time permits.

Due to the popularity of the Open Directory and its resulting impact on search engine rankings, domains with lapsed registration that are listed on ODP have attracted domain hijacking, an issue that has been addressed by regularly removing expired domains from the directory.

While corporate funding and staff for the ODP have diminished in recent years, volunteers have created editing tools, such as linkcheckers to supplement Robozilla, category crawlers, spellcheckers, search tools that directly sift a recent RDF dump, bookmarklets to help automate some editing functions, and tools to help work through unreviewed queues.

License and Requirements

ODP data is made available for open content distribution under the terms of the Open Directory License, which requires a specific ODP attribution table on every Web page that uses the data.

The Open Directory License also includes a requirement that users of the data continually check the ODP site for updates and discontinue use and distribution of the data or works derived from the data once an update occurs. This restriction prompted the Free Software Foundation to refer to the Open Directory License as a non-free documentation license, citing the right to redistribute a given version not being permanent, and the requirement to check for changes to the license.

RDF Dumps

ODP data is made available through an RDF-like dump that is published on a dedicated download server, where an archive of previous versions is also available. New versions are usually generated weekly. An ODP editor has catalogued a number of bugs that are/were encountered when implementing the ODP RDF dump, including UTF-8 encoding errors (fixed since August 2004) and an RDF format that does not comply with the final RDF specification because ODP RDF generation was implemented before the RDF specification was finalized. So while today the so-called RDF dump is valid XML, it is not strictly RDF, but an ODP-specific format. Software to process the ODP RDF dump needs to take account of this.

Content Users

ODP data powers the core directory services for many of the Web's largest search engines and portals, including Netscape Search, AOL Search, Google, and Alexa.

Other uses are also made of ODP data. For example, in the spring of 2004 Overture announced a search service for third parties combining Yahoo! Directory search results with ODP titles, descriptions and category metadata. The search engine Gigablast announced on May 12, 2005 its searchable copy of the Open Directory. The technology permits search of websites listed in specific categories, "in effect, instantly creating over 500,000 vertical search engines".

As of September 8, 2006, the ODP listed 313 English-language Web sites that use ODP data as well as 238 sites in other languages. However, these figures do not reflect the full picture of use, as those sites that use ODP data without following the terms of the ODP license are not listed.

Policies and Procedures

There are restrictions imposed on who can become an ODP editor. The primary gatekeeping mechanism is an editor application process wherein editor candidates demonstrate their editing abilities, disclose affiliations that might pose a conflict of interest, and otherwise give a sense of how the applicant would likely mesh with the ODP culture and mission. A majority of applications are rejected, but reapplying is allowed and sometimes encouraged. The same standards apply to editors of all categories and subcategories.

ODP's editing model is a hierarchical one. Upon becoming editors, individuals will generally have editing permissions in only a small category. Once they have demonstrated basic editing skills in compliance with the Editing Guidelines, they are welcome to apply for additional editing privileges, in either a broader category, or in a category elsewhere in the directory. Mentorship relationships between editors are encouraged, and internal forums provide a vehicle for new editors to ask questions.

ODP has its own internal forums, the contents of which are intended only for editors to communicate with each other primarily about editing topics. Access to the forums requires an editor account, and editors are expected to keep the contents of these forums private.

Over time, senior editors may be granted additional privileges which reflect their editing experience and leadership within the editing community. The most straightforward are *editall* privileges, which allow an editor to access all categories in the directory. *Meta* privileges additionally allow editors to perform tasks such as reviewing editor applications, setting category features, and handling external and internal abuse reports. *Cateditall* privileges are similar to *editall*, but only for a single directory category. Similarly, *catmod* privileges are similar to *meta*, but only for a single directory category. *Catmv* privileges allow editors to make changes to directory ontology by moving or renaming categories. All of these privileges are granted by admins and staff, usually after discussion with *meta* editors.

In August 2004, a new level of privileges called *admin* was introduced. Administrator status was granted to a number of long serving metas by staff. Administrators have the ability to grant editall+ privileges to other editors and to approve new directory-wide policies, authorities that had previously only been available to root (staff) editors. A full list of senior editors is available to the public, as is a listing of all current editors.

All ODP editors are expected to abide by ODP's Editing Guidelines. These guidelines describe editing basics: what types of sites may be listed and which may not; how site listings should be titled and described in a loosely consistent manner; conventions for the naming and building of categories; conflict of interest limitations on the editing of sites which the editor may own or otherwise be affiliated with; and a code of conduct within the community. Editors who are found to have violated these guidelines may be contacted by staff or senior editors, have their editing permissions cut back, or lose their editing privileges entirely. ODP Guidelines are periodically revised after discussion in editor forums.

Site Submissions

One of the original motivations for forming Gnuhoo/Newhoo/ODP was the frustration that many people experienced in getting their sites listed on Yahoo! Directory. However Yahoo! has since implemented a paid service for timely consideration of site submissions. That lead has been followed by many other directories. Some accept no free submission at all. By contrast the ODP has maintained its policy of free site submissions for all types of site — the only one of the major general directories to do so.

One result has been a gradual divergence between the ODP and other directories in the balance of content. The pay-for-inclusion model favours those able and willing to pay, so commercial sites tend to predominate in directories using it. Conversely, a directory manned by volunteers will reflect the aims and interests of those volunteers. The ODP lists a high proportion of informational and non-profit sites.

Another consequence of the free submission policy is that the ODP has enormous numbers of submissions still waiting for review. In large parts those consist of spam and incorrectly submitted sites. So the average processing time for a site submission has grown longer with each passing year. However the time taken cannot be predicted, since the variation is so great: a submission might be processed within hours or take several years. However, site suggestions are just one of many sources of new listings. Editors are under no obligation to check them for new listings, and are actually encouraged to use other sources.

Controversy and Criticism

There have long been allegations that volunteer ODP editors give favourable treatment to their own websites while concomitantly thwarting the good faith efforts of their competition. Such allegations are fielded by ODP's staff and meta editors, who have the authority to take disciplinary action against volunteer editors who are suspected of engaging in abusive editing practices.

In 2003, ODP introduced a new *Public Abuse Report System* that allows members of the general public to report and track allegations of abusive editor conduct using an online form. Uninhibited discussion of ODP's purported shortcomings has become more common on mainstream Webmaster discussion forums. Although site policies suggest that an individual site should be submitted to only one category, as of October 2007, Topix.com, a news aggregation site operated by ODP founder Rich Skrenta, has more than 10,000 listings.

Early in the history of the ODP, its staff gave representatives of selected companies, such as Rolling Stone magazine or CNN, editing access in order to list individual pages from their websites. Links to individual CNN articles have been added until 2004 and have been entirely removed from the directory in January 2008 due to being outdated and not considered worth the effort to maintain. Such experiments have not been repeated later.

Ownership and Management

Underlying some controversy surrounding ODP is its ownership and management. Some of the original GnuHoo volunteers felt that they had been deceived into joining a commercial enterprise. To varying degrees, those complaints have continued up until the present.

At ODP's inception, there was little thought given to the idea of how ODP should be managed, and there were no official forums, guidelines, or FAQs. In essence, ODP began as a free for all.

As time went on, the ODP Editor Forums became the *de facto* ODP parliament, and when one of ODP's staff members would post an opinion in the forums, it would be considered an official ruling.

Even so, ODP staff began to give trusted senior editors additional editing privileges, including the ability to approve new editor applications, which eventually led to a stratified hierarchy of duties and privileges among ODP editors, with ODP's paid staff having the final say regarding ODP's policies and procedures.

Editor Removal Procedures

ODP's editor removal procedures are overseen by ODP's staff and meta editors. According to ODP's official editorial guidelines, editors are removed for abusive editing practices or uncivil behaviour. Discussions that may result in disciplinary action against volunteer editors take place in a private forum which can only be accessed by ODP's staff and meta editors, and volunteer editors who are being discussed are not given notice that such proceedings are taking place. Some people find this arrangement distasteful, wanting instead a discussion modelled more like a trial held in the U.S. judicial system.

In the article *Editor Removal Explained*, ODP meta editor Arlarson states that "a great deal of confusion about the removal of editors from ODP results from false or misleading statements by former editors".

The ODP's confidentiality guidelines prohibit any current ODP editors in a position to know anything from discussing the reasons for specific editor removals. However, a generic list of reasons is for example given in the guidelines. In the past, this has led to removed ODP editors wondering why they cannot login at ODP to perform their editing work.

Allegations that Editors are Removed for Criticizing Policies

David F. Prenatt, Jr. (former ODP editor *netesq*) and the former editor known by the alias *The Cunctator* claim to have been removed for disagreeing with staff about changes to the policies, with special regard to the ODP's copyright policies. According to their claims, staff used the excuse that their behaviour was uncivil to remove bothersome editors.

Blacklisting Allegations

Senior ODP editors have the ability to attach "warning" or "do not list" notes to individual domains, but no editor has the unilateral ability to block certain sites from being listed. Sites with these notes might still be listed, and at times notes are removed after some discussion.

Hierarchical Structure

Recently criticism of ODP's hierarchical structure emerged. Many believe hierarchical directories are too complicated. As the recent emergence of Web 2.0, folksonomies began to appear. These people thought folksonomies, networks, and directed graph are more "natural" and easier to manage than hierarchies.

Software

Search: The ODPSearch software is a derivative version of Isearch which is open source, licensed under the Mozilla Public License.

Editor Forums

The ODP Editor Forums were originally run on software that was based on the proprietary Ultimate Bulletin Board system. In June 2003, they switched to the open source phpBB system. As of 2007, these forums are powered by a modified version of phpBB.

Bug Tracking

The bug tracking software used by the ODP is Bugzilla, and the web server Apache. Squid web proxy server was also used but it was removed in August 2007 when the storage servers were reorganized. All these applications are open source.

Interface

The ODP database/editing software is closed source, although Richard Skrenta of ODP did say in June 1998 that he was considering licensing it under the GNU General Public License. This has led to criticism from the aforementioned GNU project, many of whom also criticise the ODP content license. As such, there have been some efforts to provide alternatives to ODP. These alternatives would allow communities of like-minded editors to set up and maintain their own open source/open content Web directories. However, no significant open source/open content alternative to ODP has emerged.

Economic development is the development of economic wealth of countries or regions for the well-being of their inhabitants. This is the short definition of Economic Development.

Economic Growth & development are two different terms used in economics. Generally speaking economic development refers to the problems of underdeveloped countries and economic growth to those of developed countries.

By Economic Growth we simply mean increase in per capita income or increase in GNP. In recent literature, the term economic growth refers to sustained increase in a country's output of goods and services, or more precisely product per capita. Output is generally measured in terms of GNP. The term economic development is far more comprehensive. It implies progressive changes in the socio-economic structure of a country. Viewed in this way economic development Involves a steady decline in agricultural shares in GNP and continuous increase in shares of industries, trade banking construction and services. Further whereas economic growth merely refers to rise in output; development implies change in technological and institutional organization of production as well as in distributive pattern of income.

Hence, compared to the objective of development, economic growth is easy realize. By a larger mobilization of resources and raising their productivity, output level can be raised. The process of development is far more extensive. Apart from a rise in output, it involves changes in composition of output, shift in the allocation of productive resources, and elimination or reduction of poverty, inequalities and unemployment.

In the words of Amartya Sen "Development requires the removal of major sources of unfreedom poverty as well as tyranny, poor economic opportunities as well as systematic social deprivation neglect of public facilities as well as intolerance or over activity of repressive states...." Economic development is not possible without growth but growth is possible without development because growth is just increase in GNP It does not have any other parameters to it. Development can be conceived as Multi-Dimensional process or phenomena. If there is increase in GNP more than the increase in per capita Income then we can say that Development is possible. When given conditions of population improves then we can say that this is also an indicator of economic Development.

Economic Development of India

Post 1990 ' Economic Development of India ' can be attributed to globalization and liberalization of Indian Economy. Till the end of 1980s ' Economic Development of India ' suffered stagnation due to protectionism both internally and externally.

India was predominantly an agriculture based country and the British colonial government did not pursue any active agricultural and 'welfare of the rural population', policy. Most of the commissions which were set-up for ' Economic Development of India' were unsuccessful. The food crisis during World War II, made the Government realize the need for growing more food and to be self sufficient. Famine in Bengal in 1943 forced the government to release its first agriculture policy statement and which formed the basis of many of the policies adopted thereafter, especially in the First 5-Year Plan. The 5-year plans played a pivotal role in ' India Economic Development ' and they are summarized as follows:

- The first four 5-year plans involved a total public sector disbursement of Rs.314.1 billion. The first plan prioritized agriculture and power projects.
- The second plan focused on new industrial policy, rapid industrialization and envisaged 25% increase in national income.
- The third plan targeted rapid industrialization, with 24.6% outlay on transport and communications and 20.1% on industry and minerals.
- The fourth plan stressed on agriculture and allied sectors and received around 27%, while industry and minerals outlay was 18.5%, transport and communications stood at 18.4%, and power development at 17.8%.
- The fifth plan envisaged removal of poverty and the attainment of self-reliance. A total spent of Rs.393.2 billion was allocated, and actual expenditures amounted to Rs.394.2 billion.
- The sixth plan targeted developmental plans and the projected outlays amounted to Rs.975 billion.
- The seventh plan projected 5% overall GDP growth (which was surpassed) based on increases of 4% in agricultural and 8% industrial output. And spent amounted to Rs.1,800 billion.
- The eighth development plan laid the foundation for long-term economic gains. The eighth plan was a grand success and economic growth rose to 6% a year, generated more employment, poverty was curtailed, exports increased many folds, and inflation declined substantially.
- The ninth plan witnessed overall stupendous improvement in the GDP growth rate from an average of about 5.7% to about 6.1% and increased literacy from 52% in 1991 to 65% in 2001.

Further, the credit of ' Economic Development of India ' goes to the liberal and friendly central government, who has fundamentally altered its development paradigm and have initiated a quiet economic revolution.

Economic Development Research Group (EDR Group)-advancing the state-of-the-art in measuring economic development performance, impacts and opportunities. We provide research, consulting services and software relating to the economic and development implications of.

- Transportation and Infrastructure Investment-including roads, airports, marine ports, railroad facilities and public transportation;
- Energy Programs and Projects-including renewable energy facilities, distribution systems and energy efficiency programs;

Economic Development Programs and Strategies-including industry targeting, existing business retention and competition benchmarking. EDR Group has earned a reputation for unsurpassed technical expertise and leadership through three mechanisms:

Focus: We specialize in understanding effects of infrastructure and investment programs on economic development.

Innovation: Our state-of-the-art tools, methods and guidance documents are widely used throughout North America.

Insight: Our work directly supports policy, planning and investment decision-making.

2

Sustainable Economic Development

Sustainable Development

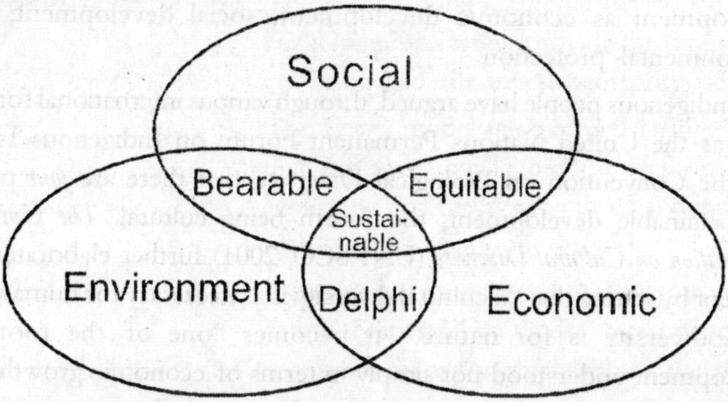

Sustainable development is a pattern of resource use that aims to meet human needs while preserving the environment so that these needs can be met not only in the present, but also for future generations. The term was used by the Brundtland Commission which coined what has become the most often-quoted definition of sustainable development as development that "meets the needs of the present without compromising the ability of future generations to meet their own needs."

Sustainable development ties together concern for the carrying capacity of natural systems with the social challenges facing humanity. As early as the 1970s "sustainability" was employed to describe an economy "in equilibrium with basic ecological support systems." Ecologists have pointed to The Limits to Growth, and presented the alternative of a "steady state economy" in order to address environmental concerns. The field of sustainable development can be conceptually broken into three constituent parts: environmental sustainability, economic sustainability and sociopolitical sustainability.

Scope and Definitions

The concept has included notions of weak sustainability, strong sustainability and deep ecology. Sustainable development does not focus solely on environmental issues. In 1987, the United Nations released the Brundtland Report, which defines sustainable development as 'development which meets the needs of the present without compromising the ability of future generations to meet their own needs. The United Nations 2005 World Summit Outcome Document refers to the "interdependent and mutually reinforcing pillars" of sustainable development as economic development, social development, and environmental protection.

Indigenous people have argued, through various international forums such as the United Nations Permanent Forum on Indigenous Issues and the Convention on Biological Diversity, that there are *four* pillars of sustainable development, the fourth being cultural. *The Universal Declaration on Cultural Diversity* (UNESCO, 2001) further elaborates the concept by stating that "...cultural diversity is as necessary for humankind as biodiversity is for nature"; it becomes "one of the roots of development understood not simply in terms of economic growth, but also as a means to achieve a more satisfactory intellectual, emotional, moral and spiritual existence". In this vision, cultural diversity is the fourth policy area of sustainable development.

Economic Sustainability: Agenda 21 clearly identified information, integration, and participation as key building blocks to help countries achieve development that recognises these interdependent pillars. It emphasises that in sustainable development everyone is a user and provider of information. It stresses the need to change from old sector-centred ways of doing business to new approaches that involve cross-sectoral coordination and the integration of environmental and social concerns into all development processes. Furthermore, Agenda 21 emphasises that broad public participation in decision making is a fundamental prerequisite for achieving sustainable development.

According to Hasna, sustainability is a process which tells of a development of all aspects of human life affecting sustenance. It means resolving the conflict between the various competing goals, and involves the simultaneous pursuit of economic prosperity, environmental quality and social equity famously known as three dimensions (triple bottom line) with is the resultant vector being technology, hence it is a continually evolving process; the 'journey' (the process of achieving sustainability) is of course vitally important, but only as a means of getting to the destination (the desired future state). However, the 'destination' of sustainability is not a fixed place in the normal sense that we understand destination. Instead, it is a set of wishful characteristics of a future system.

Green development is generally differentiated from sustainable development in that Green development prioritizes what its proponents consider to be environmental sustainability over economic and cultural considerations. Proponents of Sustainable Development argue that it provides a context in which to improve overall sustainability where cutting edge Green development is unattainable. For example, a cutting edge treatment plant with extremely high maintenance costs may not be sustainable in regions of the world with fewer financial resources. An environmentally ideal plant that is shut down due to bankruptcy is obviously less sustainable than one that is maintainable by the community, even if it is somewhat less effective from an environmental standpoint.

Some research activities start from this definition to argue that the environment is a combination of nature and culture. The Network of Excellence "Sustainable Development in a Diverse World", sponsored by the European Union, integrates multidisciplinary capacities and interprets cultural diversity as a key element of a new strategy for sustainable development.

Still other researchers view environmental and social challenges as opportunities for development action. This is particularly true in the concept of sustainable enterprise that frames these global needs as opportunities for private enterprise to provide innovative and entrepreneurial solutions. This view is now being taught at many business schools including the Centre for Sustainable Global Enterprise at Cornell University and the Erb Institute for Global Sustainable Enterprise at the University of Michigan.

The United Nations Division for Sustainable Development lists the following areas as coming within the scope of sustainable development:

> *Sustainable development is an eclectic concept, as a wide array of views fall under its umbrella. The concept has included notions of weak sustainability, strong sustainability and deep ecology. Different conceptions also reveal a strong tension between ecocentrism and anthropocentrism. Many definitions and images (Visualizing Sustainability) of sustainable development coexist. Broadly defined, the sustainable development mantra enjoins current generations to take a systems approach to growth and development and to manage natural, produced, and social capital for the welfare of their own and future generations.*

During the last ten years, different organizations have tried to measure and monitor the proximity to what they consider sustainability by implementing what has been called sustainability metrics and indices. Sustainable development is said to set limits on the developing world. While current first world countries polluted significantly during their development, the same countries encourage third world countries to reduce pollution, which sometimes impedes growth. Some consider that the implementation of sustainable development would mean a reversion to pre-modern lifestyles.

Others have criticized the overuse of the term: "[The] word sustainable has been used in too many situations today, and ecological sustainability is one of those terms that confuse a lot of people. You hear about sustainable development, sustainable growth, sustainable economies, sustainable societies, sustainable agriculture. Everything is sustainable."

Environmental Sustainability

Environmental sustainability is the process of making sure current processes of interaction with the environment are pursued with the idea of keeping the environment as pristine as naturally possible based on ideal-seeking behaviour.

An "unsustainable situation" occurs when natural capital (the sum total of nature's resources) is used up faster than it can be replenished. Sustainability requires that human activity only uses nature's resources at a rate at which they can be replenished naturally. Inherently the concept of sustainable development is intertwined with the concept of carrying capacity. Theoretically, the long-term result of environmental degradation is the inability to sustain human life. Such degradation on a global scale could imply extinction for humanity.

Consumption of renewable resources	***State of environment***	***Sustainability***
More than nature's ability to replenish	Environmental degradation	Not sustainable
Equal to nature's ability to replenish	Environmental equilibrium	Steady state economy
Less than nature's ability to replenish	Environmental renewal	Environmentally sustainable

The notion of Capital in Sustainable Development

The sustainable development debate is based on the assumption that societies need to manage three types of capital (economic, social, and natural), which may be non-substitutable and whose consumption might be irreversible. Daly (1991), for example, points to the fact that natural capital can not necessarily be substituted by economic capital. While it is possible that we can find ways to replace some natural resources, it is much more unlikely that they will ever be able to replace eco-system services, such as the protection provided by the ozone layer, or the climate stabilizing function of the Amazonian forest. In fact natural capital, social capital and economic capital are often complementarities. A further obstacle to substitutability lies also in the multi-functionality of many natural resources. Forests, for example, do not only provide the raw material for paper (which can be substituted quite easily), but they also maintain biodiversity, regulate water flow, and absorb CO_2. Another problem of natural and social capital deterioration lies in their partial irreversibility. The loss in biodiversity, for example, is often definite. The same can be true for cultural diversity. For example with globalisation advancing quickly the number of indigenous languages is dropping at alarming rates. Moreover, the depletion of natural and social capital may have non-linear consequences. Consumption of natural and social capital may have no observable impact until a certain threshold is reached. A lake can, for example, absorb nutrients for a long time while actually increasing its productivity. However, once a certain level of algae is reached lack of oxygen causes the lake's ecosystem to break down all of a sudden.

Market Failure

If the degradation of natural and social capital has such important consequence the question arises why action is not taken more systematically to alleviate it. Cohen and Winn (2007) point to four types of market failure as possible explanations: First, while the benefits of natural or social capital depletion can usually be privatized the costs are often externalized (i.e. they are borne not by the party responsible but by society in general). Second, natural capital is often undervalued by society since we are not fully aware of the real cost of the depletion of natural capital. Information asymmetry is a third reason—often the link between cause and effect is obscured, making it difficult for actors to make informed choices. Cohen and Winn close with the realization that contrary to economic theory many firms are not perfect optimizers. They postulate that firms often do not optimize resource allocation because they are caught in a "business as usual" mentality.

The business Case for Sustainable Development

The most broadly accepted criterion for corporate sustainability constitutes a firm's efficient use of natural capital. This eco-efficiency is usually calculated as the economic value added by a firm in relation to its aggregated ecological impact. This idea has been popularised by the World Business Council for Sustainable Development (WBCSD) under the following definition: "Eco-efficiency is achieved by the delivery of competitively-priced goods and services that satisfy human needs and bring quality of life, while progressively reducing ecological impacts and resource intensity throughout the life-cycle to a level at least in line with the earth's carrying capacity."

Similar to the eco-efficiency concept but so far less explored is the second criterion for corporate sustainability. Socio-efficiency describes the relation between a firm's value added and its social impact. Whereas, it can be assumed that most corporate impacts on the environment are negative (apart from rare exceptions such as the planting of trees) this is not true for social impacts. These can be either positive (e.g. corporate giving, creation of employment) or negative (e.g. work accidents, mobbing of employees, human rights abuses). Depending on the type of impact socio-efficiency thus either tries to minimize negative social impacts (i.e. accidents per value added) or maximise positive social impacts (i.e. donations per value added) in relation to the value added.

Both eco-efficiency and socio-efficiency are concerned primarily with increasing economic sustainability. In this process they instrumentalize both natural and social capital aiming to benefit from win-win situations. However, as Dyllick and Hockerts point out the business case alone will not be sufficient to realise sustainable development. They point towards eco-effectiveness, socio-effectiveness, sufficiency, and eco-equity as four criteria that need to be met if sustainable development is to be reached.

Critique of the Concept of Sustainable Development

The concept of " Sustainable Development " raises several critiques at different levels.

Purpose

Various writers have commented on the population-control agenda that seems to underlie the concept of sustainable development. Maria Sophia Aguirre writes:

> *"Sustainable development is a policy approach that has gained quite a lot of popularity in recent years, especially in international circles. By attaching a specific interpretation to sustainability, population control policies have become the overriding approach to development, thus becoming the primary tool used to "promote" economic development in developing countries and to protect the environment."*

Mary Jo Anderson suggests that the real purpose of sustainable development is to contain and limit economic development in developing countries, and in so doing control population growth. It is suggested that this is the reason the main focus of most programs is still on low-income agriculture. Joan Veon, a businesswoman and international reporter, who covered 64 global meetings on sustainable development posits that:

> *"Sustainable development has continued to evolve as that of protecting the world's resources while its true agenda is to control the world's resources. It should be noted that Agenda 21 sets up the global infrastructure needed to manage, count, and control all of the world's assets."*

Consequences

John Baden reckons that the notion of sustainable development is dangerous because the consequences are proceedings with unknown effects or potentially dangerous. He writes: "In economy like in ecology, the interdependence rules applies. Isolated actions are impossible. A policy which is not enough carefully thought will carry along various perverse and adverse effects for the ecology as much as for the economy. Many suggestions to save our environment and to promote a model of 'sustainable development' risk indeed leading to reverse effects." Moreover, he evokes the bounds of the public action which are underlined by the public choice theory: quest by the politics of their own interests, lobby pressure, partial disclosure etc. He develops his critique by noting the vagueness of the expression, which can cover anything : It is a gateway to interventionist proceedings which can be against the principle of freedom and without proven efficacy. Against this notion, he is a proponent of private property to impel the producers and the consumers to save the natural resources. According to Baden, "the improvement of environment quality depends on the market economy and the existence of legitimate and protected property rights." They enable the effective practice of personal responsibility and the development of mechanisms to protect the environment. The State can in this context "create conditions which encourage the people to save the environment."

Vagueness of the Term

The term of "sustainable development" is criticized because of its vagueness. For example, Jean-Marc Jancovici or the philosopher Luc Ferry express this view. The latter writes about sustainable development: "I know that this term is obligatory, but I find it also absurd, or rather so vague that it says nothing." Luc Ferry adds that the term is trivial by a proof by contradiction: "who would like to be a proponent of an "untenable development! Of course no one! [..] The term is more charming than meaningful. [..] Everything must be done so that it does not turn into a Russian-type administrative planning with ill effects."

Basis

Sylvie Brunel, French geographer and specialist of the Third World, develops in *A qui profite le développement durable* (Who benefits from sustainable development?) (2008) a critique of the basis of sustainable development, with its binary vision of the world, can be compared to the Christian vision of Good and Evil, a idealized nature where the human being is an animal like the others or even an alien. Nature – as Rousseau thought – is better than the human being. It is a parasite, harmful for the nature. But the human is the one who protects the biodiversity, where normally only the strong survive.

Moreover, she thinks that the ideas of sustainable development can hide a will to protectionism from the developed country to impede the development of the other countries. For Sylvie Brunel, the sustainable development serves as a pretext for the protectionism and "I have the feeling about sustainable development that it is perfectly helping out the capitalism".

"De-growth"

The proponents of the de-growth reckon that the term of sustainable development is an oxymoron. According to them, on a planet where 20% of the population consumes 80% of the natural resources, a sustainable development cannot be possible for this 20%: "According to the origin of the concept of sustainable development, a development which meets the needs of the present without compromising the ability of future generations to meet their own needs, the right term for the developed countries should be a sustainable de-growth".

Sustainable Development in Economics

The Venn diagram of sustainable development shown above has many versions, but was first used by economist Edward Barbier (1987). However, Pearce, Barbier and Markandya (1989) criticized the Venn approach due to the intractability of operationalizing separate indices of economic, environmental, and social sustainability and somehow combining them. They also noted that the Venn approach was inconsistent with the Brundtland Commission Report, which emphasized the interlinkages between economic development, environmental degradation, and population pressure instead of three objectives. Economists have since focused on viewing the economy and the environment as a single interlinked system with a unified valuation methodology. Intergenerational equity can be incorporated into this approach, as has become common in economic valuations of climate change economics. Ruling out discrimination against future generations and allowing for the possibility of renewable alternatives to petro-chemicals and other non-renewable resources, efficient policies are compatible with increasing human welfare, eventually reaching a golden-rule steady state. Thus the three pillars of sustainable development are interlinkages, intergenerational equity, and dynamic efficiency. Arrow et al. (2004) and other economists have advocated a form of the weak criterion for sustainable development – the requirement than the wealth of a society, including human-capital, knowledge-capital and natural-capital (as well as produced capital) not decline over time. Others, including Barbier 2007, continue to contend that strong sustainability – non-depletion of essential forms of natural capital – may be appropriate.

Applied Sustainability

Applied sustainability is the application of science and innovation to meet human needs while indefinitely preserving the life support systems of the planet.

Note that this is a significant difference from the standard definition of sustainability that normally is encapsulated by some version of the Brundtland Commission's concept: "development that meets the needs and aspirations of the present without compromising the ability of future generations to meet their own needs".

Just Applied Sustainability

A more refined definition would be called just applied sustainability: the application of science and innovation to ensure a better quality of life for all, now and into the future, in a just and equitable manner, whilst living within the limits of supporting ecosystems. This comes from the definition of Just Sustainability, which is "the egalitarian conception of sustainable development".

It generates an improved definition of sustainable development as "the need to ensure a better quality of life for all, now and into the future, in a just and equitable manner, whilst living within the limits of supporting ecosystems". This new form of sustainable development prioritizes justice and equity, while maintaining the importance of the environment and the global life support system.

Synonymous with Applied Science

The relationship between applied sustainability and sustainability (or sustainability science) is analogous relationship between applied science (engineering) and basic science. Whereas science is the effort to discover, understand, or to understand better, how the physical world works, with observable physical evidence as the basis of that understanding. Applied science is the application of knowledge from one or more natural scientific fields to solve practical problems.

Sustainable Engineering

Applied sustainability is essentially sustainability engineering – by utilizing natural laws and physical resources in order to design and implement materials, structures, machines, devices, systems, and processes that meets human need while preserving the environment forever. Applied sustainability is made up of work in engineering, policy, and education – whatever methods are necessary to conserve the world for our children.

Confusion over Terms

Sustainability, itself, is a term that is often confused because in its most basic form it is a characteristic of a process or state that can be maintained at a certain level indefinitely. When used in the context of development, as sustainable development, it is a pattern of resource use that aims to meet human needs while preserving the environment so that these needs can be met not only in the present, but in the indefinite future. The most evolved definition of sustainability is that of just sustainability-"the need to ensure a better quality of life for all, now and into the future, in a just and equitable manner, whilst living within the limits of supporting ecosystems".

'Sustainable Economic Development'

The term 'Sustainable economic development' acquires a major importance in the economic parlance of countries all across the globe. World has witnessed major economic development in last century. Industrial revolution of two centuries back has resulted into all round economic growth and prosperity across the nations. But the major beneficiaries of this economic boom have been western countries.

Major parts of Africa and Asia lagged behind in this context. The difference of economic chasm is so stark that, terms like 'First world countries' and 'Third world countries' were coined. On the one hand, poverty has reduced in many countries along with overall increase in income but at the same time, this economic growth has not spread equally along all spheres of economy.

To go further into the issue, inclusive growth has remained a mirage. There is a huge gap in income distribution, almost to the point that rich has become richer whereas poor have remained same. In view of such conditions, sustainable economic development plans are the need of the hour.

Sustainable economic development strives for reducing poverty and equitable use of resources. The means adopted consist of minimization of depletion of environmental dilapidation, social unsteadiness, economic resources and cultural disorder.

It also aims to use the resources in a judicious way so that present as well future needs be met. Now a day's biggest concern is rapidly diminishing of natural resources, whether it is oil, minerals, energy sources or food etc. Because of the rapid industrialization, natural resources have suffered the most.

We are also constantly struggling with environmental issues. World has taken notice to this grave scenario and has started to address the issue by focusing upon economic as well as environmental and socio-political sustainability so that future generations can meet their demands. Different means of energy conservation, alternate energy resources, nature protection and equal distribution of income have been taken to ensure sustainable economic development.

Concept

Sustainable development is defined as a pattern of social and structured economic transformations (i.e. development) which optimizes the economic and societal benefits available in the present, without jeopardizing the likely potential for similar benefits in the future. A primary goal of sustainable development is to achieve a reasonable and equitably distributed level of economic well-being that can be perpetuated continually for many human generations.

Sustainable development implies using renewable natural resources in a manner which does not eliminate or degrade them, or otherwise diminish their usefulness for future generations. It further implies using non-renewable (exhaustible) mineral resources in a manner which does not unnecessarily preclude easy access to them by future generations. Sustainable development also requires depleting non-renewable energy resources at a slow enough rate so as to ensure the high probability of an orderly society transition to renewable energy sources.

Based on similar arguments, sustainable development has been alternatively defined in various manners also, some of them are as follows:

> *"Development that meets the needs of the present without compromising the ability of future generations to meet their own needs". The World Commission on Environment and Development, Brundtland Commission 1987.*

"Sustainable development ensures that the maximum rate of resource consumption and waste discharge for a selected development portfolio would be sustained indefinitely, in a defined planning region, without progressively impairing its bio-productivity and ecological integrity. Environmental conservation, therefore, contrary to general belief, accelerates rather than hinders economic development.

Therefore, the Development plans have to ensure:

- Sustainable and equitable use of resources for meeting the needs of the present and future generations without causing damage to environment.
- To prevent further damage to our life-support systems;
- To conserve and nurture the biological diversity, gene pool and other resources for long term food security".

Key areas where the partnership works hard to address sustainable economic development issues include the following:

Economic Integration, Investment and Dialogue

The FEMISE network has been financed by the European Commission since 1997, and undertakes economic research and organises dialogue to assess the state of the EU-Med Partnership. The Barcelona Summit in November 2005 advocated the acceleration of Free Trade Agreements (FTAs) among Mediterranean partners to stimulate investment within an integrated economic zone and to achieve concrete progress towards the objective of a Euro-Mediterranean Free Trade Area by 2010.

EC support to South-South FTAs has so far materialised through a programme to support the implementation of the Agadir Agreement. Under this programme, activities such as studies/analyses in the economic and trade domain have been developed as well as support to the creation of a technical unit established in Amman, Jordan.

Investment Promotion

There is a need to improve the investment climate and to energise the reform agenda in some Mediterranean countries. Since 2002, the Commission has financed FEMIP, which aims to enhance the supply of foreign and domestic financing for both private and public investment in the region. The Commission support to FEMIP includes funding for private equity operations as well as technical assistance, and currently comprises an active portfolio of more than € 400 million.

From 2002 to June 2007, the Commission also supported the ANIMA network, which aimed to strengthen cooperation between European and Mediterranean organisations that are involved in investment promotion. Since 2008, Invest in Med is taking over and will develop investments and trade flows in the region.

Industrial Cooperation

By 2010, the Euro-Mediterranean region should become a vast free-trade area with strong development prospects for entrepreneurs. Economic integration is taking place in a global context of increasing trade and competition.

To meet this challenge, the Commission supports various regional programmes and projects:

- The Euro-Med Quality project helped Mediterranean countries to develop quality products for the international marketplace.
- Euro-Med Market aimed to help establish a seamless free-trade area between the two regions.
- MedIbtikar (Euromed Innovation and Technology Programme) aims to boost the innovative capacities of Mediterranean businesses.

Energy

The Euro-Mediterranean Partnership agreed as far back as 1998 that work on energy issues should cover the following priorities:

- Security of supply.
- Energy industry competitiveness.
- Environmental protection and sustainable development.

The Euro-Mediterranean Conferences of Energy Ministers held in Athens and Rome in the year 2003 put an increased emphasis on the necessity of ensuring security of energy supply through better interconnections and increased regional integration.

Hence in 2004, three sub-regional projects were launched to support i) the integration of the Maghreb electricity market; ii) the creation of a Euro-Mashreq gas market (EAMGM); and iii) the establishment of a Joint Office aimed to enhance energy cooperation between Israel and the Palestinian Authority.

The Euro-Med Energy Forum, held in 2006, defined some new priorities for the sector including: the need to integrate energy markets; the promotion of mutually valuable energy projects; and increasing support to sustainable energy initiatives.

A significant proportion of the EC resources available under the regional budget are also used to support the FEMIP Technical Assistance Support Fund, which helps prepare energy-related projects and to provide interest rates subsidies to the European Investment Bank.

Since 2007 and 2008, new projects have been launched:

- Electricity market integration: it aims to harmonise the legislative and regulatory framework of Algeria, Marocco and Tunisia, in line with EU standards.
- Med Emip: its objectives are to enhance the integration of the energy markets and to improve security and sustainability.
- Medreg: it strengthens the cooperation between EU energy regulators and those of the partner countries.

Transport

Over the past few years, the Commission has prioritised regional transport programmes which have addressed shared challenges and the need to develop common standards. Projects which reflect this approach include:

- Safemed, which seeks to improve maritime safety and prevent sea pollution.
- Euromed Aviation, with its emphasis on creating a common aviation area.
- Meda Motorways of the Sea, aiming to modernise maritime connections between the two sides of the Mediterranean

In parallel, the Euromed Transport project has provided an overall policy framework for establishing and maintaining sustained policy dialogue and cooperation between the two regions' transport actors, notably via the Euromed Transport Forum.

The important progress accomplished by the Euromed Transport Forum was recognised by the first Euromed Ministerial Conference, held in December 2005 in Marrakech. This meeting provided the opportunity to reaffirm the political impetus of our cooperation in the field of transport by adopting the recommendations of the Blue Paper on Euro-Mediterranean transport networks, namely the opening up of transport markets, the development of infrastructure, in particular interconnections, safety and security of transport systems, and the smooth functioning of the multimodal freight transport of chain.

Environment

The promotion and the protection of the environment is an essential dimension of the Euro-Mediterranean Partnership. The challenges related to the scarcity of water and environmental degradation should be tackled at national and regional levels to ensure the sustainable development of the region. Water and environment programmes have the objective to stop degradation and protect the particularly fragile Mediterranean eco-region. The SMAP (Short and Medium Term Priority Environmental Action Programme) and the MEDA Water Regional Programme are the most relevant environmental regional programmes under MEDA. In November 2005, during the 10th anniversary of the Barcelona Declaration Summit, it was agreed to launch the so-called Horizon 20020 Initiative for the depollution of the Mediterranean Sea. The Horizon 2020 initiative was launched the following year.

Information Society

Cooperation in the field of information society is essential to contribute to the sustainable economic and social development of an increasingly integrated Euro-Mediterranean region. In this sector, the programme Eumedis has interconnected European with Mediterranean research networks and funded 21 regional pilot information society projects in sectors such as healthcare, e-commerce, tourism and cultural heritage, research, business and innovation, and education. The NATP project (New Approaches to Telecommunications policy) in 2002 has established a Euro-Mediterranean dialogue in this field.

Statistics

The Medstat II programme aims at improving statistical information and strengthening the Mediterranean Partners' statistical systems. This programme helps to produce updated, reliable and relevant statistical data necessary for political decision-making and to ensure good governance.

The Government's overarching economic goal is to grow an inclusive, innovative economy for the benefit of all. This goal is closely related to the Government's other social and environmental goals. These include improving the skills of New Zealanders, closing the gaps for Maori and Pacific People in Health, Education, Employment and Housing and protecting and enhancing the environment.

The concept of sustainable economic development is central to the achievement of these key goals. It can be thought of in terms of policies and programmes designed to meet the needs of present generations without compromising the ability of future generations to meet their own needs.

The achievement of sustainable economic development requires a new and different approach to policy making and its implementation. The Government is looking for greater integration and coordination of policy making and its implementation across the public sector, and across social, economic and environmental policy portfolios. It is also looking for an approach characterised by greater partnership between central government, local government, Maori economic entities, private industry and other community groups.

The Ministry is being challenged to lead the production and coordination of policy advice on issues related to sustainable economic development across the public sector. It is also required to work closely with New Zealand Trade and Enterprise to design and implement policies and programmes to deliver the Government's sustainable economic policies. To meet these challenges, the Ministry will need to work proactively with other government agencies, and across policy portfolios. It will also need to develop close working relationships with industry, local government, Maori economic entities and other non-government stakeholders.

Successfully meeting this challenge will require the Ministry to develop a range of new functions, while continuing to advise the

Government on the regulation and operation of markets and industries. These new functions include those related to the:

- Development of policies and coordination of policy advice on issues related to economic development, regional development and industry development;
- Monitoring and researching trends and issues related to sustainable economic development, regional development and industry development;
- Evaluating government policies and programmes to determine their contribution to sustainable economic development, regional development and industry development goals and objectives; and
- Advising on the performance and governance of New Zealand Trade and Enterprise.

Economic Growth

Economic growth is a term used to indicate the increase of total GDP. It is often measured as the rate of change of gross domestic product (GDP). Economic growth refers only to the quantity of goods and services produced; it says nothing about the way in which they are produced. Economic development, a related term, refers to change in the way goods and services are produced; positive economic development involves the introduction of more efficient or "productive" technologies or forms of social organisation.

Economic growth is that branch of one, which deals with the study of rate of change of gross domestic product, referring to the quantity of goods and services produced. Economic growth can either be positive or negative. Negative growth can also be referred to by saying that the economy is *shrinking*. Negative growth is associated with economic recession and economic depression.

Gross national product (GNP) is sometimes used as an alternative measure to gross domestic product. In order to compare multiple countries, the statistics may be quoted in a single currency, based on either prevailing exchange rates or purchasing power parity. Then, in order to compare countries of different population sizes, the per capita figure is quoted. To compensate for changes in the value of money (inflation or deflation) the GDP or GNP is usually given in "real" or inflation adjusted, terms rather than the actual money figure compiled in a given year, which is called the nominal or current figure. GDP per capita is not the same thing as earnings per worker since GDP measures only monetary transactions for all final goods and services in a country without regard to who receives that money.

Short-term Stabilization and Long-term Growth

Economists draw a distinction between short-term economic stabilization and long-term economic growth. The topic of economic growth is primarily concerned with the long run. The short-run variation of economic growth is termed the business cycle. The long-run path of economic growth is one of the central questions of economics; in spite of the problems of measurement, an increase in GDP of a country is generally taken as an increase in the standard of living of its inhabitants. Over long periods of time, even small rates of annual growth can have large effects through compounding. A growth rate of 2.5% per annum will lead to a doubling of GDP within 28 years, whilst a growth rate of 8% per annum (experienced by some Four Asian Tigers) will lead to a doubling of GDP within 9 years. This exponential characteristic can exacerbate differences across nations.

In the early 20th century, it became the policy of most country's governments to encourage growth of this kind. To do this required enacting policies, and being able to measure the results of those policies. This gave rise to the importance of econometrics, or the field of creating measurements for underlying conditions. Terms such as "unemployment rate", "Gross Domestic Product" and "rate of inflation" are part of the measuring of the changes in an economy.

Various Theories on Economic Growth

Origins of the Concept

In 1377, the Arabian economic thinker Ibn Khaldun provided one of the earliest descriptions of economic growth in his famous *Muqaddimah* (known as *Prolegomena* in the Western world):

> *'When civilization [population] increases, the available labour again increases. In turn, luxury again increases in correspondence with the increasing profit, and the customs and needs of luxury increase. Crafts are created to obtain luxury products. The value realized from them*

increases, and, as a result, profits are again multiplied in the town. Production there is thriving even more than before. And so it goes with the second and third increase. All the additional labour serves luxury and wealth, in contrast to the original labour that served the necessity of life."

In the early modern period, some people in Western European nations developed the idea that economies could "grow", that is, produce a greater economic surplus which could be expended on something other than mere subsistence. This surplus could then be used for consumption, warfare, or civic and religious projects. The previous view was that only increasing either population or tax rates could generate more surplus money for the Crown or country.

Now it is generally recognized that economic growth also corresponds to a process of continual rapid replacement and reorganization of human activities facilitated by investment motivated to maximize returns. This exponential evolution of our self-organized life-support and cultural systems is remarkably creative and flexible, but highly unpredictable in many ways. As there are difficulties in modelling complex self-organizing systems, various efforts to model the long term evolution of economies have produced mixed results.

During much of the "Mercantilist" period, growth was seen as involving an increase in the total amount of specie, that is circulating medium such as silver and gold, under the control of the state. This "Bullionist" theory led to policies to force trade through a particular state, the acquisition of colonies to supply cheaper raw materials which could then be manufactured and sold.

Later, such trade policies were justified instead simply in terms of promoting domestic trade and industry. The post-Bullionist insight that it was the increasing capability of manufacturing which led to policies in the 1700s to encourage manufacturing in itself, and the formula of importing raw materials and exporting finished goods. Under this system high tariffs were erected to allow manufacturers to establish "factories". Local markets would then pay the fixed costs of capital growth, and then allow them to export abroad, undercutting the prices of manufactured goods elsewhere. Once competition from abroad was removed, prices could then be increased to recoup the costs of establishing the business.

Under this theory of growth, one policy attempted to foster growth was to grant monopolies, which would give an incentive for an individual to exploit a market or resource, confident that he would make all of the profits when all other extra-national competitors were driven out of business. The "Dutch East India company" and the "British East India company" were examples of such state-granted trade monopolies.

In this period the view was that growth was gained through "advantageous" trade in which specie would flow in to the country, but to trade with other nations on equal terms was disadvantageous. It should be stressed that Mercantilism was not simply a matter of restricting trade. *Within* a country, it often meant breaking down trade barriers, building new roads, and abolishing local toll booths, all of which expanded markets. This corresponded to the centralization of power in the hands of the Crown (or "Absolutism"). This process helped produce the modern nation-state in Western Europe.

Internationally, Mercantilism led to a contradiction: growth was gained through trade, but to trade with other nations on equal terms was disadvantageous.

Classical Growth Theory

The modern conception of economic growth began with the critique of Mercantilism, especially by the physiocrats and with the Scottish Enlightenment thinkers such as David Hume and Adam Smith, and the foundation of the discipline of modern political economy. The theory of the physiocrats was that productive capacity, itself, allowed for growth, and the improving and increasing capital to allow that capacity was "the wealth of nations". Whereas they stressed the importance of agriculture and saw urban industry as "sterile", Smith extended the notion that manufacturing was central to the entire economy.

David Ricardo argued that trade was a benefit to a country, because if one could buy a good more cheaply from abroad, it meant that there was more profitable work to be done here. This theory of "comparative advantage" would be the central basis for arguments in favour of free trade as an essential component of growth.

Creative Destruction and Economic Growth

Many economists view entrepreneurship as having a major influence on a society's rate of technological progress and thus economic growth.

Joseph Schumpeter was a key figure in understanding the influence of entrepreneurs on technological progress. In Schumpeter's *Capitalism, Socialism and Democracy*, published in 1942, an entrepreneur is a person who is willing and able to convert a new idea or invention into a successful innovation. Entrepreneurship forces "creative destruction" across markets and industries, simultaneously creating new products and business models. In this way, creative destruction is largely responsible for the dynamism of industries and long-run economic growth. Former Federal Reserve chairman Alan Greenspan has described the influence of creative destruction on economic growth as follows: "Capitalism expands wealth primarily through creative destruction—the process by which the cash flow from obsolescent, low-return capital is invested in high-return, cutting-edge technologies."

The Neo-Classical Growth Model

The notion of growth as increased stocks of capital goods (means of production) was codified as the Solow-Swan Growth Model, which involved a series of equations which showed the relationship between labour-time, capital goods, output, and investment. According to this view, the role of technological change became crucial, even more important than the accumulation of capital. This model, developed by Robert Solow and Trevor Swan in the 1950s, was the first attempt to model long-run growth analytically. This model assumes that countries use their resources efficiently and that there are diminishing returns to capital and labour increases. From these two premises, the neoclassical model makes three important predictions. First, increasing capital relative to labour creates economic growth, since people can be more productive given more capital. Second, poor countries with less capital per person will grow faster because each investment in capital will produce a higher return than rich countries with ample capital. Third, because of diminishing returns to capital, economies will eventually reach a point at which no new increase in capital will create economic growth. This point is called a "steady state".

The model also notes that countries can overcome this steady state and continue growing by inventing new technology. In the long run, output per capita depends on the rate of saving, but the rate of output growth should be equal for any saving rate. In this model, the process by which countries continue growing despite the diminishing returns is "exogenous" and represents the creation of new technology that allows production with fewer resources. Technology improves, the steady state level of capital increases, and the country invests and grows. The data does not support some of this model's predictions, in particular, that all countries grow at the same rate in the long run, or that poorer countries should grow faster until they reach their steady state. Also, the data suggests the world has slowly increased its rate of growth.

However modern economic research shows that this model of economic growth is not supported by the evidence. Calculations made by Solow claimed that the majority of economic growth was due to technological progress rather than inputs of capital and labour. Recent economic research has, however, found the calculations made to support this claim to be invalid as they do not take into account changes in both investment and labour inputs.

Dale Jorgenson, of Harvard University, President of the American Economic Association in 2000, concludes that: 'Griliches and I showed that changes in the quality of capital and labour inputs and the quality of investment goods explained most of the Solow residual. We estimated that capital and labour inputs accounted for 85 percent of growth during the period 1945–1965, while only 15 percent could be attributed to productivity growth... This has precipitated the sudden obsolescence of earlier productivity research employing the conventions of Kuznets and Solow.'

John Ross has analysed the long term correlation between the level of investment in the economy, rising from 5-7% of GDP at the time of the Industrial Revolution in England, to 25% of GDP in the post-war German 'economic miracle', to over 35% of GDP in the world's most rapidly growing contemporary economies of India and China.

Taking the G7 economies and the largest non-G7 economies Jorgenson and Vu conclude in considering: 'the growth of world output between input growth and productivity... input growth greatly predominated... Productivity growth accounted for only one-fifth of the total during 1989-1995, while input growth accounted for almost four-fifths. Similarly, input growth accounted for more than 70 percent of growth after 1995, while productivity accounted for less than 30 percent.'

Regarding differences in output per capita Jorgenson and Vu

conclude: 'differences in per capita output levels are primarily explained by differences in per capital input, rather than variations in productivity.'

Development Economics

The latter half of the 20th century, with its global economy of a few very wealthy nations and many very poor nations, led to the study of how the transition from subsistence and resource-based economies to production and consumption based-economies occurred. This led to the field of development economics, including the work of Nobel laureates Amartya Sen and Joseph Stiglitz. However this model of economic development does not meet the demands of subaltern populations and has been severely criticized by later theorists. PROTAP

New Growth Theory

Growth theory advanced again with the theories of economist Paul Romer in the late 1980s and early 1990s. Other important new growth theorists include Robert E. Lucas and Robert J. Barro.

Unsatisfied with Solow's explanation, economists worked to "endogenize" technology in the 1980s. They developed the endogenous growth theory that includes a mathematical explanation of technological advancement. This model also incorporated a new concept of human capital, the skills and knowledge that make workers productive. Unlike physical capital, human capital has increasing rates of return. Therefore, overall there are constant returns to capital, and economies never reach a steady state. Growth does not slow as capital accumulates, but the rate of growth depends on the types of capital a country invests in. Research done in this area has focused on what increases human capital (e.g. education) or technological change (e.g. innovation). Recent empirical analyses suggest that differences in cognitive skills, related to schooling and other factors, can largely explain variations in growth rates across countries.

Other Theories

Theories of economic growth, the mechanisms that let it take place and its main determinants abound. One popular theory in the 1970s for example was that of the "Big Push" which suggested that countries needed to jump from one stage of development to another through a virtuous cycle in which large investments in infrastructure and education coupled to private investment would move the economy to a more productive stage, breaking free from economic paradigms appropriate to a lower productivity stage.

Analysis of recent economies' success shows a close correlation between growth and climate. It is possible that there is absolutely no actual mechanism between the two, and the relation may be spurious. In early human history, economic as well as cultural development was concentrated in warmer parts of the world, like Egypt.

According to Acemọðlu, Johnson and Robinson, the positive correlation between high income and cold climate is a by-product of history. Europeans adopted very different colonization policies in different colonies, with different associated institutions. In places where these colonizers faced high mortality rates (e.g., due to the presence of tropical diseases), they could not settle permanently, and they were thus more likely to establish extractive institutions, which persisted after independence; in places where they could settle permanently (e.g., those with temperate climates), they established institutions with this objective in mind and modelled them after those in their European homelands. In these 'neo-Europes' better institutions in turn produced better development outcomes. Thus, although others economists focus on the identity or type of legal system of the colonizers to explain institutions, these authors look at the environmental conditions in the colonies to explain institutions. For instance, former colonies have inherited corrupt governments and geo-political boundaries (set by the colonizers) that are not properly placed regarding the geographical locations of different ethnic groups; this creates internal disputes and conflicts, which in turn hinders development. In another example, societies that emerged in colonies without solid native populations, established better property rights and incentives for long-term investment than those where native populations were large.

Effects of Growth

Economic growth has undeniable effects on the living conditions of the peoples of the earth. However, whether these effects are on balance positive or negative is currently open to debate.

Positive Effects

Economist Xavier Sala-i-Martin argues that global income inequality is diminishing, and the World Bank argues that the rapid reduction in global poverty is in large part due to economic growth. The decline in poverty has been the slowest where growth performance has been the worst (ie. in Africa).

Happiness has been shown to increase with a higher GDP per capita, at least up to a level of $15,000 per person.

Many earlier predictions of resource depletion, such as Thomas Malthus' 1798 predictions about approaching famines in Europe, *The Population Bomb* (1968), *Limits to Growth* (1972), and the Simon-Ehrlich wager (1980) have proven false, one reason being that advancements in technology and science have continually allowed previously unavailable resources to be utilized more economically. The book *The Improving State of the World* argues that the state of humanity is rapidly improving.

Those more optimistic about the environmental impacts of growth believe that, although localized environmental effects may occur, large scale ecological effects are minor. The argument as stated by economists such as Julian Lincoln Simon states that if these global-scale ecological effects exist, human ingenuity will find ways of adapting to them.

Economists theorize that economies are driven by new technology and ongoing improvements in efficiency — for instance, we have faster computers today than a year ago, but not necessarily computers requiring more natural resources to build. Also, physical limits may be very large if considering all the minerals in the planet Earth or all possible resources from space colonization, such as solar power satellites, asteroid mining, or a Dyson sphere. The book *Mining the Sky: Untold Riches from the Asteroids, Comets, and Planets* is one example of such arguments. However, depletion and declining production from old resources can sometimes occur before new resources are ready to replace them. This is, in part, the logical basis of the Peak Oil theory. Although individual oil wells and mines for other nonrenewable resources are often depleted, the availability of these resources has generally risen and their prices have dropped over the long-run.

Negative Effects

A number of critical arguments have been raised against economic growth. Economic growth may reflect or create a decline in the quality of life, such as crime, prisons, or pollution, in what is known as uneconomic growth Other aspects of economic growth that affect quality of life, such as its effects on the environment, are externalized, and not traded or accounted for in the market. Growth leads to consumerism by encouraging the creation of artificial needs: Industries cause consumers to develop new taste, and preferences for growth to occur. Consequently, "wants are created, and consumers have become the servants, instead of the masters, of the economy." The ecological footprint of economic growth has been shown to create an unsustainable drain on the earth's resources. The 2007 United Nations GEO-4 report warns that we are living far beyond our means. The human population is now larger and that the amount of resources it consumes takes up a lot of those resources available. Humanity's environmental demand is purported to be 21.9 hectares per person while the Earth's biological capacity is purported to be 15.7 ha/person. This report supports the basic arguments and observations made by Thomas Malthus in the early 1800s, that is, economic growth depletes non-renewable resources rapidly. Economic inequality has increased; the gap between the poorest and richest countries in the world has been growing.. Although mean and median wealth has increased globally, it adds to the inequality of wealth.

Some critics argue that a narrow view of economic growth, combined with globalization, is creating a scenario where we could see a systemic collapse of our planet's natural resources. Other critics draw on archaeology to cite examples of cultures they claim have disappeared because they grew beyond the ability of their ecosystems to support them. Concerns about possible negative effects of growth on the environment and society led some to advocate lower levels of growth, from which comes the ideas of uneconomic growth and de-growth, and Green parties which argue that economies are part of a global society and a global ecology and cannot outstrip their natural growth without damaging them.

The Austrian School argues that the concept of "growth" or the creation and acquisition of more goods and services is dependent upon the relative desires of the individual. Someone may prefer having more leisure time to acquiring more goods and services, but this fulfilment of desires would have a negative effect on GDP increase. Also, they claim that the notion of growth implies the need for a "central planner" within an economy. To Austrian economists, such an ideal is antithetical to the concept of a free market economy, which best satisfies the wants of consumers. As such, Austrian economists believe that the individual should determine how much "growth" she desires.

Canadian scientist, David Suzuki stated in the 1990s that ecologies can only sustain typically about 1.5-3% new growth per year, and thus any requirement for greater returns from agriculture or forestry will necessarily cannibalize the natural capital of soil or forest Some think this argument can be applied even to more developed economies.

Growth 'to a Point'

The two theories can be reconciled if it is recognised that growth improves the quality of life to a point, after which it doesn't improve the quality of life, but rather obstructs sustainable living. Historically, sustained growth has reached its limits (and turned to catastrophic decline) when perturbations to the environmental system last long enough to destabilise the bases of a culture.

Implications of Global Warming

Up to the present there are close correlations of economic growth with carbon dioxide emissions across nations, although considerable divergence in carbon intensity (carbon emissions per GDP). The Stern Review notes that "under business as usual, global emissions will be sufficient to propel greenhouse-gas concentrations to over 550ppm CO2e by 2050 and over 650-700ppm by the end of this century is robust to a wide range of changes in model assumptions". This is in contrast with scientist consensus that planetary ecosystem functioning without incurring dangerous risks requires stabilization at 450-550ppm.

As a consequence, growth oriented environmental economists propose massive government intervention into switching sources of energy production, favouring wind, solar, hydroelectric and nuclear. This would largely confine use of fossil fuels to either domestic cooking needs (such as for kerosene burners) or where carbon capture and storage technology can be cost-effective and reliable. The Stern Review, published by the United Kingdom Government in 2006, concluded that an investment of 1% of GDP per annum would be sufficient to avoid the worst effects of climate change, and that failure to do so could risk global GDP being 20% lower than it otherwise might be. Because carbon capture and storage is as yet widely unproven, and its long term effectiveness (such as in containing carbon dioxide 'leaks') unknown, and because of current costs of alternative fuels these policy responses largely rest on faith on technological change.

On the other hand, Nigel Lawson claimed that people in a hundred years' time would be "seven times as well off as we are today", therefore it is not reasonable to impose sacrifices on the "much poorer present generation".

Defining Economic Growth

The simplest definition of economic growth is an increase in real gross domestic product (GDP) (that is, GDP adjusted for inflation). The growth rate of real GDP is the percentage change in real GDP from one year to the next. We can express the rate of growth in, for example, the period 2004-2005, as follows:

Growth rate of GDP = [GDP (2005)-GDP (2004)]/ GDP (2004) × 100 U.S. real GDP in 2004 was 10.76 trillion and in 2005 it was 11.13 trillion. Thus the growth rate of real U.S. GDP from 2004 to 2005 was (11.13 – 10.76) / 10.76 = (0.37) / 10.76 = 0.034 or 3.4%. For purposes of evaluating how economic growth can feed into economic development it is often helpful to focus on the growth rate of GDP per capita—that is, output per person—rather than simply on overall output. Mathematically, GDP per capita is expressed as:

GDP per capita = GDP / Population.

The growth rates of GDP, population, and GDP per capita are related in the following way:

Growth Rate of GDP = Growth Rate of Population + Growth Rate of GDP per capita or:

Growth Rate of GDP per capita = Growth Rate of GDP – Growth Rate of Population.

Economic Growth in the ADE/ASR model. Economic growth increases the maximum capacity of the economy. It involves both supply-side and demand-side expansions, and does not necessarily involve a change in the rate of inflation. Thus, for example, an economy that has a GDP growth rate of 4% and a population growth rate of 2% would have a per capita GDP growth rate of 2%. The per capita GDP growth rate is especially important because it indicates the actual increase in average income being experienced by the people of the country. If a country had a 2% GDP growth rate, but a 3% population growth rate, its per capita GDP growth rate would actually be negative, at - 1%. The people would on average be getting poorer each year, even though the overall economy is growing. A more positive way of putting it is that, for people's incomes on average to increase over time, the GDP growth rate must exceed the rate of population growth.

In terms of the Aggregate Supply and Demand (ASR/ADE) graphs, economic growth can be shown as a rightward shift of the ASR, increasing the economy's maximum capacity. If this kind of increase in aggregate supply took place without any shift in ADE, its effects would include growth in output and a declining rate of inflation. In practice, however, economic growth is usually accompanied by, and at least in part is often caused by, an increase in aggregate demand. Thus a more typical pattern for economic growth would be for both the ADE and ASR curves to shift to the right. In this case output clearly rises, but the effect on inflation is ambiguous.

Modelling Economic Growth

What causes economic output to increase? One way that output can increase is if there is an expansion in the inputs used to produce it. There are five kinds of capital. Human-produced capital is called manufactured capital to distinguish it from the other kinds of capital. Land and natural resources are natural capital, and all the skills and knowledge possessed by humans are also a kind of capital – human capital. We also note the importance of social and financial capital, which both refer to institutional arrangements that make production possible.

Economists sometimes think about output as being generated according to a "production function," which is a mathematical relation between various inputs and the level of output. In the most general sense we might say that the output of an economy should be expressed as a function of flows from all the different types of capital that make production possible. The inputs to the production function are commonly referred to as factors of production. In the production functions most commonly used by economists, the factors that are emphasized are manufactured capital and labour. Sometimes, but not always, natural resources also are included.

One very influential, and more specific, model of economic growth was developed by economist Robert Solow in 1957. In his model, he assumed that an economy-wide production function can be written in the simple form:

$$Y = A\ K^{0.3}\ L^{0.7}$$

where Y is aggregate output, A is a number based on the current state of technology as described below, K is a quantitative measure of the size of the stock of manufactured capital, and L the quantity of labour used during the period of time. K and L are the only factors of production explicitly included in the model. Both capital and labour are needed for the production of output, with the exponents in the equation reflecting their relative contributions.

A is called total factor productivity, and includes all contributions to total production not already reflected in levels of K and L. Often, "total factor productivity" has been interpreted as reflecting the way in which technological innovation allows capital and labour to be used in more effective and valuable ways. For example, the development of computer word-processing greatly increased efficiency compared to the use of typewriters. Typewriters, which seem antique to us today, were themselves a huge productive advance over clerical work using pen and paper. This process of improved technological methods has resulted in an increase in labour productivity – more output can now be produced with fewer labour-hours.

After some mathematical manipulations, the production function above can be converted to an equation for the growth rate of output per worker as a function of "total factor productivity" and the growth rate of manufactured capital per worker: Growth rate of output per worker = growth rate of total factor productivity + 0.3 (growth rate of manufactured capital per worker) For example, if "total factor productivity" grows at 1% per year and capital per worker grows at 2% per year, this equation says that output per worker will grow at 1.6% per year (1% + (0.3)2% = 1.6%). This became known as the "growth accounting" equation.

Note that output per worker is what is commonly referred to as "labour productivity". While labour productivity and GDP per capita are not quite equivalent (some people in the population do not work, for example), they are obviously closely related. Thus, this model implies that the way to raise income per capita—to achieve economic growth—

is to increase the amount of capital that each person works with (the second term) and improve technology.

The use of the Solow growth model served to highlight some important factors in economic growth. In particular, the model led to much discussion of the role of savings in providing the basis for growing levels of manufactured capital per worker. Technological change also received attention, since this was thought to be the main driver behind growth in the value of "A." For many years, economists tended to treat growth as primarily a matter of encouraging savings, investment, and the creation and dissemination of technology.

In more recent years, other economists have suggested that perhaps this model has directed too much attention to savings and technology. Some have argued that other factors such as good institutions that support markets, innovations in the organization of work, or access to global markets should be thought of as equally important in promoting economic growth. It is not helpful, they suggest, to fold all issues of social, human, financial and natural capital into just one, rather vague, "A" term.

Country Per Capita Income, Country GDP Per Capita

In common parlance, news reports and economic forecasts, country per capita income is considered as an indicator of a country's economic well being. Gross domestic product or GDP is an approximate measure of the market value of all goods and services produced in a country during a specific period.

How to Calculate Country per Capita Income

When country GDP per capita is calculated, it is done by dividing the nominal or real GDP by the country's population. When the GDP is adjusted for inflation, it is called nominal GDP.

One method of calculation is to consider GDP at its purchasing power parity (PPP). The alternate method includes making inferences from nominal GDP figures.

Country per Capita Income as Economic Indicator

Country per capita is used to measure a country's financial well being, particularly in comparison with other regions or nations. That is one reason why per capita income figures are expressed in terms of international currencies, such as US dollars. For a country, it goes beyond being a mathematical formula of economic growth as it also reveals the quality and standard of living of its people. For economists, however, an increase in country per capita income signifies national economic growth.

Economists and policy planners use country per capita income figures to:

- estimate future trends of national economy.
- use these figures to devise apt strategies to tackle potential fiscal threats to the economy.
- use favourable figures to propel a country's monetary activities.
- strengthen a country's economic climate.
- devise structural adjustments to avert rising inflation in the wake of high purchasing power.

Drawbacks of Country per Capita Income

Just as a coin has two sides, the merits and drawbacks of country per capita income are highly debated.

Drawbacks include:

- Gives no exact figure pertaining to domestic income levels.
- Excludes the effects of economic differences existing in the society.
- Prevailing economic differences threaten national stability even as it maintains high per capita income figures.
- Excludes unregulated economic transactions such as black money and bartering.
- Excludes production activity or reconstruction work due to natural disasters.
- Tax evaders can easily hamper per capita income data.

Drawbacks are many but its benefits outweigh them, which is why it continues to be used by experts as a key economic indicator of a country's economic progress.

Compound Rates of Growth

In the modern version of an old legend, an investment banker asks to be paid by placing one penny on the first square of a chessboard, two pennies on the second square, four on the third, etc. If the banker had asked that only the white squares be used, the initial penny would have doubled in value thirty-one times, leaving $21.5 million on the last square. Using both the black and the white squares would have made the penny grow to $92 million billion.

People are reasonably good at forming estimates based on addition, but for operations such as compounding that depend on repeated multiplication, we systematically underestimate how quickly things grow. As a result, we often lose sight of how important the average rate of growth is for an economy. For an investment banker, the choice between a payment that doubles with every square on the chessboard and one that doubles with every other square is more important than any other part of the contract. Who cares whether the payment is in pennies, pounds, or pesos? For a nation, the choices that determine whether income doubles with every generation, or instead with every other generation, dwarf all other economic policy concerns.

Growth in Income per Capita

You can figure out how long it takes for something to double by dividing the growth rate into the number 72. In the twenty-five years between 1950 and 1975, income per capita in India grew at the rate of 1.8 percent per year. At this rate, income doubles every forty years because 72 divided by 1.8 equals 40. In the twenty-five years between 1975 and 2000, income per capita in China grew at almost 6 percent per year. At this rate, income doubles every twelve years.

These differences in doubling times have huge effects for a nation, just as they do for our banker. In the same forty-year time span that it would take the Indian economy to double at its slower growth rate, income would double three times—to eight times its initial level—at China's faster growth rate.

From 1950 to 2000, growth in income per capita in the United States lay between these two extremes, averaging 2.3 percent per year. From 1950 to 1975, India, which started at a level of income per capita that was less than 7 percent of that in the United States, was falling even farther behind. Between 1975 and 2000, China, which started at an even lower level, was catching up.

China grew so quickly partly because it started so far behind. Rapid growth could be achieved in large part by letting firms bring in ideas about how to create value that were already in use in the rest of the world. The interesting question is why India could not manage the same trick, at least between 1950 and 1975.

Growth and Recipes

Economic growth occurs whenever people take resources and rearrange them in ways that make them more valuable. A useful metaphor for production in an economy comes from the kitchen. To create valuable final products, we mix inexpensive ingredients together according to a recipe. The cooking one can do is limited by the supply of ingredients, and most cooking in the economy produces undesirable side effects. If economic growth could be achieved only by doing more and more of the same kind of cooking, we would eventually run out of raw materials and suffer from unacceptable levels of pollution and nuisance. Human history teaches us, however, that economic growth springs from better recipes, not just from more cooking. New recipes generally produce fewer unpleasant side effects and generate more economic value per unit of raw material.

Take one small example. In most coffee shops, you can now use the same size lid for small, medium, and large cups of coffee. That was not true as recently as 1995. That small change in the geometry of the cups means that a coffee shop can serve customers at lower cost. Store owners need to manage the inventory for only one type of lid. Employees can replenish supplies more quickly throughout the day. Customers can get their coffee just a bit faster. Although big discoveries such as the transistor, antibiotics, and the electric motor attract most of the attention, it takes millions of little discoveries like the new design for the cup and lid to double a nation's average income.

Every generation has perceived the limits to growth that finite resources and undesirable side effects would pose if no new recipes or ideas were discovered. And every generation has underestimated the potential for finding new recipes and ideas. We consistently fail to grasp how many ideas remain to be discovered. The difficulty is the same one we have with compounding: possibilities do not merely add up; they multiply.

In a branch of physical chemistry known as exploratory synthesis, chemists try mixing selected elements together at different temperatures and pressures to see what comes out. About a decade ago, one of the hundreds of compounds discovered this way—a mixture of copper, yttrium, barium, and oxygen—was found to be a superconductor at temperatures far higher than anyone had previously thought possible. This discovery may ultimately have far-reaching implications for the storage and transmission of electrical ENERGY.

To get some sense of how much scope there is for more such discoveries, we can calculate as follows. The periodic table contains about a hundred different types of atoms, which means that the number of combinations made up of four different elements is about 100 × 99 × 98 × 97 = 94,000,000. A list of numbers like 6, 2, 1, 7 can represent the proportions for using the four elements in a recipe. To keep things simple, assume that the numbers in the list must lie between 1 and 10, that no fractions are allowed, and that the smallest number must always be 1. Then there are about 3,500 different sets of proportions for each choice of four elements, and 3,500 × 94,000,000 (or 330,000,000,000) different recipes in total. If laboratories around the world evaluated one thousand recipes each day, it would take nearly a million years to go through them all. (If you like these combinatorial calculations, try to figure out how many different coffee drinks it is possible to order at your local shop. Instead of moving around stacks of cup lids, baristas now spend their time tailoring drinks to individual palates).

In fact, the previous calculation vastly underestimates the amount of exploration that remains to be done because mixtures can be made of more than four elements, fractional proportions can be selected, and a wide variety of pressures and temperatures can be used during mixing.

Even after correcting for these additional factors, this kind of calculation only begins to suggest the range of possibilities. Instead of just mixing elements together in a disorganized fashion, we can use chemical reactions to combine elements such as hydrogen and carbon into ordered structures like polymers or proteins. To see how far this kind of process can take us, imagine the ideal chemical refinery. It would convert abundant, renewable resources into a product that humans value. It would be smaller than a car, mobile so that it could search out its own inputs, capable of maintaining the temperature necessary for its reactions within narrow bounds, and able to automatically heal most system failures. It would build replicas of itself for use after it wears out, and it would do all of this with little human supervision. All we would have to do is get it to stay still periodically so that we could hook up some pipes and drain off the final product.

This refinery already exists. It is the milk cow. And if nature can produce this structured collection of hydrogen, carbon, and miscellaneous other atoms by meandering along one particular evolutionary path of trial and error (albeit one that took hundreds of millions of years), there must be an unimaginably large number of valuable structures and recipes for combining atoms that we have yet to discover.

Objects and Ideas

Thinking about ideas and recipes changes how one thinks about economic policy (and cows). A traditional explanation for the persistent poverty of many less-developed countries is that they lack objects such as natural resources or capital goods. But Taiwan started with little of either and still grew rapidly. Something else must be involved. Increasingly, emphasis is shifting to the notion that it is ideas, not objects, that poor countries lack. The knowledge needed to provide citizens of the poorest countries with a vastly improved standard of living already exists in the advanced countries. If a poor nation invests in EDUCATION and does not destroy the incentives for its citizens to acquire ideas from the rest of the world, it can rapidly take advantage of the publicly available part of the worldwide stock of knowledge. If, in addition, it offers incentives for privately held ideas to be put to use within its borders—for example, by protecting foreign patents, copyrights, and licenses; by permitting direct investment by foreign firms; by protecting property rights; and by avoiding heavy regulation and high marginal tax rates—its citizens can soon work in state-of-the-art productive activities.

Some ideas such as insights about public health are rapidly adopted by less-developed countries. As a result, life expectancy in poor countries is catching up with that in the leaders faster than income per capita. Yet governments in poor countries continue to impede the flow of many other ideas, especially those with commercial value. Automobile producers in North America clearly recognize that they can learn from ideas developed in the rest of the world. But for decades, car firms in India operated in a government-created protective time warp. The Hillman and Austin cars produced in England in the 1950s continued to roll off production lines in India through the 1980s. After independence, India's commitment to closing itself off and striving for self-sufficiency was as strong as Taiwan's commitment to acquiring foreign ideas and participating fully in world markets. The outcomes—grinding poverty in India and opulence in Taiwan—could hardly be more disparate.

A poor country like India can achieve enormous increases in standards of living merely by letting in the ideas held by companies from industrialized nations. With a series of economic reforms that started in the 1980s and deepened in the early 1990s, India has begun to open itself up to these opportunities. For some of its citizens, such as the software developers who now work for firms located in the rest of the world, these improvements in standards of living have become a reality. This same type of opening up is causing a spectacular transformation of life in China. Its growth in the last twenty-five years of the twentieth century was driven to a very large extent by foreign investment by multinational firms.

Leading countries like the United States, Canada, and the members of the EUROPEAN UNION cannot stay ahead merely by adopting ideas developed elsewhere. They must offer strong incentives for discovering new ideas at home, and this is not easy to do. The same characteristic that makes an idea so valuable—everybody can use it at the same time—also means that it is hard to earn an appropriate rate of return on investments in ideas. The many people who benefit from a new idea can too easily free ride on the efforts of others.

After the transistor was invented at Bell Laboratories, many applied ideas had to be developed before this basic science discovery yielded any commercial value. By now, private firms have developed improved recipes that have brought the cost of a transistor down to less than a millionth of its former level. Yet most of the benefits from those discoveries have been reaped not by the innovating firms, but by the users of the transistors. In 1985, I paid a thousand dollars per million transistors for memory in my computer. In 2005, I paid less than ten dollars per million, and yet I did nothing to deserve or help pay for this windfall. If the government confiscated most of the oil from major discoveries and gave it to consumers, oil companies would do much less exploration. Some oil would still be found serendipitously, but many promising opportunities for exploration would be bypassed. Both oil companies and consumers would be worse off. The leakage of benefits such as those from improvements in the transistor acts just like this kind of confiscatory tax and has the same effect on incentives for exploration. For this reason, most economists support government funding for basic scientific research. They also recognize, however, that basic research grants by themselves will not provide the incentives to discover the many small applied ideas needed to transform basic ideas such as the transistor or Web search into valuable products and services.

It takes more than scientists in universities to generate progress and growth. Such seemingly mundane forms of discovery as product and process engineering or the development of new business models can have huge benefits for society as a whole. There are, to be sure, some benefits for the firms that make these discoveries, but not enough to generate innovation at the ideal rate. Giving firms tighter patents and copyrights over new ideas would increase the incentives to make new discoveries, but might also make it much more expensive to build on previous discoveries. Tighter intellectual property rights could therefore be counterproductive and might slow growth.

The one safe measure governments have used to great advantage has been subsidies for education to increase the supply of talented young scientists and engineers. They are the basic input into the discovery process, the fuel that fires the innovation engine. No one can know where newly trained young people will end up working, but nations that are willing to educate more of them and let them follow their instincts can be confident that they will accomplish amazing things.

Meta-ideas

Perhaps the most important ideas of all are meta-ideas—ideas about how to support the production and transmission of other ideas. In the seventeenth century, the British invented the modern concept of a patent that protects an invention. North Americans invented the modern research university and the agricultural extension service in the nineteenth century, and peer-reviewed competitive grants for basic research in the twentieth. The challenge now facing all of the industrialized countries is to invent new institutions that encourage a higher level of applied, commercially relevant research and development in the private sector.

As national markets for talent and education merge into unified global markets, opportunities for important policy innovation will surely emerge. In basic research, the United States is still the undisputed leader, but in key areas of education, other countries are surging ahead. Many of them have already discovered how to train a larger fraction of their young people as scientists and engineers.

We do not know what the next major idea about how to support ideas will be. Nor do we know where it will emerge. There are, however, two safe predictions. First, the country that takes the lead in the twenty-first century will be the one that implements an innovation that more effectively supports the production of new ideas in the private sector. Second, new meta-ideas of this kind will be found.

Only a failure of imagination—the same failure that leads the man on the street to suppose that everything has already been invented—leads us to believe that all of the relevant institutions have been designed and all of the policy levers have been found. For social scientists, every bit as much as for physical scientists, there are vast regions to explore and wonderful surprises to discover.

The Size and Functions of Government and Economic Growth

From the standpoint of economic stability, the U.S. economy has performed very well in recent years. The current expansion is now into its eighth year, and the economy continues to grow. It has been 15 years since the United States has experienced a serious recession. This is the good news. But there is also another story that has been largely ignored: The real growth rate of the United States has persistently declined during the last three decades. Even with the expansion of the 1990s, the average growth rate during the current decade is less than half that of the 1960s, and only about two-thirds of the figure achieved during the instability of the 1970s.

The experience of other developed nations has been similar—their economies have been expanding, but at much slower rates than was previously the case. The sluggish growth of developed economies is particularly surprising in light of another trend. Following the collapse of central planning and fall of the Berlin Wall, economic liberalism has become much more acceptable. In recent years, the world has moved toward greater economic freedom in several areas. Many countries have reduced their tariff rates, liberalized (or eliminated) interest rate and exchange rate controls, lowered their top marginal tax rates, and followed monetary policies more consistent with price stability. Economic theory indicates and a number of studies have shown that these moves toward economic freedom have promoted economic growth.

Despite these encouraging trends, however, one major component of economic freedom—size of government expenditures has generally been moving in the opposite direction. In recent decades, there has been substantial growth in the size of government as a share of the economy, particularly in high-income industrial nations. This study examines this expansion in the size of government and its impact on economic growth.

Exhibit 1 illustrates the growth of government in countries that are members of the Organization for Economic Cooperation and Development (OECD). Data are presented for all 23 countries that were OECD members during 1960-96. *Measured as a share of gross domestic product (GDP)*, total government expenditures have grown substantially in every one of the OECD countries.

In 1960, the government expenditures of the group averaged 27 percent of GDP; by 1996 they had grown to 48 percent of GDP. This is a staggering increase, especially because Exhibit 1 measures government growth very conservatively.

Why do Government Expenditures Affect Economic Growth?

In theory the relationship between government expenditures and economic growth is ambiguous. Long ago, Thomas Hobbes (1651) described life without government as "nasty, brutish, and short" and argued that the law and order provided by government was a necessary component of civilized life. Taking the Hobbesian view, certain functions of government such as the protection of individuals and their property and the operation of a court system to resolve disputes should enhance economic growth. Viewed from another angle, secure property rights, enforcement of contracts and a stable monetary regime provide the foundation for the smooth operation of a market economy.

Governments can enhance growth through efficient provision of this infrastructure. In addition, there are a few goods—economists call them "public goods"—that markets may find troublesome to provide because their nature makes it difficult (or costly) to establish a close link between payment for and receipt of such goods. Roads and national defence fall into this category. Government provision of such goods might also promote economic growth.

However, as government continues to grow and more and more resources are allocated by political rather than market forces, three major factors suggest that the beneficial effects on economic growth will wane and eventually become negative. First, the higher taxes and/or additional borrowing required to finance government expenditures exert a negative effect on the economy. As government takes more and more of the earnings of workers, their incentive to invest, to take risks, and to undertake productivity-enhancing activities, decreases. Like taxes, borrowing will crowd out private investment and it will also lead to higher future taxes. Thus, even if the productivity of government expenditures did not decline, the disincentive effects of taxation and borrowing, as resources are shifted from the private sector to the public sector, would exert a negative impact on economic growth.

Second, as government grows relative to the market sector, diminishing returns will be confronted. Suppose that a government initially concentrates on those functions for which it is best suited (for example, activities such as protection of property rights, provision of an unbiased legal system, development of a stable monetary framework, and provision of national defence).

By performing these core functions well, the government provides the framework for the efficient operation of markets and thereby enhances economic growth. As it expands into other areas, such as the provision of infrastructure and education, the government might still improve performance and promote growth, even though the private sector has demonstrated its ability to effectively provide these things. If the expansion in government continues, however, expenditures are increasingly channeled into less and less productive activities. Eventually, as the government becomes larger and undertakes more activities for which it is ill suited, negative returns set in and economic growth is retarded. This is likely to result when governments become involved in the provision of private goods—goods for which the consumption benefits accrue to the individual consumers. Goods like food, housing, medical service, and child care fall into this category. There is no reason to expect that governments will either allocate or provide such goods more efficiently than the market sector. Finally, the political process is much less dynamic than the market process. While competition rewards alertness, it also imposes swift and sure punishment on those who make bad decisions and thereby reduce the value of resources. Adjustment to change is much slower in the public sector. By way of comparison with markets, the required time for the weeding out of errors (for example, bad investments) and adjustments to changing circumstances, new information, and improved technologies is more lengthy for governments. This is a major shortcoming as it relates to economic growth. To a large degree, growth is a discovery process. As entrepreneurs discover new and improved technologies, better methods of production, and opportunities that were previously overlooked, they are able to combine resources into goods and services that are more highly valued. This is the central element of wealth creation and growth. Reliance on markets and the presence of economic freedom facilitate this process. Clearly, the expansion of government relative to the market sector slows this important source of economic growth.

In summary, government provision of both (a) an infrastructure for the operation of a market economy and (b) a limited set of public goods can provide a framework conducive for economic growth. However, as the size of government continues to grow, the (a) disincentive effects of higher taxes and borrowing, (b) diminishing returns, and (c) a slowing of the discovery and wealth-creation process will become more and more important. Eventually, these factors will dominate and the marginal government expenditures will exert a negative impact on growth.

Exhibit 2 illustrates the relationship between size of government and economic growth, *assuming that governments undertake activities based on their rate of return.* As the size of government, measured on the horizontal axis, expands from zero (complete anarchy), initially the growth rate of the economy—measured on the vertical axis—increases. The A to B range of the curve illustrates this situation. As government continues to grow as a share of the economy, expenditures are channeled into less productive (and later counterproductive) activities, causing the rate of economic growth to diminish and eventually decline. The range of the curve beyond B illustrates this point. In the real world, governments may not undertake activities based on their rate of return and comparative advantage. Small government by itself is not an asset. When a small government fails to focus on and efficiently provide core functions such as protection of persons and property, a legal system that helps with the enforcement of contacts, and a stable monetary regime, there is no reason to believe that it will promote economic growth. This has been (and still is) the case in many less developed countries. Governments—including those that are small—can be expected to register slow or even negative rates of economic growth when these core functions are poorly performed. Unless proper adjustment is made for how well the core functions are performed, the empirical relationship between size of government and economic growth is likely to be a loose one, particularly when the analysis involves a diverse set of economies.

A fundamental model of economic growth developed by Robert Solow (1956) suggests that while some economies may be wealthier than others, in the long run they should all grow at the same rate. More recent work has suggested that not only do economies actually have substantially different growth rates over lengthy time periods, there are also good theoretical reasons for believing that countries can maintain the different rates same), the long-term consequences of economic policies that impede growth are less severe. This study will examine the issue empirically by looking at how the size of government has affected economic growth.

Government Expenditures and Economic Growth in the United States

Exhibit 3 A looks at this growth in government expenditures in the United States, and shows that the increase in government expenditures is primarily due to the growth of transfers and subsidies, rather than in the core areas of government. The bars in Exhibit 3A show average government expenditures for all years in each decade, or in the case of the 1990s, partial decade.

In the 1960s government expenditures at all levels of government averaged 29.9 percent of GDP, and increased to 32.8 percent of GDP in the 1970s, 34.7 percent of GDP in the 1980s, and 35.3 percent of GDP in the 1990s. The breakdown of components in Exhibit 3A shows that while net interest expenditures almost doubled as a percent of GDP, even in the 1990s interest expenditures amounted to only 2.2 percent of GDP. National defence expenditures declined substantially over the entire period, and there was a slight increase in non-defence purchases.

While non-defence purchases were higher in the 1970s than the 1960s, they have been virtually unchanged during the last three decades. *As a share of GDP*, transfers and subsidies have more than doubled since the 1960s. They have risen from 6.4 percent of GDP in the 1960s to 13.5 percent of GDP during the 1990s. Thus, transfers and subsidies consumed an additional 7.1 percent of GDP in the 1990s than during the 1960s. The share of GDP devoted to total government expenditures rose by 5.4 percent over that same period (and 6.2 percent between 1960 and 1996). Thus, transfers and subsidies by themselves fully account for the growth of government as a share of GDP in the United States. This expansion in the size of the transfer sector is likely to reduce economic growth. Transfers and subsidies that enlarge the size of government will require higher tax rates, which will reduce productive incentives. Compared to expenditures in core areas, additional government expenditures on transfers will exert little positive impact on growth. Transfers and subsidies also bring with them the problem of rentseeking. Rent-seeking (or subsidyseeking) occurs when people attempt to enhance their wealth by trying to direct government benefits to themselves rather than by engaging in productive activity. Rent-seeking benefits the recipient of the rents, but it is a drain on the economy as a whole. The terminology is somewhat unfortunate because, in this context, "rent" does not mean a payment to a property owner, as it does in common language.

Rather, it is referring to transfers received by the recipient that are paid for by others. When people try to obtain income by having the government transfer benefits to themselves rather than by providing goods and services to others, economic growth suffers. Exhibit 3B shows gross investment as a percentage of GDP for the same time periods covered in Exhibit 3A.

While government expenditures increased as a share of GDP during every decade, gross investment fell. Of course, other factors may be at work here, but there are several reasons to expect that the growth of transfers and subsidies will retard investment. The increased availability of transfers and subsidies will increase the incentive of both businesses and organized interest groups to seek gains through government largess rather than increases in productivity. Since the direction of transfers is generally either from those with high income to those with lower levels of income, or from working people to retired people, they shift income away from people with high savings rates and toward those who save less of their income. The predictable effects are a reduction in total savings, higher real interest rates and a decline in the rate of investment, particularly investment financed by Americans. In addition, much of the growth in the transfer sector (and overall size of government) has been financed with government borrowing. This too is likely to place upward pressure on interest rates and reduce the level of investment.

Evidence From Oecd Countries

Compared to most other countries around the world, the institutional arrangements and income levels of the 23 long-standing OECD members are relatively similar. Politically, all OECD countries are stable democracies. Their legal structures generally reflect a commitment to the rule of law. Monetary arrangements have been stable enough to avoid hyperinflation during the post World War II era. In the area of international trade, OECD members have been at the forefront of those promoting more liberal trade policies within the framework of GATT and the World Trade Organization. The homogeneity among these countries adds to the significance of comparisons within this group.

Despite their similarities, the size of government as a share of the economy has varied substantially among OECD countries (and across time periods). What impact has this variation had on economic growth? This section views relevant data from several perspectives in an effort to answer this question.

More International Evidence

In order to add breadth, data were assembled on size of government and other factors thought to influence growth for 60 countries, including both less developed and high-income industrial economies. Because this is a more diverse group than OECD members, adjustment for differences in political economy characteristics is important. Because of the unavailability of some of the required variables for years prior to 1980, our analysis covers the 1980-95 period.

Exhibit 8 summarizes the statistical results for this larger and more diverse data set. Results are presented for four different regression models. All countries for which the required data could be obtained are included in the analysis. The average annual growth rate of real GDP during 1980-95 is the dependent variable.

The first four independent variables are measures of government expenditures and their changes. In addition to these size of government variables, alternative models also consider the impact of (a) security of property rights, (b) variability in the rate of inflation, (c) schooling (investment in human capital), and (d) investment in physical capital. These "control variables" are included in order to help us better isolate the independent effects of size of government.

The data on security of property rights come from the *International Country Risk Guide,* a private rating service that has tracked the political, financial and economic risks accompanying business and investment activities in various countries since 1982. The credibility of these ratings is enhanced by the fact that the business has survived by marketing them to investors and businesses over a lengthy time period. While the ratings cover several areas, three of them pertain specifically to the security of property rights and presence of rule of law. These three factors are (a) risk of expropriation, (b) risk of contact violation, and (c) presence of rule of law.

We placed the ratings on a scale of one to ten; a higher rating is indicative of more secure property rights and stronger support for rule of law principles. Because the data series begins in 1982, the initial rating is for 1982 (or earliest available year) rather than 1980. Components for both the property rights rating in 1982 and the *change in the rating* during the 1982-1995 period are incorporated into the analysis. High and variable rates of inflation may also retard economic growth. Higher inflation rates reduce the value of a nation's currency and encourage people to shift resources away from production and toward activities designed to protect themselves from inflation. Inflation also lowers the informational content of prices. Nations with high levels of inflation also tend to have high variability in their inflation rates, but there is a slightly stronger statistical relationship between the variability of the inflation rate (as measured by its standard deviation) and GDP growth than is true for the level of inflation. Thus, the standard deviation of the inflation rate was used to measure the impact of inflation on economic growth. Both economic theory and prior research suggest that investment in both human and physical capital can be expected to enhance economic growth.

We use data on increases between 1980 and 1995 in the mean years of schooling for persons age 25 and over as a measure of improvements in the level of human capital. The physical investment component is the average investment rate as a share of GDP during 1980-95. Of course, increases in both of these variables are expected to positively impact economic growth. In addition to the size of government variables, Equation 1 of Exhibit 8 includes the initial property rights rating in 1982, the *change* in the rating between 1982 and 1995, and standard deviation of the inflation rate in the model. Both property right variables are highly significant and the inflation variable is also significant at the 90 percent level. With regard to the size of government variables, the coefficients for the *level* of government expenditures as a share of GDP, and the *changes* between 1980 and 1985 and between 1985 and 1990 were all negative and highly significant. The adjusted. R2 of Equation 1 indicates that the variables incorporated into this model explain 48 percent of the variation in growth rates among this diverse set of countries.

What do the coefficients for the size of government variables indicate about the impact of government expenditures on the growth of economies? The coefficient for the *level* variable indicates that a 10 percentage point increase in size of government *at the beginning of the period* was associated with approximately a six-tenths of a percentage point reduction in annual growth during the entire 15-year period. The coefficients for the *change* in size of government variables between 1980 and 1985 and between 1985 and 1990 indicate that a 10 percentage point increase during each of these periods reduced the annual growth of real GDP by 1.15 percentage points during the 1980-95 period. While the change in size of government between 1990 and 1995 is negative, it is insignificant. The larger coefficients (and greater significance) of the variables reflecting the changes in the size of government for the earlier five-year periods compared to the five years of the 1990s make sense. After all, the expansion in government between 1980 and 1985 (and 1985 and 1990) will influence growth for a decade or more of the 1980-95 period, whereas the government growth of the 1990s will exert an impact over only a short portion of 1980-95 period. The schooling variable to the model. The changes in the years of schooling between 1980 and 1995 exert the expected positive impact and the variable is significant at the 95 percent level of confidence. With the exception of the inflation variable, all of the other variables remain significant. Equation 3 deletes the schooling variable from the model and inserts the investment rate. The investment variable has the expected sign and it is significant at the 90 percent level of confidence.

Finally, Equation 4 incorporates both the schooling and investment variables into the model along with the property rights, inflation, and size of government measures. In this more comprehensive model, both the initial level of government expenditures and the change during both of the five-year periods of the 1980s continue to be significant at the 90 percent level or more. The property rights and schooling variables are also highly significant. While the inflation and investment variables have the expected signs, they are no longer significant. The R2 for Equation 4 indicates that the variables of this model explain 54 percent of the variation in the ratings among this diverse set of countries.

The results of Exhibit 8 illustrate that there is a strong positive correlation between the security of property rights and economic growth. This relationship highlights the importance of a legal structure that protects property rights, helps with the enforcement of contacts, and provides a fair mechanism—rule of law—for the settlement of disputes between parties. As we previously discussed, core functions of government in this area are vitally important for the smooth operation of a market economy. Many governments—particularly those of less developed nations—perform this function poorly. Economic stagnation and poverty are the highly visible side effects. Exhibit 8 also indicates that improvements in human capital are an important source of growth. Increases in educational attainment consistently lead to increases in the growth rate of GDP. While the statistical links between growth and the price level stability and investment variables were weaker, their significance may well have been reduced because of their correlation with other variables in the model.

The primary reason for including the "control variables" of Exhibit 8 was to see whether size of government exerted a strong independent impact on the growth of real GDP. The results indicate that it does.

Even after accounting for differences across countries in protection of property rights, inflation, education, and investment, the level of government expenditures at the beginning of the period and the growth of those expenditures during the first decade of the 15- year period exerted statistically significant effects on the growth of GDP during 1980-95. As in the case of the OECD nations, the magnitude of these coefficients indicates that the negative impact of size of government on growth is sizeable.

Evidence from OECD Nations with Shrinking Government

The growth of government has been so pervasive in the last half of the twentieth century that there have been only a few instances where nations have substantially reduced its size. This is particularly true for the high-income industrial economies. Exhibit 9 isolates the only three instances of a substantial decline in government expenditures as a share of the economy among OECD countries during the 1960-96 period. The first case is that of Ireland, which saw government expenditures as a share of GDP go from 28 percent in 1960 to 52.3 percent in 1986.

This situation was reversed during the 1987-96 period. As a share of GDP, government expenditures declined from the 52.3 percent level of 1986 to 37.7 percent in 1996, a reduction of 14.6 percentage points. From 1960 to 1977 government expenditures increased from 28 percent to 43.7 percent, and Ireland's real GDP growth rate was 4.3 percent. It declined to 3.4 percent during 1977-86, as the government further expanded to 52.3 percent of GDP. During the recent decade of shrinking government, the annual growth rate in Ireland's real GDP rose to 5.4 percent. As government expenditures shrank in Ireland, Ireland's economic growth increased.

The experience of New Zealand is also revealing. Between 1974 and 1992, New Zealand's government expenditures as a share of GDP rose from 34.1 percent to 48.4 percent. Its average growth rate during this period was 1.2 percent. Recently New Zealand began moving in the opposite direction. The percentage of GDP devoted to government expenditures was reduced from 48.4 percent in 1992 to 42.3 percent in 1996, a reduction of 6.1 percentage points.

Compared to the earlier period, New Zealand's real GDP growth has increased by more than two percentage points to 3.9 percent. The United Kingdom provides additional evidence. Government's share of

GDP rose from 32.2 percent in 1960 to 47.2 percent in 1982. During this period, UK's GDP growth rate was 2.2 percent and there was widespread reference to the "British disease." Between 1982 and 1989, government's share of GDP declined by 6.5 percentage points to 40.7 percent. Responding, UK's rate of GDP growth increased from 2.2 percent to 3.7 percent. While shrinking government has been rare in the past few decades, evidence from places where government has shrunk is consistent with the hypothesis that larger government lowers economic growth. The evidence illustrates that if the size of government is reduced, higher rates of economic growth can be anticipated.

The Size of Government in High-growth Nations

The data in Exhibit 4 for OECD countries suggests that smaller government is correlated with faster rates of economic growth. While in theory government could be too small to provide the necessary environment for economic growth, the data in Exhibit 4 give no indication that any OECD government was excessively small at any time during 1960-96. Within the size of government range of this period, smaller government was consistently associated with more rapid economic growth.

Exhibit 10 probes this issue further by looking at government expenditures as a share of GDP for the 10 nations with the fastest rates of economic growth during 1980-95. The average annual per capita GDP growth of these countries ranged from 7.4 percent for South Korea to 4.2 percent for Malaysia. There are no OECD members in this group of fastest-growing economies.

The numbers in the table show total government expenditures as a share of GDP at five-year intervals during the 1975-95 period. The numbers in parentheses show non-investment government expenditures in cases where these figures are available. South Korea, the world's fastest-growing economy during this period, had government expenditures that were relatively stable at between 20 and 21 percent of GDP. Non-investment government expenditures in South Korea showed a steady decline from just over 15 percent of GDP to just over 10 percent during the two decade period, indicating that South Korea has increasingly been devoting government expenditures toward investment. The total government expenditures of Thailand, the second fastest-growing economy, were generally less than 20 percent of GDP throughout most of the period, and they also showed a trend toward increased government investment. Taiwan, third on the list, showed a substantial increase in total government expenditures, from 21.5 percent of GDP to 30.1 percent, but still ended the period with government expenditures well below the world average. Taiwan's non-investment government expenditures were still less than 20 percent of GDP. Singapore and Hong Kong, the next two countries, saw substantial declines in government expenditures as a percentage of GDP, and both countries had 1995 government expenditures well below 20 percent of GDP.

The average level of government expenditures of the 10 fastest-growing economies was 24.7 percent of GDP in 1995, compared to 25.2 percent in 1975. Thus, these economies were characterized by small and relatively stable government expenditures as a share of the economy. These characteristics were even more pronounced among the Top Five. Except for Taiwan, none of the five fastest-growing economies had government expenditures greater than 21 percent of GDP in 1995. The average level of government expenditures for the five fastest-growing economies was 20.1 percent of GDP in 1995, lower than the average for the Top 10.

The non-investment government expenditures of the five fastest-growing economies averaged less than 13 percent of GDP in 1995. Once again, the size of government figures from the world's fastest-growing economies are consistent with the hypothesis that the smaller the level of government expenditures, the higher the rate of GDP growth. Furthermore, in contrast with OECD countries, the tendency toward the growth of government was absent among the fast-growing economies.

The Growth-maximizing Level of Government Expenditures

A persuasive argument can be made for designing government policies in order to maximize the economy's rate of growth. In the long run, a strong economy is the best way to benefit all citizens. One need only look at the progress of the 20th century to see how economic growth has helped even those least well-off in the economy or compare the well-being of those in poverty in the United States with the typical standard of living in less-developed economies, to see why policies that foster economic growth are the key to long-term prosperity. If one wanted to design a government that maximized economic growth, how large would that government be? The data examined earlier give no indication because for every nation examined, none had governments so small that they impeded economic growth, even though there were several instances in which total government expenditures were less than 20 percent of GDP.

Because there is no evidence that any existing government is smaller than the growthmaximizing size of government, some other method must be used to surmise what size of government would maximize an economy's growth rate. One way to address the question would be to look at the size of the government within the framework of the theory discussed earlier in the paper. There are certain core functions of government that assist economic growth by protecting property rights and creating an environment conducive to growth. As economies expand beyond these core functions, larger government impedes growth because of: (a) the disincentive effects of taxes, (b) the tendency of government to expand into areas that are better suited for private sector production, (c) increased rent-seeking (rather than productive) activities, and (d) the crowding out of private investment.

Thus, one way to conjecture what level of government would maximize economic growth is to examine the size of public sector expenditures on these core functions.

What might fall into these core functions is itself a matter of debate. Exhibit 11 indicates the size of federal, state, and local government expenditures in the United States for various years for six categories that many would consider the core functions of government. Protection of persons and property would come high on the list, and the top section of Exhibit 11 shows the percentage of GDP devoted to this area, broken out to show several sub-components. Expenditures on the protection of persons and property have been expanding over the years, rising from 0.64 percent of GDP in 1960 to 1.5 percent of GDP in 1992. Despite this growth, these expenditures consumed a relatively small share of GDP even in the 1990s.

National defence and international affairs is another area that might be considered a core function of government. In most years it is the largest of the functions listed here, but has shown a considerable decline since the 1960s. The national security category was 9.3 percent of GDP in 1960, and after the end of the Cold War has fallen to approximately 5 percent in 1992.

One might debate whether education should even be included as a core function of government, because the private sector has shown itself quite capable of providing high-quality education. Nevertheless, education is a key component in economic growth, and most education in the United States (and around the world) is produced by government. Education's share of GDP increased substantially in the 1960s, from 3.69 percent in 1960 to 5.38 percent in 1970. It was only slightly more than that in 1992. Infrastructure is another area in which government might foster economic growth, even though the private sector has the capability to produce infrastructure without government.

Exhibit 11 shows government expenditures on (a) highways and (b) sewage, sanitation, and environmental protection. The combined government expenditures in these categories summed to less than two percent of GDP in 1992. The expenditures of the Federal Reserve System, which only constitute a tiny fraction of GDP, are also included.

3

Transition Economy

A transition economy or transitional economy is an economy which is changing from a centrally planned economy to a free market. Transition economies undergo economic liberalization (letting market forces set prices and lowering trade barriers), macroeconomic stabilization where immediate high inflation is brought under control, and restructuring and privatization in order to create a financial sector and move from public to private ownership of resources. These changes often may lead to increased inequality of incomes and wealth, dramatic inflation and a fall of GDP.

Transition process is usually characterized by the changing and creating of institutions, particularly private enterprises; changes in the role of the state, thereby, the creation of fundamentally different governmental institutions and the promotion of private-owned enterprises, markets and independent financial institutions.

Transition Indicators

The existence of private property rights may be the most basic element of a market economy and therefore implementation of these rights is the main indicator of transition process. According to the IMF the main ingredients of the transition process are:

- *Liberalization*–the process of allowing most prices to be determined in free markets and lowering trade barriers that had shut off contact with the price structure of the world's market economies.
- *Macroeconomic stabilization*–bringing inflation under control and lowering it over time, after the initial burst of high inflation

that follows from liberalization and the release of pent-up demand. This process requires discipline over the government budget and the growth of money and credit (that is, discipline in fiscal and monetary policy) and progress toward sustainable balance of payments.

- *Restructuring and privatization*–the creation of a viable financial sector and reforming the enterprises in these economies to render them capable of producing goods that could be sold in free markets and of transferring their ownership into private hands.
- *Legal and institutional reforms*–redefining the role of the state in these economies, establish the rule of law, and introduce appropriate competition policies.

According to Oleh Havrylyshyn and Thomas Wolf of the IMF, transition in a broad sense implies:

- liberalizing economic activity, prices, and market operations, along with reallocating resources to their most efficient use;
- developing indirect, market-oriented instruments for macroeconomic stabilization;
- achieving effective enterprise management and economic efficiency, usually through privatization;
- imposing hard budget constraints, which provides incentives to improve efficiency; and
- establishing an institutional and legal framework to secure property rights, the rule of law, and transparent market-entry regulations.

The EBRD developed set of indicators to measure the progress in transition. The classification system was originally created in the EBRD's 1994 Transition Report, but has been refined and amended in subsequent Reports. The EBRD's overall transition indicators are:

- Large-scale privatisation.
- Small-scale privatisation.
- Governance and enterprise restructuring.
- Price liberalisation.
- Trade and foreign exchange system.

- Competition policy.
- Banking reform and interest rate liberalisation.
- Securities markets and non-bank financial institutions.
- Infrastructure reform.

Process

Transition trajectories can be idiosyncratic. Some nations have been experimenting with market reform for several decades, while others are relatively recent adopters (e.g., Republic of Macedonia, Serbia and Montenegro). In some cases reforms have been accompanied with political upheaval, such as the overthrow of a dictator (Romania), the collapse of a government (the Soviet Union), a declaration of independence (Croatia), or integration with another country (East Germany). In other cases economic reforms have been adopted by incumbent governments with little interest in political change (China, Laos, Vietnam). Transition trajectories also differ in terms of the extent of central planning being relinquished (e.g. high centralized coordination among the CIS states) as well as the scope of liberalization efforts being undertaken (e.g. relatively limited in Romania).

According to the World Bank's "10 Years of Transition" report "... the wide dispersion in the productivity of labour and capital across types of enterprises at the onset of transition and the erosion of those differences between old and new sectors during the reform provide a natural definition of the end of transition." Mr. Vito Tanzi, Director of the IMF's Fiscal Affairs Department, gave definition that the transformation to a market economy is not complete until functioning fiscal institutions and reasonable and affordable expenditure programs, including basic social safety nets for the unemployed, the sick, and the elderly, are in place. Mr. Tanzi stated that these spending programs must be financed from public revenues generated—through taxation—without imposing excessive burdens on the private sector.

Countries in Transition

Although the term "transition economies" usually covers the countries of Central and Eastern Europe and the Former Soviet Union, this term may have a wider context. There are countries outside of Europe, emerging from a socialist-type command economy towards a market-based economy (e.g. China). Moreover, in a wider sense the definition of transition economy refers to all countries which attempt to change their basic constitutional elements towards market-style fundamentals. Their origin could be also in a post-colonial situation, in a heavily regulated Asian-style economy, in a Latin American post-dictatorship or even in a somehow economically underdeveloped country in Africa.

In 2000, IMF listed following countries as transitions economies: Albania, Armenia, Azerbaijan, Belarus, Bulgaria, Cambodia, China, Croatia, Georgia, Czech Republic, Estonia, Hungary, India, Laos, Latvia, Lithuania, Kazakhstan, Kyrgyz Republic, Republic of Macedonia, Moldova, Poland, Romania, Russia, Slovak Republic, Slovenia, Tajikistan, Turkmenistan, Ukraine, Uzbekistan and Vietnam. In addition, in 2002 the World Bank defined Bosnia and Herzegovina, and Federal Republic of Yugoslavia (later Serbia and Montenegro) as transition economies. Some World Bank studies also include Mongolia.

Eight countries, which joined the European Union on 1 May 2004 (Czech Republic, Estonia, Hungary, Latvia, Lithuania, Poland, Slovakia, Slovenia) have completed the transition process.

Branch of Economics

Transition economics is a special branch of economics dealing with the transformation of a planned economy to a market economy. It has become especially important after the collapse of Communism in Eastern Europe. Transition economics investigates how an economy should reform itself in order to endorse capitalism and democracy. There are usually two sides: one which argues for a rapid transformation and one which argues for a gradual approach. Gerard Roland's book *Transition and Economics. Politics, Markets and Firms* (MIT Press 2000) gives a good overview of the field.

Transition and Economics

The transition from socialism to capitalism in former socialist economies is one of the main economic events of the twentieth century. Not only does it affect the lives of approximately 1.65 billion people, but it is contributing to a shift in emphasis in economics from standard price and monetary theory to contracting and its institutional environment. Economic research in transition shows not only that institutions matter but also how their evolution toward higher efficiency depends on initial conditions and on sustained political support.

Unlike early policy literature on transition economics, which focused on the so-called Washington consensus, this book provides an overview of current research, analysing issues raised by transition for which economic theorists and policy makers had no ready answers. It shows how research on transition contributes to our understanding of capitalism as an economic system and of the dynamics of large-scale institutional change.

The book is divided into three parts. The first part looks at how large-scale reforms are decided dynamically through the political process. The second part looks at the general equilibrium and macroeconomic effects of liberalization in economies without preexisting markets. The third part looks at the economic behaviour of firms in the transition from state to private ownership and compares the effects of privatization, restructuring, and financial reform. Although focused on transition economics, the discussions are relevant to topics in political economics, development, public economics, corporate finance, and micro-and macroeconomics.

Transition Economics

The small town of Hohenwald Tennessee, population of around 4000 people, is taking small steps at greening up the community and region. Since 2006 a group of dedicated volunteers have been hosting events building on Hohenwald's efforts to make Lewis County, population of around 12,000 people, greener, safer, and more economically viable. This group, the Sonnenschein Green Initiative (SGI), focuses on proactively supporting local economic and community development strategies (LECD). SGI strives to support the following areas: local business owners, farmers, artisans and service providers; the creation of quality and long-term local employment; community networking opportunities and social events; creating an economy that has a total and sustainable economic return; and increasing goods and services exported rather than imported. SGI also focuses on 'green' development, as we see that creating a 'green' economy and 'greening up' our production and consumption will be the quickest and most effective way to achieve sustainable economic and community development. To SGI the word 'green' equals efficiency and less waste.

What does LECD have to do with energy efficiency? Every time an average US citizen consumes 1 lb. or resources, it took 15 times that amount of resources to produce that 1 lb. On average goods travel thousands of miles to get to your home. By localizing production of goods and services, communities can cut down on their power drain. The less travelling for consumers and employees and less freight shipping for producers means that we don't need to be such energy hogs.

The growing trend toward localization of food, energy, goods & services, and entire economies, away from a dependency on a teetering, global non-renewable energy based economy, exemplifies the transition culture's response to massive resource depletion, global energy crises, rising fuel and food prices, plummeting markets, and the threat of global climate change. Towns, organizations, and entire governments are finding that localization is a "win" for the economy, environment, community development, and for quality of life. The Transition Town Movement— one example of localization — was founded in 2005, in Kinsale, Ireland and then Totnes England; and has since spread throughout Europe, and into the Americas. Towns across the world are asking questions related to energy decent planning and transitioning away from a centralized petroleum-and other non-renewable energy based economy. Our community of Hohenwald, TN began similar conversations in 2006.

The Making of Transition Town Hohenwald

Being a rural community, we found that the best way to communicate with local residents about energy efficiency was to talk about economics. We're trying to invent or grow something locally that's positive and within the existing boundaries. People have enough problems already and this makes them sensitive to talking outside their boundaries. The 2009 unemployment rate of Hohenwald and Lewis County is above 17% and our neighbour, Perry County has above 25%. With unemployment so high, people within our current cultural context, don't want to talk about protecting ecosystems, they want to talk about jobs and saving money.

The Earth had become a dirty word over the past decades. As Permaculture Designer Stefan Geyer in his Spring 2009 Permaculture Activist article Permaculture in Business points out, "Permacultures potential applications in business have largely been passed over due ...

to its gems hidden under the dirty fingernails of radical tree huggers." Hohenwald's Vice Mayor Dustin Flowers, an active supporter of SGI and LECD recently spoke at a local Transition Town meeting, he shared, "In the past, green tended to cause fear. Green meant taking away our toys and telling us what to do. "Now," he said, "Green equals gold." Flowers believes that there are a number of opportunities for green economic development. He stated, "We are not the first to realize the beauty of a marriage of a sustained environment with the boost of opportunities from a green economy. We as a city realize these opportunities and those are a few reasons why the City supports becoming a Transition Town. Our first true step is renaming an industrial park on Swan Avenue the Hohenwald Eco-Industrial Park... In a green economy we're all doing the right thing." SGI is supporting the City and County in their efforts to target new green industries to our city and county industrial parks.

SGI would rather that green businesses seed from within the community, but the City and County are already focused on attracting outside businesses. SGI being proactive, tries to work with existing infrastructure and aims to have a three tiered approach to local business development: 1. Green existing businesses, 2. Educate and support locals in starting new green businesses, 3. Attract new green jobs to the area. To accomplish these three goals SGI in partnership with the Financial Permaculture Institute offers monthly green educational gatherings, quarterly green business tradeshows and an annual green business summit that focuses on participatory learning through business design charettes. SGI is also working with the local Tennessee Technology Centre and Tennessee Career Centre to create a Green Jobs Technical Training Program for residents of Southern Middle Tennessee. SGI is also partnering with the local Chamber of Commerce to green-up existing businesses.

Mark Graves, Chamber President and City Recorder gave his support and encouragement for the local Government and Chamber to partner with SGI in developing a local green economy. Graves, as Chamber President, recently formed a Green Business Development Committee for the Chamber. The goal of this new Development Committee is to educate current businesses to capitalize on green energy and efficiency. Graves stated, "Our current environmental situation can become our greatest economic opportunity, if we seize the moment." He shared that his definition of Green equaled efficiency, hope, invention, ingenuity, entrepreneurialism, capital markets, commerce and profit. "There is a global investment to reinvent most of the things we do to become more efficient," Graves said. He added words of encouragement: " My hope is that the Chamber of Commerce become a key force in inspiring Lewis County to embrace a new, exciting and prosperous economic environment and not be afraid of it."

The most effective and energy efficient strategy or "right thing" for SGI's transition initiative has been to marry Permaculture with financial and economic literacy. Permaculture design and system thinking is at the core of SGI's transition strategy. Our project development incorporates Permaculture design principles and ethics of earth care, people care and fair share. Over the years we've accessed and have shared a wealth of information on ecological design principles and community development tools, but found a lack of information on sustainable financial and economic development. In 2008, SGI through the Centre for Holistic Ecology (CHE) and a partnership with Solari Inc. and other local organizations gave birth to the Financial Permaculture Institute (FPI).

Through FPI we're both discovering and creating language, tools and design models towards transition economics or what I also like to call whole ecosystem economics. We're using our home, Hohenwald as our base camp and grounds for proactive experimentation. While SGI is our local face, FPI is our international face. FPI aims to create and add value to existing templates for community economic development. Right now we're working on some crosscutting mapping of the financial ecosystem of Lewis County and surrounding region. We'll be holding the second Financial Permaculture Green Business Summit in Hohenwald September 22-26, 2009 where we will have trainings and then break out sessions on food and farming, building and housing, energy and fuel, solid waste and recycling, green business, community development and on mapping financial ecosystems.

The two greatest success of the 2008 Summit were that it: 1. Ignited the interest of our local residents, thus catalyzing our transition efforts, and 2. Brought together an interdisciplinary coalition of individuals from the government, business, non-profit and education sectors. Some useful catalysts were that we firstly, had about 14 local residents, aside from the organizers, attend the Summit and that we secondly, did well in our documentation of the event and post event process. This was like a mycelium effect. As these 14 people went back into the community, just two months later the word Permaculture and Transition Towns had permeated the culture and my friend heard people using the words as she got her hair cut at the local beauty salon. Overhearing conversations like these are a telltale sign of cross-pollination.

On documentation, we had about 12 people live blogging the Summit, Byron Palmer graciously volunteered to make a 30 minute documentary about the event and after the Summit I and others have been blogging about our local Transition efforts. This documentation toolbox has really helped catalyze our local transition efforts. We've given about 200 copies of the documentary to local residents and have shown it several times at public events. The documentary, which can be viewed on www.financialpermaculture.com has been like a huge business card or portfolio that locals are using to gauge our worth. The results are in and folks who see the documentary generally want to either get involved or find out more. The blogging on www.financialpermaculture.org has been really useful also because we've seen our blogs connected to several local links. Some of the links are positive and some negative. On the negative, a few people view our efforts as trying to take over the government. For their own reasons, they are aggravated and restimulated. Even negative input on our efforts is useful as it creates opportunities for conversations and educational moments.

We had a team of people organizing a course on complimentary currency and this provoked a number of local residents and city officials. Rather than force something that wasn't ready to fit, we simply removed that project from the table and put it on the shelf. Our goal is to be effective community organizers and that means that we may need to occasionally reprioritize our projects due to community opinion. There are so many possible projects that we've learned to stack functions, be opportunistic and go with the flow to get the highest yield (long term sustainability) with the least waste of our efforts (total economic return).

We know that many people have different opinions on core issues like politics, religion, climate change and the economy. To us, diversity of opinion is very welcome and encouraged. We appreciate working with diverse demographics of age, gender, level of education and income – plus a wide dissimilarity in our shades of green. Our aim is to collaborate with as many types of people as possible.

We also seek to bring as many conversations to the table as needed to move forward with our own unique transition efforts, while looking for key crosscutting patterns applicable to other communities. Our goal for Hohenwald is not to mimic other successful communities, but to learn about working solutions and adapt our findings to our own unique circumstances.

This process of design from pattern to detail moves us forward, with occasional trials and errors. With every problem that we encounter we strive to find a useful solution. To stay proactive and effective, we regularly check in with the local group to discuss our core vision, objectives and to evaluate our process.

In March and April of 2009 SGI created a Transition Proclamation. The County and City Government and the local Chamber signed the Proclamation. The Proclamation has had both its high's and lows. The high is that there are now key community leaders who consider themselves engaged and supportive of our LECD initiative.

It has also motivated a lot of formally uninvolved 'green' folks to get active. On the low, getting the government involved now means that our initiative is in the political arena. Once something gets in the arena it's a thing to take sides on and judge. Again, being proactive, we're looking for opportunities to arise out of any and all challenges. We hope to share the ups and downs of our learning journey.

This transition effort is a life long process and we want the community to embrace and feel empowered by change. Following are some tips that we've found useful in our transition efforts:

1. Become familiar with what is already being accomplished in the community and familiarize yourself with local history, plus it's strengths and weaknesses;
2. Look to what people really need and want, and then match your actions and language to implement strategies that meet both their needs and yours. Remember we all share the same innate needs;

3. Find a common language that you can assist you in communicating with diverse groups of people;
4. Empower people to come up with their own answers and create opportunities for them to use their own voice at meetings, in writing, during interviews and at public events;
5. Identify the community stakeholders and survey their potential risks and opportunities. Figure out ways to engage or cooperate with potential stakeholders by identifying how they could benefit from involvement, let them know how they can get involved or how you can add value to one of their existing projects or goals;
6. Collaboratively identify your core vision for your initiative and your desired public image. Be sure that other members of the group can express this. Best to keep it simple and short or in easy to remember bullet points;
7. Be inclusive and identify many portals of entry into your initiative. Integrate rather than segregate and do not discernment. Every member of a community can be a potential collaborator. Avoid creating a separation between them and us. One thing I've learned is that for the most part, we all share a similar core set of values – we just often have different totems, thus we have different languages and actions around the messages we stand behind, or signs we carry and platforms we preach on. We're all more a like than I've ever imagined;
8. Identify the skill sets and resources with in the active group and utilize them wisely, also become aware of people's overall vision and purpose for being part of the group – be sure that they're getting their needs met;
9. *Be proactive* – focus on working solutions and opportunities: Don't tell people that what they're doing is wrong, instead find something that they're doing well and help them do it even better and stack functions by helping existing groups organize around these accomplishments;
10. Utilize non-violent communication;
11. Listen closely to the communities context and needs: be willing to reprioritize your projects and be ready to jump on new opportunities as they arise;

12. Value diversity but avoid taking political or religious positions– that way more people will be comfortable being a part of the initiative;
13. Hold frequent public social events where people can learn about and discuss topics related to your initiative;
14. Encourage and train up leaders within the initiative so that each project has a leader and an engaged support group;
15. Give attention to only those projects and tasks that have a clear working group;
16. Allow participants the opportunity to frequently evaluate group process;
17. Don't throw around words like Permaculture and Transition Towns until people are ready to hear them – in the meanwhile talk in their language – and you'll find that all combined people already have a lot of the answers and knowledge. It took us 2 years of outreach before we used our own language.

Georgia—A Transition Economy

Georgia is one of the countries that used to be part of the USSR- many students following A' levels and at first year undergraduate level will not be able to remember the USSR and will have no first hand recollection of what the world was like prior to the break up of the Union.

Georgia was a former satellite of the all-powerful Russian authorities that were at the heart of the USSR. The USSR enjoyed control, both economic and political, over such satellites and for many years the ethnic diversity in Russia's republics was kept firmly in check with regards to political and national aspirations.

When the USSR broke up, countries like Georgia sought independence. Georgia broke away from the USSR in 1991. Since that time it has experienced a number of political and economic difficulties as it has come to terms with its independence. Like many of the former Soviet republics, Georgia's independence has not been without its problems.

The economic system prior to 1991 was essentially a centrally planned command economy with Moscow doing the planning. All aspects of life would be determined by the planners-what is to be produced, how it is to be produced, who gets what is produced-all these key questions that are at the heart of any economic system were decided by the bureaucrats at the state planning authority, Gosplan. This was economic management by the state. Markets as it is understood in the West did not exist and prices did not fulfil the function that they do in Western market economies.

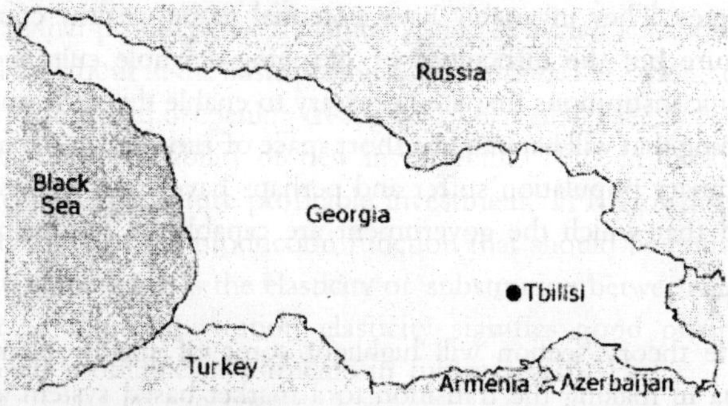

Image: The map of Georgia shows its strategic position linking Russia with Turkey which is currently in negotiations to become a member of the EU. How long will it be before Georgia joins the growing band of countries that are seeking membership of the EU?

It is difficult for those who have not lived under such a system to understand this important point. Prices were merely a means of indicating how much had to be given up to acquire what you needed, price did not have any relationship to value. Value in part, relates to notions of scarcity-the scarcer something is the more it is valued and the higher its price tends to be as a result.

In Soviet republics like Georgia this was simply not the case. Wages were determined by the planners on the basis of how much would be needed to be able to access the basics of life but since prices were determined also by the planners, wage rates meant nothing either. Imagine this scenario:

To live the average family needs to pay rent on their flat, buy 5 loaves of bread, 12 eggs, 1kg of cheese and 1/2kg of butter and also travel to work using a metro system (10 journeys per working week). If that is what is needed then wages need to be set so that this could be afforded.

Let's set wages at £5 per month. Not much you might say and compared to Western levels absolutely right. But if rent is set at 50p, bread at

5p, eggs per dozen at 75p, cheese per Kg at 50p, butter per kg 50p and a metro ride 1p per journey then £5 is more than enough to enable the family to get what they need.

When independence came, there came with it the shift to a market based economic system. The transition from planned to market is not an easy one and this is why these states are referred to as transition economies. They invariably have potential to be wealthy countries in the future but the difficulties of changing a whole culture plus the economic institutions that are necessary to enable this to happen is not something that will happen in a short space of time and in the meantime the ordinary population suffer and perhaps have expectations that are beyond that which the government are capable of producing.

Theory

The theory section will highlight some of the problems facing Georgia in making the transition to a market based system and offer a brief outline of the state of its economy.

One of the main problems facing transition economies is how to remove price controls and expose the population to market forces. The President after independence was Zviad Gamsakhurdia. Price controls are invariably associated with rationing. Gamsakhurdia attempted to maintain his political position by attempting to control the price of basic supplies and public transport-what this means is fixing prices below market levels.

Look at the diagram below to see what effect this has. Basic market economics tells us that if we try to restrict price below market equilibrium then demand will exceed supply and there will be a shortage. To cope with this shortage the state has to ration supplies. In 1991, Gamsakhurdia did just this by restricting the population to buy only from local shops!

The problem faced by all transition economies is that this merely stores up the shortage. When price liberalisation occurs as it did when the President was ousted in 1992 the shortage comes into the open and prices begin to rise sharply. Georgia faced this exact problem-not only from food prices but also the prices of basic raw materials needed to boost manufacture.

In these circumstances, the ordinary member of the public has to find a way around this or go without. Even now over half the population live below the poverty line. The new opportunities that arise in a market economy mean that those who take the opportunities can become very wealthy but that the business activities they are involved in are half legal and half not! What we mean by this is that the restrictions on business activity that existed in the planned economy era have not all been swept away at the same time and so business people find it hard to carry out normal business activity in such circumstances. Where rules still exist they have to be 'bent' and this tends to lead to an underground economy which fuels other problems, notably corruption.

Inflation during the early years of independence rose by 79% in 1991, 887% in 1992, 3,125% in 1993 and 15,606% in 1994! Such alarming inflation rates are typical of transition economies after price controls are removed. When inflation is this bad confidence in the economy drains away and people look at other ways of getting what they need-possibly through bartering-and avoid using money. In such circumstances output is also affected as unemployment rises and GDP is affected. In 1991, GDP fell by 21% then a further 45% in 1992, -29% in 1993 and yet another 10% drop in 1994.

Georgia has limited natural resources. It is a fairly mountainous country but does produce some metals, machinery and chemicals and has manganese and copper mines. 20% of the economy is agriculture with 40% of the population employed in this sector. Products include grapes, citrus fruits, hazelnuts and tea. Its main energy source is hydroelectric power and it has to import most of its oil and gas supplies.

Given this situation the problems facing a transition economy are even greater. Some transition economies have large natural gas and oil supplies that can be used to help drive economic growth and wealth generation but Georgia does not have this luxury. In addition to these difficulties, civil strife caused much disruption as regions sought greater independence-particularly in Abkhazia and Ossetia. The wars in these areas tended to have the effect of stifling foreign direct investment (FDI) further hindering the pace of economic development.

The difficulties of transition alluded to above have meant that a significant proportion of the economy is now underground. It has been estimated that over a quarter of Georgia's output is accounted for by the black economy and two-thirds of its trade. This then creates another problem. The existence of a black economy means that production and exchange are not declared and thus taxes are not paid. This puts pressure on the government who need tax revenue to invest in infrastructure to help boost economic growth that will benefit everyone.

Examples of this are clear from the demonstrations that have occurred about the lack of electricity in the country. In early 2000, only six hours of electricity was available each day. Not only does this affect the standard of living but also limits the potential for growth as businesses find it difficult to operate.

One of the tasks of the government is to try to make key industries like the electricity supply industry efficient. The answer to this seems to be attempts to try and privatise them. This in itself is a problem-to privatise them implies that some organisation is going to take over the running of the industry from the state and attempt to run it to make a profit. The extent of the dilapidation of the industry and the amount of investment that would be needed to make it profitable and efficient is often prohibitive.

However, one of the major obstacles facing this country is that of corruption. It is partly due to the way in which the transition has been handled and also something to do with the geographical and historical position of Georgia. Its geographical position meant that during the Soviet years much illegal trade occurred across the difficult terrain of the borders both North and South. The government of Gamsakhurdia and his replacement, Eduard Shevardnadze, who at one stage was the Soviet Foreign Minister, was expected to be a moderating influence on the country but he was unable to get to grips with the corruption problem and was 'forced' to resign after popular protest at vote rigging in elections in November 2003.

The current president is Mikhail Saakashvili who was elected on a mandate of solving the corruption problem that has so blighted the country. He is making inroads into the problem but it is a long and difficult, not to mention dangerous process.

There are two potential areas where Georgia can look to its longer-term economic development. One is tourism. Part of Georgia is situated on the Black Sea coast and the country used to be popular with Soviet tourists. The potential for developing the tourist industry could generate large revenues but the investment needed into the infrastructure to support tourism is again likely to pose a problem.

The other main area is again linked to its geography. The Caspian Sea and a number of countries surrounding Georgia have good supplies of oil and natural gas and the development of these supplies may see Georgia benefiting from the economic activity that will result. Already a $2.9 billion 1,650km pipeline has been laid connecting the oil fields of Azerbaijan with ports on the Black Sea coast of Georgia and Turkey. Other pipeline projects are in construction and the jobs and economic activity that this will generate is also a cause for some optimism but again, there are concerns that such investment will be short lived if the corruption problems cannot be solved.

The path of transition to market economy from planned economy is not easy for any of the countries involved. The remarkable thing is that there have been a number of similarities in the way in which all of the former Soviet republics have gone through the transition to market economies. This allows us to look at how such economies develop and also learn something about what we, in the West, may take for granted about the way a market economy works and what is needed to ensure it works smoothly-well as smoothly as possible anyway!

Tasks

1. Explain why corruption is a major obstacle to economic development in countries like Georgia.
2. To what extent is the change in culture from a planned to a market based system necessary to ensure successful transition?
3. Georgia's President has suggested that Georgia could become a member of the EU by 2008. Assess the strength of the case for Georgia joining the EU.

Transition Economies of Russia

The Russian Federation is what remains of the former Soviet Union following the collapse of the communist regime and the break up of the Union of Soviet Socialist Republics (USSR). Russia is symptomatic of a country that, in the space of ten years, has had to make massive adjustments to its economic and political system as it seeks to move away from a planned economic system to a more market orientated one. The problems it has faced has been mirrored by the countries that have gained independence but which used to be dependent on Russia for its economic survival. In the week 20th-27th November one of those former republics, Georgia, saw further political upheaval as the President, Eduard Sheverdnadze, was forced to resign in the face of protests about poverty, lack of economic opportunity and alleged election rigging. Such problems exist throughout the former Eastern European bloc countries.

The move to a market based economy from a planned system brings many problems. Russia's Gross Domestic Product (GDP) is currently around $1.35 trillion ($1,350,000,000,000) (£81 billion) compared to the UK which stands at $1.52 trillion (£91 billion). The population of Russia is over 144 million compared to that of the UK which is 60 million. The GDP per capita for Russia is $9,300 (£5,580) whereas for the UK the figure is $25,300 (£15,180).

Following the collapse of the communist regime, many price controls were removed which led, in 1992, to inflation rates of 2,520%. Current rates of 15% seem to be small by comparison and is a measure of the progress that Russia has made in adapting to a market system. Unemployment also rose following the introduction of market reforms; the very notion of unemployment was not something many Russians were used to under panning system and as such represented a massive culture shock and a source of resentment. Unemployment rates currently stand at around 7% but it is difficult to be precise about the true extent of such problems because of the widespread existence of an informal economy. Many of the governments problems have stemmed from corruption and an inability to impose a sufficiently robust taxation system that is adhered to by the population as a whole.

The unmistakable land mark of St Basil's Cathedral in the heart of Moscow has witnessed dramatic and historical upheaval in Russia over the past century.

Other problems that have been a feature of the transition involve the removal of all manner of restriction on trade both within and outside Russia. Much of the trade under the planned system was with Russia's satellite republics-Poland, Ukraine, Georgia and so on; the market system has meant that western powers can now seek to invest in Russia, engage in trade and equally Russia has to find its way into a financial and trading world which many Russians simply did not have any experience of. The notion of marketing products was alien and the extensive privatisation that has had to be undertaken has necessitated a very steep learning curve for those involved-the Russian stock exchange for example is still relatively new!

The problems faced by Russia are typical of those being experienced by most of the so-called 'transition economies'. Potentially they represent burgeoning new markets with massive resources and economic potential but the problems along the way also make for a very volatile political and economic mix that can, as highlighted in Georgia over the past week, lead to explosive situations.

Theories

Command Economies. Command economies or Planned economies were a feature of those countries referred to as 'communist' regimes-mostly in Eastern Europe centred on the Union of Soviet Socialist Republics (USSR) a collection of states under the economic and political control of Russia. The planned aspect referred to the process of resource allocation. The needs of the population and the country were effectively planned and resources allocated to achieve desired production in capital and consumer goods. The notion that 'communism' means 'equality' is far too simplistic. It is true to suggest that income disparities were far less than in most western countries. In Russia in 1991, the average wage ranged between £18 and £40 per month, those at the top end may have been doctors, professors at universities, engineers and computer technicians and those at the lower end cleaners, factory workers and so on, but such differences in wages are significantly less than we might expect in the west!

It is this type of culture that is so different to that which those brought up on a diet of markets are used to. Investment in the USSR may have been directed towards projects that would bring benefits for the nation as a whole rather than for certain individuals or the few. The staging of the Olympics' in 1980 for example, was designed in part to show off the ability of Russia and the Soviet Union to stage a major event and to demonstrate the athletic prowess of its sports men and women.

Effectively, central planning meant that production units were given targets for output and resources were given that should allow those targets to be met. Economic growth would be achieved through progressive increases in the targets and reductions in the inputs. In reality it appeared that the targets were often not met and if not there was very little by way of retribution! In addition, all manner of manipulation to the targets could be achieved partly because there was little personal incentive for anyone to achieve beyond the target, in fact if the targets were not met it meant that there was less work to do! It seemed that the link between individual performance and the impact on the nation as a whole ('the common wealth'?) was lost.

Inefficiency was rife, waste and pollution at alarming levels, the lack of high quality information for the planners and the ability to be able to communicate the plans effectively all led to economic decline and, as the eighties drew to an end, the gap between the wealth and economic power of the west and that of the Soviet Union was rapidly widening. Incomes were set at a level that allowed people to be able to afford the items necessary to live, the prices of which in turn, were set by the planners. So, visiting Moscow in 1991, it was revealing to note that the price of an underground trip in Moscow worked out at 1/10th of 1p! This makes travel affordable for all but takes no account of the relative demand and supply of the items. It was estimated that some 40% of all Soviet agricultural output was wasted; in the supply chain from planting to purchase by the consumer it had rotted, been lost or wasted in some way!

A classic example of the mismatch of information in the system centred on the need for shoes and an excess of rubber. Shoes were in short supply so it made logical sense to use the surplus of rubber to make shoes. Production was geared up but it would come as no surprise to learn that rubber shoes are not the most elegant or functional of items. The result was a 'shoe mountain' and a waste of all the resources that went into the planning and manufacture of the shoes! The combined effect of all these factors led to immense pressures on the economy. Many people in the Soviet Union would not have recognised the notion of being paid for a job well done or the idea of customer service. In the west the penalty for poor customer service and inefficiency is, in the end, bankruptcy and loss of jobs; in the Soviet Union this did not happen because unemployment was, to all intents and purposes zero.

A housing development in the suburbs of St Petersburg in Russia, 1992. Housing can be made available for everyone but some would question the quality of life of its residents under a planned economic system.

After the collapse of the 'communist regimes' and the break up of the Soviet Union, the Eastern part of Europe became a patchwork of nation states who rapidly gained independence from Russia but who, having been dependent for so long on Moscow, found the transition from a planned to a market economy an intensely painful experience. The massive structural changes needed, regardless of the cultural adjustments, have proved a massive challenge to governments throughout the region. Some, like Poland, the Czech Republic and Hungary have emerged from the process with some credit while others are still struggling to adjust. The events of the week 20th-27th November 2003 in the former Soviet Republic of Georgia are testament to the problems these countries face.

Transition Economies: An IMF Perspective on Progress and Prospects

The race to transform centrally planned economies into market economies has led, ten years later, to one group of countries approaching the finish line, others languishing at various points along the track, and a few barely off the starting blocks. Some Central and Eastern European economies (CEE) and the Baltics are knocking on the doors of the European Union. But in many economies in the Commonwealth of Independent States (CIS), including Russia, there has been uneven progress and prospects remain murky.

Why have the CEE and Baltic economies outpaced those of the

CIS? And what is the way forward for Russia and the others? These are the broad questions addressed in the following sections. The focus in the main text is on the countries in transition in Europe and the former Soviet Union; developments in China and transition economies of Southeast Asia are discussed only briefly.

The Ingredients of the Transition Process

The main ingredients of the transition process were agreed upon fairly early. They were:

- *Liberalization*: the process of allowing most prices to be determined in free markets and lowering trade barriers that had shut off contact with the price structure of the world's market economies.
- *Macroeconomic stabilization*: primarily the process through which inflation is brought under control and lowered over time, after the initial burst of high inflation that follows from liberalization and the release of pent-up demand. This process requires discipline over the government budget and the growth of money and credit (that is, discipline in fiscal and monetary policy) and progress toward sustainable balance of payments.
- *Restructuring and privatization*: the processes of creating a viable financial sector and reforming the enterprises in these economies to render them capable of producing goods that could be sold in free markets and of transferring their ownership into private hands.
- *Legal and institutional reforms*: These are needed to redefine the role of the state in these economies, establish the rule of law, and introduce appropriate competition policies.

It was envisaged that the liberalization and macroeconomic stabilization could be undertaken fairly quickly, as could the privatization of small-scale enterprises. The privatization of large-scale enterprises and legal and institutional reforms would intensify at a later stage of the transition process and take a longer time.

The Taming of Inflation and the Recovery of Output

At the start of the transition, most economists agreed that, to get market price mechanisms working, liberalization and macroeconomic stabilization should proceed quickly, despite the economic hardship they might impose. The view was that the hardship would be temporary and less severe than if the process were dragged out over time.

The transition thus started in most economies with prices being rapidly liberated from artificially low levels, which led to an immediate burst of corrective inflation. The pent-up demand that had built up during the period of central planning sustained the inflation. Early in the transition inflation averaged 450 percent a year in CEE, nearly 900 percent in the Baltics and over 1000 percent in the CIS. By 1998, however, annual inflation had been lowered to the single digits in the first two groups and around 30 percent in the third.

Along with the burst in inflation, the transition began with another shock: output fell in all three groups of countries at the start of the transition, on average by 40 percent before it bottomed out, far more than was expected.

It is likely that the pre-transition level of output was overestimated by faulty statistics. If value added had been measured correctly at market prices, the pre-transition output, and therefore the collapse of output, would have been much lower. By 1998, output was growing in all three, though pre-transition levels of measured output had not been surpassed in most countries.

Figure 1
Output in Transition Economies

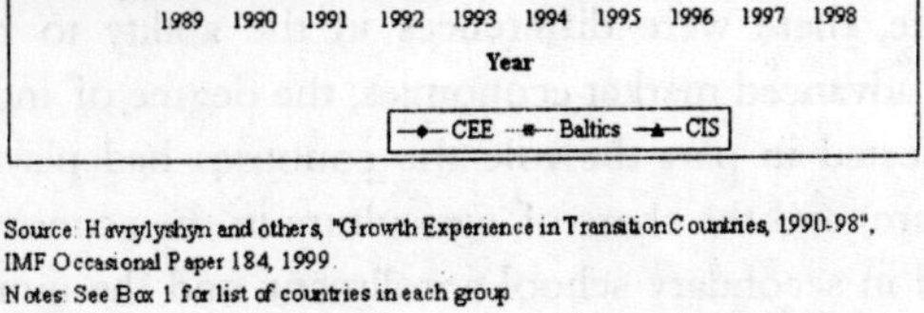

Source: Havrylyshyn and others, "Growth Experience in Transition Countries, 1990-98", IMF Occasional Paper 184, 1999.
Notes: See Box 1 for list of countries in each group

How was inflation tamed? Most of the early reformers adopted an explicit or implicit exchange rate peg. In other words, the country's government promised to stand ready to exchange its currency for a 'hard' currency, an internationally held currency with relatively stable value. Since too rapid a rate of money expansion, e.g., due to excessive government spending, would make it difficult to maintain the peg, this was essentially a promise to follow tight macroeconomic policies. These policies, and the effect they had on the private sector's expectations of inflation, helped bring inflation down. However, mechanisms other than exchange rate pegs have also succeeded in lowering inflation. For instance, many countries adopted charters giving their central banks considerable independence to pursue tight monetary policies or accepted the discipline of IMF-supported macroeconomic programs. This too helped check inflation.

Why did output fall initially and so markedly, why did the pattern of collapse differ across countries, and what explains the recovery of output? These questions have been the subjects of much econometric investigation.

The results suggest that relatively little of the initial decline in output was due to the tight macroeconomic policies used to tame inflation. Instead, 'disorganization'-associated with shocks such as the collapse of the Council for Mutual Economic Assistance (CMEA)-was an important factor. Disorganization refers to disruption in the production network, particularly in the provision of materials and intermediate inputs, resulting from the collapse of central planning and the dismantling of vertically integrated conglomerates that operated under the old system. Such disruption led to a loss in output.

'Adverse initial conditions' in some countries are generally invoked to explain why the pattern of collapse differed across countries. This is a reference to the fact that the characteristics of the economies differed at the start of the transition, and, in many countries, the characteristics made the task of maintaining economic activity difficult. For instance, there were differences in the ability to reorient trade toward the advanced market economies, the degree of industrialization (which reflected in part the role the countries had played under the Soviet system) and the share of agriculture in the economy, skill levels as reflected in secondary school enrollment, and the number of years under communism. Not surprisingly, countries where initial conditions were more adverse experienced a sharper initial decline in output.

What explains the subsequent recovery in output? One important factor was progress made in lowering inflation. Countries that tamed inflation quickly and sustained the gains experienced a speedier and stronger recovery in output.

This is illustrated in Figure 2, which shows the relationship between the change in output in a country, on the one hand, and the progress it made in reducing inflation, on the other. Each "diamond" on the graph represents a country; the country names are not listed on the graph to avoid cluttering it. Countries appearing in the lower right-hand corner of the graph had low inflation (relative to other transition economies) and experienced a recovery of output; countries appearing in the upper right-hand corner had high inflation and suffered output losses. In general, the graph shows that countries that kept a lid on inflation were better able to maintain economic activity than countries where inflation was unchecked.

Figure 2: Inflation and Growth in Transition Economies

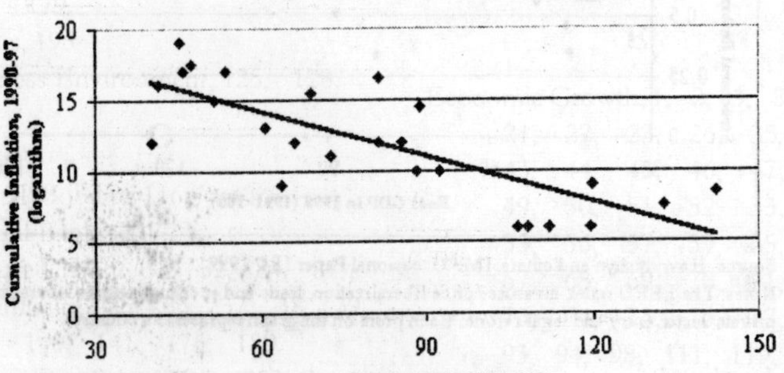

Sources: Havrylyshyn and others, IMF Occasional Paper 184, 1999 and Havrylyshyn, Izvorski and van Rooden, IMF Working Paper 98/141.
Notes: Each point on the graph represents a country.

Though progress with lowering inflation proved necessary for the revival of growth, it was not sufficient. Structural reforms were key in bringing about sustained recovery by facilitating the growth of the private sector. Where structural reforms were put in place early and firmly, new production networks developed quickly to counter the disorganization in the early years of transition.

This is illustrated in Figure 3. Output, relative to its pre-transition level, was higher in countries where structural reforms, as measured by an index constructed by the European Bank for Reconstruction and Development (EBRD), were the most far-reaching. These countries tended to belong to the CEE and Baltic groups. As in the earlier figure, each "diamond" on the graph represents a country. Countries appearing in the upper right-hand corner of the graph pursued structural reforms more vigorously (than other transition economies) and experienced a recovery of output; countries appearing in the lower left-hand corner of the graph lagged in the implementation of structural policies and suffered output losses.

Figure 3: Structural Reforms and Growth in Transition Economies

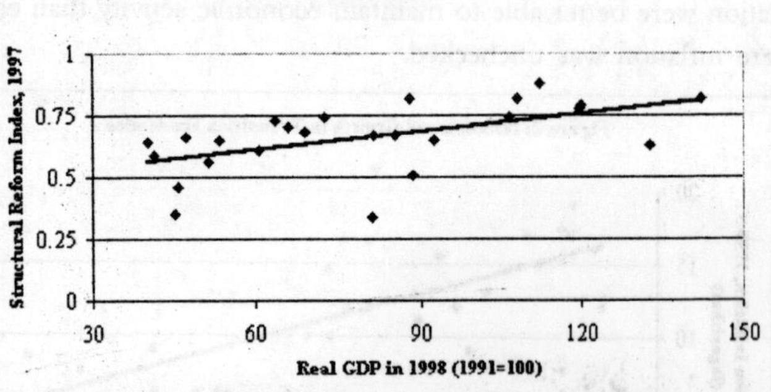

Source: Havrylyshyn and others, IMF Occasional Paper 184, 1999.
Notes: The EBRD index measures price liberalization, trade and exchange regime liberalization private sector entry and legal reform. Each point on the graph represents a country.

Privatization

As noted above, economists generally agreed on the need for speed in carrying out liberalization and stabilization. But on privatization of large enterprises, there was a debate on whether to have a rapid transfer of assets from the state to the private sector or to adopt a more gradual approach.

Advocates of rapid privatization called for eliminating state ownership by giving assets to citizens, for instance through vouchers that gave their holders the right and means to purchase state-owned companies on sale. They were motivated by considerations of fairness, a desire to give ordinary citizens a stake in the economy. They also perceived a need to seize the window of opportunity that had opened for privatization before the state bureaucracies regrouped and resisted the process.

Others advocated a more gradual scaling back of state enterprises as new private sector firms emerged in the economy. They were in favour of the privatization of enterprises through the sale of assets to those likely to work on improving the performance of the companies. They also stressed the imposition of 'hard budget constraints' on enterprises so that chronic loss makers would be forced out, leaving the more profitable enterprises to attract investors. Hungary followed this gradualist approach to privatization, and it appears to have proved more conducive to genuine restructuring of enterprises.

By contrast, experience has shown some of the pitfalls of the rapid privatization approach. In the Czech Republic, for instance, the assets transferred to millions of ordinary citizens in the first phase of rapid privatization were sold by the recipients and ended up being consolidated in investment funds. But there was no genuine restructuring of enterprises, either because the investment funds lacked the capital to develop them or because the funds were in turn controlled by state-owned banks that did not impose hard budget constraints. The weak growth performance of the Czech Republic in the late-1990s, relative to other CEE countries, is attributed in part to its weak enterprise reforms.

Rapid privatization fared even worse in Russia. The country's mass privatization program of 1992-94 transferred ownership of over 15,000 firms into private hands. However, contrary to expectations, insider privatization did not lead to self-induced restructuring of firms. It was hoped that secondary trading would introduce outside ownership, and that transparent methods would be used in the second wave of privatization of remaining firms still in state hands. Neither hope was fulfilled. Insiders were wary of relinquishing control; workers feared the cost-cutting that might occur under outside control, and managers found it easier to keep enterprises alive by lobbying the state for subsidies than to foster competitive performance through involvement of outsiders. The second wave of privatization, in particular the so-called "loans-for-shares" scheme, was non-transparent and systematically excluded foreign investors and banks in favour of parties with ties to government interests.

Overall, the experience of the transition economies suggests that privatized firms tend to restructure more quickly and perform better than comparable firms that remain in state ownership, but only if complementary conditions are met. These conditions include the presence of hard budget constraints and competition, effective standards of corporate governance, and an effective legal structure and property rights.

In contrast to the mixed experience on privatization of large enterprises, the privatization of small-scale enterprises has been generally successful and has been completed in all but five countries.

Capital Flows

The move to a market economy required substantial amounts of finance to facilitate the reallocation of investment into productive sectors, modernize antiquated machinery, enhance public infrastructure, and provide financing for emerging firms. But, it was difficult, in the initial years of transition, for governments in these countries to raise the requisite capital. A 'Marshall Plan' for the transition economies never materialized. Rather, external assistance on a much smaller scale was provided primarily by the international financial institutions, the European Union, and individual countries.

Another factor contributing to a capital scarcity was that private capital fled the countries in response to the uncertain circumstances at the start of transition. However, once the direction of reforms was clearly established in many CEE and Baltic economies, private capital returned quickly. Chart 1 summarizes the evidence by comparing average annual estimates of capital flight, the inflation rate, real GDP growth, fiscal balances and the quality of reforms in the initial years of transition with those in the later years.

In the CEE economies, a decline in inflation and improvements in the quality of structural reforms were associated with a reversal of capital flows, from net outflows of $15 per capita to net inflows of $75 per capita. Likewise, progress in the Baltics on inflation and structural reforms, along with a check on fiscal balances, turned a net outflow of $30 per capita into a net inflow of $70 per capita. Russia's experience stands in sharp contrast. Several years into its transition, Russia is still experiencing massive capital flight. Though inflation has been brought under control, Russia has lagged in the implementation of structural reforms.

Inequality

Inequality in incomes has increased, not surprisingly, over the period of transition. A commonly-used measure of inequality is the Gini coefficient for income, which takes on values between zero and one; a value of zero would indicate perfect equality of incomes. Pre-transition Gini coefficients were around 0.25, close to those of Scandinavian countries and far below that of the United States (0.4). Post-transition Gini coefficients have increased, ranging from 0.2 in Slovenia to 0.5 in Ukraine. Countries with better growth performance—as measured by cumulative GDP growth in the first eight years of transition—experienced a smaller increase in inequality, as shown in Figure.

Figure 4: Inequality and Growth in Transition Economies

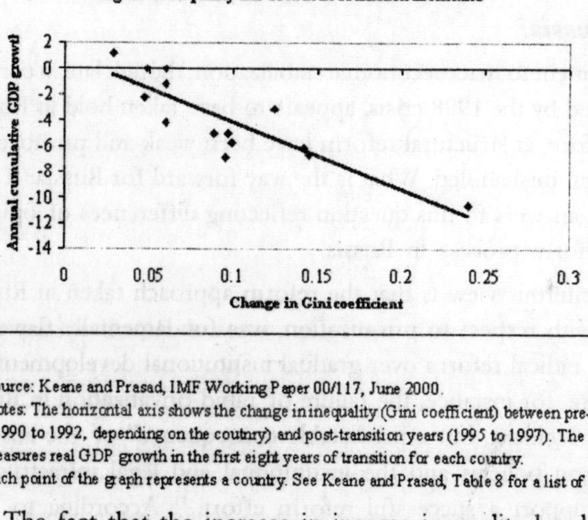

Source: Keane and Prasad, IMF Working Paper 00/117, June 2000.
Notes: The horizontal axis shows the change in inequality (Gini coefficient) between pre-transition years (1990 to 1992, depending on the coutnry) and post-transition years (1995 to 1997). The vertical axis measures real GDP growth in the first eight years of transition for each country.
Each point of the graph represents a country. See Keane and Prasad, Table 8 for a list of countries.

The fact that the increase in income inequality has been modest in many countries does not mean that the process of transition has not generated winners and losers. The case of Poland proves this point. Poland did experience a substantial increase in inequality of *labour earnings*. But social transfers played a role in mitigating this shift, so that the rise in *income* inequality was far more modest. Interestingly, the transfers were targeted at the people who had lost or stood to lose the most from the transition. These people tended to be middle class rather than the poor; that is, they were not the ones who would have been targeted had the goal been to help those whose absolute need was the greatest. But they may have helped the reform effort by bolstering political support for the reforms among the people most likely to block them.

This brief discussion of inequality is by no means a complete account of the often wrenching social changes under transition. For instance, one major aspect of the increase in inequality is the deterioration in the relative position of retirees (although this was not the case in Poland). With the demographic pressures facing these countries, this is a very hard problem to address in the framework of existing pay-as-you-go pension systems. The pension reforms in most of these countries will improve the situation, but this will unfortunately be too late for the current generation of retirees. Furthermore, several other social indicators have deteriorated in some of the transition economies.

Whither Russia?

Commitment to macroeconomic stabilization, though late in coming and threatened by the 1998 crisis, appears to have taken hold in Russia. However, efforts at structural reform have been weak and privatization has been often mishandled. What is the way forward for Russia? There is a range of answers to this question reflecting differences of opinion about the reform process in Russia.

One vociferous view is that the reform approach taken in Russia, particularly with respect to privatization, was fundamentally flawed in emphasizing radical reform over gradual institutional development. To Joseph Stiglitz, for instance, the failure of rapid privatization in Russia "was not an accident, but a predictable consequence" of the absence of competition policies and the institutional and legal infrastructure needed to support a successful reform effort. [11] According to him, Russia should now proceed very gradually with privatization (or re-privatization of any assets that may fall back into state hands), with due recognition of the need for establishing institutional pre-conditions, and making good use of such social and organizational capital as Russia possesses. Stiglitz suggests that Russia could learn in this regard from the "enormous success of China, which created its own path of transition, rather than just using a blueprint or recipe from Western advisors".

An opposing view, associated with some Russian observers and policy makers such as Boris Fedorov and Andrei Illarionov, is that the reform strategy was the correct one, but never implemented, in part because of the leniency shown by the advanced market economies and international financial institutions. For instance, Illarionov writes that "... the IMF's attitude towards economic policy carried out by the Russian authorities was and remains timid, inconsistent and subject to permanent compromise... For several years, the Russian government and Russian society as a whole turned out to be effectively spoiled, as they have been granted unearned financial assistance. As a result, Russian economic policy has not only been inconsistent, but it has seriously diverged from the economic policy conducted in a majority of countries in transition..."

In a similar spirit, Fedorov's "recommendations for the West" are not to grant Russia "concessions, but rather apply the rules as you would to any country. Western capital should flow to the private sector, not the government. Only this will help to change the country, create jobs and increase efficiency."

While acknowledging that greater attention ought to have been given to institutional reforms, the view from the IMF is that the basic strategy pursued in Russia was sound but derailed by special factors. For instance, Fischer and Sahay write that the source of Russia's current problems lies largely in the "failure to drive ahead with reforms after the 1996 elections, when powerful vested interests strengthened their hold on political and economic power, deepening corruption". What is needed is not a fundamental change in reform strategy, but a decision by the political authorities "to renew reforms and improve governance." Evidence from CEE and Baltic countries, summarized earlier, suggests that once a commitment to reform takes root, capital returns to the country, providing a basis for sustained growth.

Can the power of vested interests be overcome? Havrylyshyn and Odling-Smee hold out hope. The vested interests themselves might become willing to accept reforms if they decide that their future profits would be higher in an economy in "which property rights are protected and the rule of law obtains, rather than one ruled by lawlessness, like much of the CIS today. Such a shift from predator to conserver has been seen in market economies...". Change could also come through the emergence of a strong leader willing to take on the vested interests, or from the political clout of a growing middle class, or pressure from foreign competitors and international financial institutions.

A Summing-up

The transition has yielded notable successes. Though the focus of this brief has been on economic developments, the first major achievement is the widespread, though far from universal, commitment to democracy and to the establishment of a market-based economy. The transition to a market economy has been associated with increased political freedom in most countries.

All but six of the countries are classified as "free" or "partly free" by the human rights organization Freedom House; periodic elections in these countries have served to give citizens a voice in the transition process. Politicians advocating a retreat from the path to a market economy have never captured power, though unreformed Communist parties have on occasion captured as much as a third of the popular vote. It appears, therefore, that despite the economic hardships imposed by the transition, citizens have viewed turning back the clock as a worse outcome.

Second, a commitment to macroeconomic stability appears to have taken hold, with inflation brought under control in most cases. An example of this is Russia's determination to prevent an inflationary spiral in the aftermath of the ruble's devaluation in 1998.

Third, many of the basic structural underpinnings of market economies have been put in place in most countries, at least in a *de jure* sense. These include bankruptcy procedures, competition policy and anti-monopoly regulations, improvements in accounting standards, and legislation for regulating financial markets.

In the countries of Central Europe and the Baltics, commitment to macroeconomic stabilization came sooner and implementation of structural reforms was firmer.

These countries have re-joined the ranks of middle-income countries and can claim to have transition*ed.* These countries now face the challenges posed by accession to the EU, and, more generally, by the process of catching-up with the richer nations.

The mainstream view is that Russia and other countries of the CIS can and ought to follow a similar path, but there is increased appreciation of the difficulties of institution-building and of the power of vested interests to derail the process of reform in the interim.

Business Strategy in China's Transition Economy: Problems and Perspectives

Context

Institutional reform is a main feature of China's transition from a planned to a market economy which started in the 1980s, and is a major influence on economic growth. Specialists have published numerous studies on the process of institutional reform, such as research by Fan Gang on incremental reform (1991, 1993 and 1996), Yang Ruilong's theory of three-stage institutional change (1998) and Zhou Ye'an's take on trends in China's institutions (2000). To a certain extent, this research describes the transformation process of China's economic system. Substitution, transformation and exchange in institutional change leads to the transformation of a country's institutional framework. The way different institutional arrangements interact has a significant impact on how well institutions operate. As reform towards a market economy continues and expands to the social realm, numerous inconsistencies are appearing in the country's institutional system-notably the influence of Chinese culture, in which personal contacts take precedent over official means. Institutional change as a result of economic transition usually leads to the gradual elimination of older institutional arrangements and their replacement in stages by modern ones. During the switch from a planned to a market system, three economic models exist (as defined by John Hicks) that together form a mixed economy: the natural economy, planned economy and the developing market economy. In terms of the institutional impact on economic activity, three principles apply to each of these models, respectively: the principle of 'relations', the principle of intrinsic regulation in statedirected economic reform, and the principle of market-steered activity with the judiciary as a third component of its implementation. This last principle is the goal of economic transition.

Complex patterns are emerging between the above-mentioned principles due to poor communications, institutional shortcomings and the limitations of government control in the transformation, concept and reorganisation of public institutions. As a result, the three following situations may occur: new institutional arrangements replace old ones, old arrangements in certain sectors are not replaced by new ones thus leading to a rupture in the institutional framework, and the inertia of old institutions impacts the new ones. The existence of old institutional arrangements as substitutes can undermine the work of new ones. The principles of relations and intrinsic regulation can similarly weaken the effect of newly operational formal institutions and re-enforce their own laxity. The co-existence of old and new institutional arrangements may also lead to opposition and conflict.

In this context, Chinese businesses are faced with a highly complex institutional environment. They must also deal with varying degrees of institutional pressure and consequently address a number of strategy issues.

Issues

State-owned Enterprise Reform: Tangible goods form the basis of public sector activity in a planned economy. In China, this activity is carried out by state-owned enterprises (SOEs). Every process in a SOE is influenced by the country's former planned economy, from theoretical to practical aspects, from management methods to workers' identities.

SOEs are not only extremely inefficient, but also an unlimited liability for the State, which must attribute public resources to them. State-owned national resources must be flexible, not only because this quality determines their worth but also because flexibility makes economic restructuring, sector-specific policies and national economic strategies possible. In China however, the public sector economy consists mainly of SOEs, and the public spending they require strongly contradicts the need for flexibility.

Currently, SOEs are in a transitional phase where old and new institutions co-exist. One the one hand, modernising reforms mean that SOEs must develop market-based strategies while on the other, close ties with government and State provide them with numerous privileges and additional responsibilities that reduce efficiency and put SOEs in a difficult position. Maintaining a wellbalanced relationship with government and State bodies has become a significant challenge for Chinese SOEs.

Creation of Private Businesses

Management: Should a business be managed by its owner or an organised management structure? In China, private business owners traditionally participate in the research, production and sales activities of their companies. The entrepreneur invests a lot of time in acquiring technology and improving product quality and management.

This model, in which the skills and drive of the owner plays a key role in the performance of his/her business, is known as "entrepreneur-based management".

However, as both businesses and market uncertainties grow, the pace of development stabilises, and individual entrepreneurs can no longer single-handedly steer company growth. Despite the need for an organised management system in this type of situation, most Chinese private businesses still operate using "entrepreneur-based management» methods, even if the business has reached maturity.

Stagnation and even bankruptcy can occur as a result. In cases where a company does set up a real management structure, the entrepreneur and career manager may hold opposing views on management; if the latter quits, then an entrepreneur-based management system is restored within the company.

Senior Management: Should senior management positions be filled by people who are close to the company owner, or by career managers?

A newly-created private business is often managed by individuals who have close relations with the entrepreneur. However, when the business reaches a certain size, the quality and skills of these managers is no longer sufficient to pilot growth, and externally-hired professional managers are necessary. But China's private businesses are faced with a difficult dilemma: the extra-economic nature of capital ownership makes entrepreneurs wary of professional managers and the lack of an external market regulated by competition, means that professional managers do not perform at satisfactory levels overall.

Orientation of Business Activities: Should efforts focus on "quick profit" or "sustainable development"? Private entrepreneurs in China are often laid-off employees or farmers with limited education and experience, whose motivation is often purely speculative. But China's entry into the WTO and the surge in the new information economy has made entrepreneurs aware of the need for long-term investment to boost the competitiveness of their core activities. They soon learnt that sustainable development comes at a very high cost and yields poor short-term returns. Those entrepreneurs who are determined to invest with a long-term perspective, are unable to compete with large foreign companies.

Management Philosophy: Should strategy focus on developing famous brands or on waging price wars? Because of the high cost of resources and a lack of preferential measures, many private Chinese businesses rely on product sales to cover investment costs. As a result, companies are rapidly drawn into price wars as soon as they are created, and end up using known brands merely to bring in short-term profits.

Management Methods: Should they be about product performance or non-productive activities? In recent years, private Chinese businesses have stubbornly continued to focus efforts on nonproductive activities at the expense of R&D, production and quality control. Although aware of the importance of performance, businesses using a management strategy based on product performance are currently yielding poor short-term results, thereby putting their own survival at risk.

Business Strategy: Should companies go for globalisation or localisation? Many private businesses on the Chinese market have broken into the international markets while others have failed because they were unable to develop an effective globalisation strategy. Others still have failed to seize on opportunities despite being sufficiently competitive and having a good chance at going international.

Development Strategy: Should a company diversify or specialise? It is commonly acknowledged that many of China's flourishing private businesses developed by using the reform process and institutional privileges to their advantage. Entrepreneurs of transition-phase companies expand their business considerably by diversifying, but unfortunately most do so blindly, leading to inefficiency and a poor distribution of capital.

Other companies continue to adopt risky strategies based on specialisation in sectors experiencing a decline or downturn. Managing for the future – Is it better to expand production or boost R&D? Thanks to its abundant, cheap labour pool and massive levels of fixed investment, China has become the "world's factory". But becoming a country that invents requires investment in science and technology in addition to improved R&D capacity. China's private businesses are faced with the difficult decision of whether to expand production or increase investment in research and development.

In-depth Analysis

The issues discussed above show that both state-owned and private businesses are strongly affected by their institutional environment. Moreover, previous development patterns will heavily influence future ones due to a "path-dependence" effect. The disadvantages created by this phenomenon in a market economy multiply as China's economy becomes increasingly international.

To transform Chinese business strategies, institutional impediments to new methods must be eliminated and replaced by reforms to improve the socialist market economy and build the institutional basis of intensive growth. More specifically, reform should focus on:

The continuing improvement and restructuring of the property system At one end of the spectrum, greater efficiency is needed in public spending; SOEs and companies in which the State is a shareholder need to be improved through institutional reform and better governance. At the other end, private sector development should be encouraged. To improve access to the market, the rule of law must be diligently upheld so that all citizens may exercise their rights to engage in any kind of legal activity without seeking permission from the government.

Improving education and culture, and establishing new regulations One purpose of the education system is to supply the country with a specialised and skilled work force. But rather than simply providing businesses with researchers, the main goal of education in China is to develop a market-oriented culture in the work force, particularly in high-level management and shareholders.

Improving the education level can also help the public to obtain objective knowledge about networking and market competition. We must abandon our cultural and intellectual prejudice against private shareholding (excepting where the state is a shareholder) so that new institutional frameworks become the point of reference for all shareholders. Business across all sectors must realise that their survival and expansion depends on their ability to compete on the market. Further improving property laws and related regulations Our analysis shows that legislation and public policy exert considerable influence on how a business develops and carries out its strategy.

Efforts by the State to add flexibility to the legal environment would encourage businesses to respect the rules of the market. Much needs to be done to improve and complete policy intended to encourage market-oriented development. For example, the success of venture capital depends on the free movement of investment capital; in China however, corporate legislation limits the number of shares a company may buy back and prohibits the floating of company shares on the market. These restrictions have a negative effect on capital mobility and prevent shareholders from influencing a business's strategy by modifying the size of their stake in that company.

The government must also adjust its policies to accompany legal change. Businesses must be encouraged to develop market-oriented strategies, and their earnings protected as a means of reassurance. Upholding and applying intellectual property laws not only protects the well-earned rewards of inventors, it also encourages innovation.

Key Issues

The Need for Institutional Legitimacy: For a business to survive and grow, it not only needs to perform well, it must also be 'legitimate', with management methods and goals that conform to society's expectations, customs and values.

Legitimacy confers a certain status in the social environment and makes it easier for a business to attract resources and the solid support of stakeholders. Conversely, a lack of legitimacy can badly affect a company's capacity to achieve its goals and accumulate resources. Institutional theory identifies three types of pressure for legitimacy: coercive, normative and mimetic. Each type of pressure influences different companies in different ways. Companies must meet a wide-range of criteria to acquire legitimacy in countries with a transition economy and a complex institutional environment.

This kind of pressure affects the strategies of public and private companies alike. Further research is required to understand the exact effect of each type of institutional pressure on businesses. *Changing business strategies in a changing institutional environment* – Change is a constant feature of the economic transition that involves a shift from a planned to a market economy. Business strategies must therefore also evolve according to changes in environments, and influence the direction of those institutional changes.

As institutional pressures evolve, should business strategies do the same? How? Should businesses follow change or resist it? Should a new institutional framework be created to encourage business, or should current policy be maintained?

Further research is needed to answer these questions. *Main institutional factors in business strategy* – Organisations vary across sectors but only a few of the differences between them have an effect on business strategy. These institutional factors need to be studied further. Current research shows that the size of a firm plays an important role. Large firms with greater resources and a higher degree of specialisation are more sensitive to environmental change and benefit more from public policy measures. The greater the public stake in that company, the more a company feels institutional pressure – legal and regulatory in particular. Moreover, certain institutional factors lead to differences in the way a company obtains information and how fast it circulates. The relationship between businesses may also affect the strategies they adopt. Again, further research is needed to understand how institutional factors influence business strategy.

Financial Inflows Cause Problems for Transition Economies

Contrary to common belief, large financial inflows* to a country can cause undesirable and costly economic side effects. A study by the Economic Transition and Integration (ETI) Project at the International Institute for Applied Systems Analysis (IIASA) is analysing how policy makers and economists in the transition economies of Central and Eastern Europe (CEE) can best grapple with these problems.

The study, titled "Financial Investments in Transition Economies," is based on the cooperative work of IIASA scholars and experts from CEE (mostly from Central Banks) and other international institutions (IMF, ECE, EIB, World Bank, etc.). The study covers eight transition countries (Czech Republic, Hungary, Poland, Russia, Slovenia and the three Baltic republics) and the developments in these countries are compared with experiences of several Latin American and Asian economies.

"The 1990s mark a major change from previous decades in which countries in the process of development constantly felt themselves short of foreign exchange. Now, these countries find themselves attracting too much foreign exchange at once," states Richard Cooper, scientific advisor of the IIASA study. He adds, "In principle, this is good, but every new situation brings new problems. At least in the short term, policy makers in the former communist countries now must deal with the undesirable, side effects of otherwise cherished major inflows of foreign money."

As part of the IIASA/ETI research, international experts met in Laxenburg in search of a consensus on how to deal with the most pressing issues, including real currency appreciation, higher inflation and excessive reserves of foreign currencies. In Poland, the Czech Republic and Hungary economists and policy makers are in the midst of dealing with the effects of large short-term and fluctuating financial inflows.

In Poland, most signs regarding financial inflows are positive. The investments from abroad are steadily increasing even though these have caused the real value of the Zloty to increase. Foreign exchange reserves are now equivalent to 6.5 months of imports. Because recent financial inflows are primarily in the form of foreign direct investment, Polish experts do not expect a drain on the reserves or a short term reversal of inflows. The major problem from the Central Bank's perspective is dealing with the rising amount of domestic credit facilitated by an increasing money supply fuelled by the inflows.

The situation regarding financial inflows in the Czech Republic is partially successful and partially problematic. After a record year in 1995, with financial inflows at 18 per cent of gross domestic product (GDP), Czech policy makers are trying to keep the economic system credible enough to continue attracting capital inflows while reducing the swings in short-term flows. To combat the upward pressure on the national currency, the Koruna, the Central Bank increased the band of fluctuation around the fixed exchange rate in early 1996, causing a significant amount of short-term capital to leave the country.

However, recent developments in the Czech Republic reveal the difficulties in identifying the true amounts of short-term capital. Government indecisiveness in dealing with growing trade deficits and budgetary problems induced business and households to rid themselves of holdings in Korunas, eventually forcing the financial authorities to let the currency substantially fall in value. In only a few months, the Czech situation abruptly changed from calm and stable to one with massive financial outflows (from business and official reserves) and the threat of triggering a Mexico-like financial crisis (which happened in late 1994 and early 1995).

In Hungary, the increase in financial inflows since 1995 resulted in no direct macroeconomic effects (i.e., output, investment, consumption, inflation, etc.) due to extensive Central Bank intervention (change of foreign currency to domestic currency) and sterilization (withdrawing part of the unplanned money supply through various financial instruments). The actual costs of these policies are presently being analysed. Also, little has been done to discourage financial inflows due to memories of the need to raise foreign capital to finance national debt. In fact, net financial inflows went from 16 per cent of GDP in 1995 to practically zero in 1996 because the government used its significant share of total inflows to pay off the large outstanding debt incurred during Hungary's communist past. Financial inflows, mainly as foreign direct investment, remain stable to the private sector of the economy. "Financial inflows are a mixed blessing for the transition countries-benefits are offset by uncertainties and fluctuations. Even a combination of complex policies will only mitigate but can never eliminate the unavoidable side effects of participating in the global economy," summarizes János Gács, leader of the ETI Project. The international group at the IIASA meeting agreed that:

1. High financial inflows to the transition economies in Central and Eastern Europe are primarily a reward for significantly improved economic performance following a long period of poor economic achievements and uncertain prospects.
2. Financial inflows have positive implications and outflows have negative implications for economic development from the point of view of catching up with developed market economies and establishing a base for long term economic growth. There

is little consensus that emerging economies should resist financial inflows.

3. Financial inflows can have destabilizing short term effects. However, the reasons for this have to be carefully analysed. If inflows are responding to market failures or weak banking, these weaknesses have to be remedied, rather than applying other costly treatments. Rules of bank supervision, for instance, have to be more stringent in transition economies than in mature market economies. Although Latin American and Asian experiences are useful to compare, one should not forget that Eastern European countries operate with less developed financial markets and banking systems.
4. Exchange rates should be made more flexible: wider bands around the central rate make exchange rate movements more volatile and deter short term speculative flows. In contrast, there was little agreement about the use of capital control measures: there is no conclusive experience on whether controls should be applied temporarily or permanently, against short term or long term flows, or if controls are effective at all in dealing with the inflows.

In the IIASA/ETI study, financial inflows are foreign funds/foreign exchange used to buy domestic property, businesses, stocks, bonds, treasury bills and speculative investments ("hot money"), or foreign funds taken as credits by domestic enterprises or commercial banks.

The International Institute for Applied Systems Analysis (Laxenburg, Austria) is a non-governmental research institution sponsored by a consortium of National Member Organizations in 17 nations. The Institute's research focuses on sustainability and the human dimensions of global change. The studies are international and interdisciplinary, providing timely and relevant information and options for the scientific community, policy makers and the public.

Economic Policy for Transition to Market Economy

There are at least three basic challenges that governments must tackle in countries pursuing a transition to market economies. The first is the market economy policy that governments in economies in transition have tackled and will have to continue to tackle. The second is the economic independence. Especially, countries that have won political independence must obtain their economic independence as well. The third is the economic development.

This is because most economies in transition are low-income or lower-middle-income countries. The economic development is important particularly for the governments of Central and East European countries pursuing their accession to the European Union. Here, I consider the economic policy experiences of Russia and other former Soviet republics, and East European countries from the viewpoint of these challenges facing economies in transition.

As a decade has passed since the former Soviet republics and East European countries launched their transition to market economies, these countries have created market economy institutions and organizations.

For example, market-oriented legal institutions have been established to provide for private ownership, central and commercial banks, securities markets, new fiscal and tax systems, enterprises, bankruptcies, free trading and monetary systems. A great number of private enterprises have emerged, including commercial banks and securities companies. They are clearly the fruits of transition efforts.

At the same time, however, some countries have developed phenomena that are unsuitable for market economies. The Russian economy's seven mysteries are often cited as examples: 1) Amid efforts for a transition to a market economy, barter trading has been dominant with various prices established for a single product. 2) The number of loss-laden enterprises has remained high and non-performing loans have expanded. Nevertheless, there has been no chain of bankruptcies and the number of bankruptcies has been limited to a very small amount. 3) The unemployment rate has remained below 10% while industrial production has been halved with gross domestic product plunging 40%. 4) Although Russia has been in transition to a market economy, business managers have tried only to maintain employment and production volume as in the past, instead of maximizing profits. While enterprises have been transformed into private stock companies, their managers have pursued their personal interests and ignored systematic corporate governance. 5) While people have hoarded massive cash, deposits at commercial banks have remained scarce. These banks have thus failed to mediate between savings and investment. 6) Voucher privatization has been forced to create tens of millions of shareholders and a securities market. But stock trading has been extremely limited. 7) The president and legislators are publicly elected to establish a democratic government. But the government has failed to strictly collect tax.

Russia thus features frequent phenomena that are inconsistent with a market economy. The purpose of this paper is not to analyse the status quo and problems of these transition efforts, but to shed a light on policy problems behind the status quo from the viewpoint of basic economic policy challenges for economies in transition.

4

Policy for Transition to Market Economy

The policy for transition to a market economy is one of the challenges that the governments of countries pursuing market economies have tackled and must continue to tackle. But questions still exist on what the transition to a market economy is and on what the right understanding of the transition is.

Transition to Market Economy

What is Transition to Market Economy? What Is Market Economy? The transition here is from a planned socialist economy to a market economy. In the market economy, the market works as a major adjustment mechanism between production and consumption, or between demand and supply. Its core consists of the pricing and free capital flow mechanisms. At least the following conditions are required for the establishment of the market economy:

Development of Social Division of Labour: In economies in transition where modern industries have developed, the social division of labour has well been established. From the viewpoint of a market economy, they have had distortions including monopolized industrial organizations and underdeveloped small and medium enterprises. But we can conclude that they have had established the social division of labour.

Economic Units' Decentralized Decision-Making: Various market transactions are based on agreements between economic units that emerge from their respective independent decisions. Therefore, enterprises, households and other economic units' rights to make economic decisions must be guaranteed. Subject to such decision-making are not only trading in goods or services but also capital transactions. In order to guarantee individual economic units' free decision-making, private ownership must basically be established. Disclosure and free flows of information are also indispensable. The systems for private ownership and compliance with contracts are the base for a market economy.

Free Competition: Free competition is required for the market to adjust production to consumption. At the same time, freedom of participation in the market must be guaranteed.

The government is Required for the Market Economy to Work Well: The government must serve as a "watchman state" to establish the rules of the game and guarantee compliance with the rules. In a modern society, the government is also required to carry out other functions including covering market failures, establishing social security and promoting social development. It must create taxation systems to meet these functions.

Policy Challenges for Transition to Market Economy

In a planned socialist economy, economic decision-making powers had substantially concentrated in its government, which had conducted economic management by directing and encouraging other economic units to implement plans.

Therefore, state ownership had been dominant, with enterprises deprived of powers to make their business management decisions. Free transactions and free competition had been eliminated usually. Any capital market had been eliminated and enterprise management had been linked to state finance. Any monetary system had been merely complementary to state finance. The following challenges are required for the transition from such planned economy to a market economy:

a. Privatization of state-run enterprises.
b. Liberalization of domestic and foreign trade, introduction of exchangeability for currencies, establishment of free competition.
c. Creation of the banking sector consisting of a central bank and commercial banks.

d. Creation of securities markets.

e. Establishment of state finance and tax systems based on a market economy.

f. Development of bankruptcy law, enterprise law and other institutions for a market economy to work well.

In order to build these market institutions and organizations, human resources must be developed to make up such institutions and act under the institutions and for market organization purposes. People who have used to a planned socialist economy for a long time have no experience, knowledge or know-how for a market economy. In transition to a market economy, these people must jump into an unknown world that they have never seen.

This is the case with Russia that has maintained a centralized, planned economy for 60 years. In a country like Russia, the development of human resources suitable for a market economy is indispensable during the transition, especially in its initial phase. The government in each economy in transition must create market economy institutions and organizations through efforts to develop people as market economy players or actors. This can be summarized below.

Goals of Policy for Transition to Market Economy

Each economy in transition must tackle the above challenges one by one. At the same time, its government must allow the economy to work well even during the transition. The construction of a new society has no choice but to build on the heritage of the old society. Even amid the transition, the society must remain. Therefore, any transition policy must be based on the maintenance of business activities for most of existing enterprises. The conditions and business environment must be secured for a great number of existing domestic enterprises to engage in free competition to make profit.

What Is Liberalization?

Liberalization is one of important policies for the transition to a market economy. Governments of economies in transition, the International Monetary Fund and the World Bank all emphasize the necessity of liberalization. Nevertheless, the liberalization has not necessarily been understood correctly. This is the reason why we here discuss what liberalization is.

Direct Meanings of Liberalization

The first important area for liberalization is domestic trade. The area's liberalization means the elimination of administrative regulations on choices of sellers and buyers. This should leave buyers and sellers to make choices freely. The liberalization in this area also includes a fundamental expansion of free trade. Prices are the second important area for liberalization. A socialist economy had fixed or restricted prices. Its government had fixed or restricted prices. Price liberalization means the elimination of such price regulations. The third area for liberalization is foreign trade. Soviet republics had typically featured a state's monopoly of foreign trade.

State agencies had undertaken foreign trade in most cases. Hungary had featured milder state regulations allowing producers to directly participate in foreign trade. But it had not eliminated state regulations on foreign trade. Liberalization of foreign trade means the thorough relaxation or elimination of regulations imposed on individuals' and enterprises' foreign trade. In order to allow free foreign trade, the introduction of domestic exchangeability for currencies is indispensable. Furthermore, a ban must be lifted on market units' capital transactions. The fourth area for liberalization involves production, investment and income distribution at enterprises. Government regulations on these business activities must be eliminated.

Therefore, liberalization directly means the elimination of business management regulations that had been dominant in a socialist economy. The direct result of such liberalization allows enterprises and other market units to make business decisions on their own.

What Is Freedom in Market Economy?

Having decision-making powers must be separated from making decisions. Market units, though having decision-making powers, frequently lack the ability to make reasonable decisions in various respects. In this case, market units are not necessarily free. Therefore, the elimination of regulations, though being a necessary condition for liberalization, is not necessarily a sufficient condition. Conditions must be developed for enterprise managers to make reasonable decisions from the market economy viewpoint. There are two kinds of conditions that must be considered in this respect.

The first are subjective conditions. A market unit that has the power to make its own business decisions may fail to make decisions, if without market information, funds, assets or good judgment. It may not have business freedom. Without funds, freedom of investment does not exist. Any market unit lacking market information or good judgment lacks business freedom. In this way, liberalization as conceived generally gets market units free from regulations, but fails to bring about freedom of business activities. In a country that had maintained a Soviet-type centralized, planned economy for a long time, economic information required for trade had concentrated at central planning and management agencies, and enterprise managers had lacked any ability to make market-based business decisions. Many economies in transition have had remarkable investment fund shortages. In such circumstances, the elimination of regulations does not necessarily lead to liberalization. Such countries' governments must not only eliminate regulations but also make positive policy efforts to promote the creation of subjective conditions.

Second, objective conditions must be met. They include competitive industrial organizations. If one producer exists in a certain industry sector, buyers will have no choice but to accept any request by the producer. This case is called a monopoly or an oligopoly. In Russia, a monopolistic or oligopolistic organization exists for each specific product, rather than for each industrial category. Furthermore, transportation ranges are long and transportation costs are massive, resulting in regional monopolies. Consumers have no freedom of choice. In such case, government regulations are required on monopolistic companies. In other words, regulations are required for liberalization.

The final conditions are for competitiveness. For example, a first-grade elementary school boy and an adult man compete in a 100-meter race. Fathers usually set such stage in a bid to tell their children of a joy in running or train them. However, the boy may get aware of his defeat soon and lose an incentive for running. If the boy is allowed to run only 40 meters and the adult man is forced to run 100 meters, a fair competition may be established between the boy and adult. Some adjustments are thus required to ensure fair competition. This is the same case with a situation where there are considerable competitiveness gaps between economic units. Weak units, though having business decision-making powers, lack their willingness to make decisions. Effectively, weak units have no freedom. If weak units are massive, therefore, the government must make adjustments. Depending on objective conditions, liberalization itself may require government intervention. Russia's experiences in the past years provide a good example in this respect.

Liberalization for a transition to a market economy thus means that the government should not only eliminate and relax regulations, but also develop subjective and objective conditions to allow economic units to make reasonable decisions. Liberalization promoters tend to overlook this important point.

What is Privatization?

A market economy cannot work smoothly in a country where most of enterprises are nationalized. In a transition to a market economy, privatization of enterprises is a basic problem facing the government. However, privatization should be designed to ensure conditions and the business environment that allow most of existing enterprises to freely compete for private profit. We must not overlook this point.

Significance of Privatization

Privatization means the transfer of enterprises from the public to the private sector. The transfer itself is a revision to a certain law and can be implemented if the government is willing to make such change and gets social consensus to such change.

However, the transfer is only the first step of privatization. This is because the transfer itself is separated from the problem of whether a new owner of a privatized enterprise can manage the enterprise as a private-sector owner. The essential problem with privatization rests on this point from the economic viewpoint. We must not overlook the point that any privatized enterprise requires people who have the ability and incentives to manage the enterprise reasonably. In this respect, the government must develop a business environment encouraging enterprise owners to manage their enterprises reasonably, establish corporate and other laws providing for reasonable activities of privatized enterprises, and train enterprise owners as market economy actors. These are key challenges for privatization. As a matter of fact, people can learn much from their daily activities and such daily learning is significant. But managers of privatized enterprises must be trained to develop their daily experiences into good management.

Incentives for Privatization

As for the legal aspect of privatization, political leaders and bureaucrats may be reluctant to implement privatization that could lead to their loss of economic powers.

On the other hand, privatization revamps the socialist power structure and could face strong resistance in a country like any former Soviet republic where a vested interest structure has been firmly established under a long-lasting planned economy. Privatization is politically significant to overcoming resistance to the promotion of a transition to a market economy. The Yeltsin-Gaidar regime had tried to promote a transition to a market economy and had been isolated from people who had vested interests in the socialist system. Its top priority might have been the elimination of resistance from people who had vested interests in the national ownership system and the state management structure. It was reasonable for the regime to accelerate privatization in order to eliminate the resistance. The Yeltsin regime had to create a group of private enterprise owners and obtain social support. But any significant political challenge may not always be reasonable from the economic viewpoint. This is the point we must understand in the context of social and political preparations for the transition in Russia in 1991. Political leaders of an economy in transition, who may be reluctant to implement privatization, may have to realize that privatization is indispensable for their economy in transition to become independent and develop well amid the growing globalization. We must remember that the Hungarian Socialist Workers' Party paved the way successfully for a transition to a market economy on its own when the serious external debt problem was forcing the country to implement fundamental reforms in the 1980s.

Managers of state-run enterprises may oppose their privatization, concerned that they could lose their vested powers. Conflict of interests between social groups may halt progress in privatization. In other words, the motivation of enterprise managers to promote privatization is especially important. Any mistakes in this respect could affect corporate governance after privatization. Therefore, any economy in transition must develop reasonable incentives for privatization.

Privatization Methods

None of former Soviet republics and East European countries has depended 100% on selling or granting of state assets to the private sector for privatization of enterprises. In fact, they have combined the standard method of asset sales with grants through voucher coupons. But the weight of asset sales or grants in the combination is very important and has a great influence on the resulting private ownership and corporate management systems. Hungary primarily used the sale of state assets for privatization, while Russia and the Czech Republic have placed a greater emphasis on grants. Accelerated privatization amid domestic capital shortages may depend on grants, external liberalization and foreign funds. Privatization through grants fails to lead to fund-raising operations and tends to slow corporate restructuring.

Russia has adopted the so-called voucher method for privatization. Every citizen received a 10,000-ruble voucher that could be used for making bids for enterprise ownership through auctions to promote privatization. In order to eliminate enterprise managers' resistance to privatization, Russia introduced preferential treatments for enterprise employees. The first and second variants of the preferential treatments have played a great role in promoting privatization. The first variant gave employees of an enterprise registered preferred shares equivalent to up to 25% of its fixed capital on a free-of-charge basis and allowed them to buy up to 10% of total shares at 30% discount from face value with installment payments within three years.

It also allowed managerial employees to purchase up 5% of the fixed capital. In this way, this variant allowed insiders to acquire up to 40% of the fix capital. The second variant allowed employees to purchase common stock shares equivalent to up to 51% of the fixed capital before others acquire shares. In the privatization through vouchers, some 75% of enterprises chose the second variant. Most of the others adopted the first variant. Furthermore, managers of each enterprise purchased vouchers and took advantage of all legal and illegal possible tools to put as many as shares possible under their control and avoid any control by outsiders. For example, managers of an enterprise used corporate funds to establish their own investment fund to purchase vouchers. And these managers sold shares of their enterprise to such fund. As a result, none can find outsiders' real equity stakes in many

Russian enterprises. Russian privatization has thus featured insiders' rigid pursuit of enterprise ownership and control.

The result in Russia has been a birth of quasi-private enterprises that are owned by insiders and the state. Similar results emerged in the initial phase of privatization in other former Soviet republics that adopted grants and preferential treatments for employees. The Russian government has had no policy on managing enterprises as their partial shareholder and has played little role in their management.

The Russian privatization has allowed employees of privatized enterprises, or part of the people, to enclose state assets. Especially, employees of natural resources-related enterprises have acquired massive assets. On the other hand, government agency employees, pensioners and employees of declining enterprises have become losers. The Russian privatization policy has created a great asset gap.

Formation of Enterprise Ownership Structure and Corporate Governance

The Russian privatization has resulted in a loss of corporate governance. The government had no intent to exercise its rights as the shareholder of many enterprises and left insiders to dominantly control enterprises. Their managers have used various means to avoid the influence of outside shareholders on management. It has been impossible for outside shareholders to monitor corporate management. On the other hand, economic and corporate management crises, excessive employment and threats of dismissals have discouraged employees of enterprises from monitoring their management. In this way, enterprises have effectively lost corporate governance. Enterprise managers have become dictators engaging in illegal acts. They sold good parts of enterprise assets at discounts to private firms that their families have founded. They also transferred enterprise funds to their own accounts at home and abroad. Enterprise managers have thus pursued their individual profit rather than profit for their enterprises. As a result of such privatization, the Russian economy has become a "barter economy (G. B. Kleiner)" instead of a corporate economy. The meanings of equity ownership have been lost for most of the people and a great asset gap has emerged. This has prompted the people to doubt the advisability of private ownership, destabilizing the private ownership system itself.

Legal System Development for Privatization (Rights of Shareholders)

The results of privatization vary depending on the development of legal systems for privatization and activities of privatized enterprises. For privatized enterprises, laws must be established to provide for shareholders' rights, legal status of enterprise managers, legal treatments of bankruptcies and many other aspects. If legal system development lags behind privatization, corruptions will become dominant with rights of outside shareholders ignored, as seen in Russia.

Coordination between Privatization and Macroeconomic Policy

Macroeconomic conditions involving business management may be able to exert a greater influence on the result of privatization than a choice of privatization methods or the degree of legal system development. If reckless anti-inflation tightening leads to operating fund shortages for enterprises and plunges massive enterprises into effective bankruptcies during privatization, stocks will lose their values to prompt business managers to lose interest in corporate system management and pursue their personal interests.

The Russian "barter" economy can be viewed as the result of tight macroeconomic policy. Import liberalization, if stepped up recklessly, could force uncompetitive industrial sectors, like the Russian textile sector, to cut production sharply and disappear, resulting in massive bankruptcies.

Business managers, as inside shareholders for their enterprises, would then see their shareholdings becoming meaningless. This would be the same case with outside shareholders. A great asset gap would emerge between industrial sectors that have and do not have international competitiveness, for example, between oil, natural gas and other natural resources-related sectors, and light and machinery sectors in Russia. Such gap would lead many people to view the privatization result as unequal. A precondition for private ownership is that some people consider others' ownership to be justifiable. If social approval of such precondition were shaken, the private ownership system itself would be destabilized. For example, calls have emerged in Russia for reprivatization of natural resources-related enterprises. Privatization had been designed to bring about the formation of a middle-income class and private entrepreneurs. But Russian privatization has failed to do so.

If privatization alone were pursued, its significance could be halved and its goal of the private ownership system could be distorted in some cases. Therefore, we must pay attention to coordination between privatization and macroeconomic policy. It must be reiterated that the fundamental policy goal should be ensuring conditions and business environments that allow most of existing domestic enterprises to conduct free competition for profits. This is a key point that policy makers must remember even a decade after the transition was launched.

Economic Independence and Development

From the international viewpoint, the transition to a market economy means the integration of economies in transition into the global market. Former Soviet republics and East European countries, even though with very low technological and economic development levels, have lost COMECON (Council for Mutual Economic Assistance) as their exclusive closed market and have been forced to compete with leading enterprises in the world. As a result, whether economies in transition could become independent internationally is now questioned again. Especially, former Soviet republics, the Czech Republic, the Slovak Republic and former Yugoslav republics have gained political independence upon the collapse of their respective unions and have been faced with economic independence challenges.

Economic Independence

What is Economic Independence?

Economic independence means that a country's relations with others and international organizations are stably maintained on a commercial basis. In other words, one country's economic management must work well without depending on economic assistance from abroad. To this end, a country must stably maintain equilibrium in its international balance of payments and must be able to avoid default and other results running counter to commercial rules. Specifically, a country must have strong international competitiveness and must be able to make exports meeting its imports. One country's economic independence is usually supported by the independence of domestic industries and enterprises and depends heavily on the efforts of enterprises.

International Balance of Payments in Economies in Transition

An outline of trade and current account balances in economies in transition indicate that most of economies in transition excluding Russia, Turkmenistan and other resources-rich countries have persistently run trade and current account deficits, failed to cover annual deficits with foreign direct investment and accumulated external debt.

Some have seen changes worthy of attention, including changes in external debt mixes, cuts in government debt, and rises in private-sector debt. The expansion of external debt does not necessarily means that debt-ridden economies in transition may default immediately. In fact, however, these economies have no current account or trade balance improvement in sight. This means that whether most of economies in transition can achieve economic independence is still uncertain.

Japan's Postwar Experiences

History repeats itself. After World War II, colonies winning independence as well as war losers had to achieve economic independence. Resources-poor Japan lost its markets with its economy devastated by the war.

Amid the difficulties, Japan had double challenges to achieve economic development and a transition from a government-controlled wartime economy to a free market economy. A basic policy goal was then to construct an independent economy requiring no American assistance. Indicating this is an outline of the government's postwar economic programs. Here is a brief introduction to these programs and their goals related to international relations:

1) "5-Year Program for Economic Independence" (December 1955): Enhancement of export competitiveness amid growing trade liberalization.
2) "New Long-Term Economic Development Program" (December 1957): Expansion of exports under the spirit of a trading-oriented country.
3) "National Income Doubling Program" (December 1960): Economic assistance to least developed countries and promotion of import liberalization plans.
4) "Medium-Term Economic Development Program" (January 1965): Improvement of Japan's international position and a

transition to an open economy, export expansion and import liberalization, achievement of current account equilibrium.

5) "Economic and Social Development Program" (March 1967): Liberalization of capital transactions.
6) "New Economic and Social Development Program" (May 1970): Contributions to the global economy and society, positive promotion of trade and capital liberalization.
7) "Basic Economic and Social Program" (February 1973): International cooperation under stable international payments balance surpluses, foreign aid at 1% of GNP, basic international payments balance equilibrium.

The above history indicates that the Japanese government in pursuit of economic independence had tried to enhance the nation's international competitiveness and expand exports until the mid-1960s. We may have to prudently consider whether

Japan's various policies taken then, including prolonged import curbs and other protectionist policies, could be applied to economies in transition at a time when economic liberalization has made global progress. Undoubtedly, however, positive export promotion policies are indispensable to most of economies in transition. In this respect, these economies can learn lessons from Japan's experiences.

Economic Development

Planned socialist economies of the 20th century emerged in underdeveloped regions of the world and played a great role in industrialization there to help these regions catch up with industrialized nations. However, they had lacked indigenous technological innovation capability and failed to get on an innovation track. Since the 1970s, they have remarkably lagged behind other economies in the world. None of economies in transition has developed into a high-income economy. Again, therefore, they have been considering the challenge to intentionally pursue economic development and catch up with industrialized economies.

Economic Policy Problems

The discussions above demonstrate great roles that governments must play in economies in transition. First, the governments must ensure right incentives for enterprise managers and create appropriate conditions and environments for competition. Second, they must enhance international competitiveness and accelerate economic growth. Third, they must train people as market economy actors. In fact, economic policies in economies in transition do not necessarily indicate a persistent pursuit of these goals.

Importance of Macroeconomic Policy

As known well, the Russian financial crisis in 1998 paradoxically created conditions for later economic growth. The 50% devaluation of the ruble amid the crisis has served to push up prices of imports, enhance domestic products' competitiveness against imports in the domestic market and stimulate production of goods replacing imports. As a result, imports' share of domestic retail sales has dramatically declined.

The ruble devaluation has also served to promote exports and boost export\ sales, and a substantial fall in real wages amid fast inflation has reduced production costs at enterprises. These developments have led to improvements in financial performance of Russian enterprises and prompted them to expand investment, stimulating their production of investment goods for domestic use. The Russian government had not designed these improvements, which are attributable to external factors. But they indicate the importance of macroeconomic policy for improving economic performance. In turn, they also indicate negative effects on the Russian economy of thorough import liberalization since 1992 and incomplete revisions to the liberalization since 1995.

Another point we must not overlook in the economic recovery course is a change in the policy stance of the Central Bank of the Russian Federation. Anti-inflation measures have emerged as an urgent challenge again since the 1998 financial crisis. The central bank has tried to hold down inflation while easing liquidity shortages after the crisis. Such monetary policy is indicated in Russian Central Bank Governor Viktor Gerashchenko's report on "Transition to New Currency and Credit Policy in 1999." His report emphasizes a transition to a balanced policy that prevents anti-inflation money supply restrictions from hurting the revitalization of production.

The stance of the Russian Central Bank is close to the monetary policy stance that the National Bank of Hungary had maintained in

1990. The Hungarian central bank then adopted the policy of guaranteeing money supply required for economic functions and anti-inflation monetary tightening that enterprises and citizens could tolerate. It rejected any one-sided, rough monetary tightening policy. The balanced monetary and credit policy that gave priority to the real economy could successfully prevent any excessive increase in overdue debt and deficit-ridden enterprises and made the implementation of a bankruptcy law (a new bankruptcy law established in 1991) feasible. Russia was too late in departing from a rough money supply restriction policy.

The Russian economy's remarkable recovery is indicated in the next table. Noteworthy is basic investment that recovered in 1999 after a persistent decline since 1992 and scored substantial growth in 2000. Russia has resumed economic growth even in the absence of effective improvements in the transparency of the enterprise ownership structure, commercial banks' malfunctions and other structural microeconomic problems. This indicates how great the impact of macroeconomic conditions and the central bank's monetary and credit policy on the economy is. In respect to Russia, macroeconomic conditions include the exchange rate and terms of trade. The purpose of macroeconomic policy must thus be to set a normal economic environment where most of existing enterprises can usually compete for profit.

Macroeconomic Policy and Enterprise Reform

The Russian economy has featured the prevalence of deficit-ridden enterprises, overdue debt and barter trade, as well as irresponsible corporate governance that has led to the "barter economy." These problems involving acts of enterprises and their managers have frequently been attributed to defects of privatization methods, lagging development of law, insufficient enterprise reform, etc. They have also been interpreted as factors to explain Russia's deteriorating macroeconomic performance. Such interpretation is right in a sense. At the same, we can also note that macroeconomic policy has deteriorated the enterprise management environment and caused the problematic acts of enterprises and their managers, as indicated by the Russian economy's recovery since the latter half of 1998. Enterprise bankruptcies and other negative incentives, as well as acquisition of profit, private obtainment of wealth and other positive incentives, are required for a market economy to work well. If macroeconomic policy is too rough and forces a great number of enterprises to go bankrupt, implementation of bankruptcies will become impossible to prevent negative incentives working well and will cause malpractices in enterprise management. We cannot overlook such great negative effect of rough macroeconomic policy.

Policy Mix

During the transition to a market economy, the government must abolish or relax various regulations set by a socialist regime. Also as noted earlier, liberalization itself requires appropriate government regulations.

In Hungary, for example, price liberalization was promoted as outline. Hungary took three years to increase liberalized-price products' share of consumer goods transactions from 41% in 1987 to 77% in 1990, while maintaining reports and consultations on prices to fight against monopoly or oligopoly. It also adopted rules to link prices of raw and other materials for massive consumption to global market prices. The basic idea behind such approach was that the introduction of an overall free market price system must be gradual to prevent inflation and other negative effects from outdoing positive effects of a market price system. Hungary mixed gradual price liberalization with administrative intervention.

Hungary also implemented gradual trade liberalization. Imports free from import licenses or quotas accounted for only 40% of total imports in value in 1989. The percentage was raised to 65% in 1990, 90% in 1991 and 95% in 1995. Hungary, which joined the Central Europe free trade agreement in 1993, has been a member country of the General Agreement on Tariffs and Trade and the World Trade Organization. In March 1995, however, it introduced an 8% import surcharge in the face of trade balance deterioration. In this way, trade liberalization was accompanied by government regulations. We must remember that if a great competitiveness gap exists between domestic and foreign enterprises, any reckless import liberalization can effectively deprive domestic enterprises of freedom in management and fail to lead to real liberalization.

Policy Sequencing

From 1991 to 1992, Russia was dominated by excess liquidity on one hand and by monopolistic industrial organizations on the other.

In such circumstances, thorough price liberalization was unreasonable. Some economists then insisted that Russia should begin with sales of state assets to absorb excess liquidity. This was reasonable.

A reasonable argument may be that values of goods including state assets cannot be determined unless prices are liberalized. However, there is no guarantee that price liberalization could result in reasonable prices under a distorted market structure. Price liberalization, including a price system formation process, should be gradual. It may also be reasonable that antimonopoly measures should be enhanced before price liberalization.

It was unreasonable for Russia to promote privatization before developing law to govern enterprise management after privatization. It was also problematic for Russia to liberalize trade before taking measures to enhance the competitiveness of domestic industry. These Russian experiences indicate that policy sequencing is very important for the course of transition to a market economy.

Industrial Policy

Most of economies in transition have prepared government programs for economic development and are trying to implement industrial policy. Russia has introduced a development budget and created the Russian Development Bank. But its industrial policy is still in embryo. Most of economies in transition have to enhance international industrial competitiveness, promote exports and accelerate economic development in order to achieve economic independence. An industrial policy approach may be effective for such challenges. But many of these economies have yet to develop information flows, organizations, policy tools and other things to ensure the preparation and implementation of industrial policy. Economies in transition that are trying to join the EU may have to narrow their scope of industrial policy because the EU has authorized industrial policy limited to the promotion of small and medium enterprises, technological development, regional development and some other areas.

These economies could have difficulties implementing policies that are required in accordance with their economic realities and development levels. The EU's approach on industrial policy tends to exclude sector-specific promotion. In the circumstances, governments of Central and East European countries may be required to give practical and pragmatic considerations to industrial policy. Financial difficulties have prevented some of them from developing sufficient policy tools. These problems exist regarding industrial policy of economies in transition. But Hungary has implemented and is systematizing industrial policy, as indicated below:

(Basic Government Documents):

1) Industrial Policy in 1990s (January 1993).
2) Industrial Policy for Enhancing Competitiveness (drafted in November 1995).
3) Hungary in New Europe (1997).
4) Szechenyi Plan (2000).

(Policy):

1) A 50% corporate tax cut for export-expansion investment (just before the accession to the WTO in January 1996).
2) Exemption of corporate tax for investment in recession-hit regions (since 1996).
3) Accelerated depreciation (since 1996).
4) Technology Development Fund (National Technology Development Commission).
5) Industrial Development Fund (Ministry of Industry and Trade, marketing aid).
6) Financing for equipment investment at small and medium enterprises.
   a. Start loan.
   b. Reorg Start loan.
   c. Export-Import Bank of Japan loan.
   d. Energy-saving investment loan.
   e. "25%" Loan System.
   f. Phare loan.
   g. Micro Credit.
7) Credit guarantee for small and medium enterprises.
   a. Credit Guarantee Co. Ltd.
   b. Start Guarantee Fund.
   c. Tariff-free zone.

Tariff-free zone enterprises numbered 116 in 1999, accounting for 43% of foreign trade.

(Organizations):

1) Ministry of Industry and Trade, Ministry of Economic Affairs.
2) Enterprise Promotion Foundation of Hungary (SME promotion, 1990)
3) Hungarian Investment and Trade Development Corp.
4) National Technology Development Commission.
5) Hungarian Investment and Trade Information Centre.
6) Hungarian Export-Import Bank (1994).
7) Hungarian Export Insurance Corp. (1994).
8) Hungarian Investment Development Bank (1991).
9) Hungarian Productivity Centre.

Hungary, which has been leading in making a transition to a market economy, has thus positively implemented industrial policy. As indicated by the tariff-free zone, industrial policy has some economic development effects.

Conclusion

The need for liberalization has been emphasized since former Soviet republics and East European countries launched their transition to market economies. The International Monetary Fund and other international financial institutions have frequently forced radical liberalization as the conditionality for credits to economies in transition.

Liberalization has also been adopted as the benchmark to assess progress in transition. For example, "World Development Report-from Planned Economy to Market Economy" argued that "Central and Eastern European economies, which won independence seven years ago, and newly industrializing economies are leading" and that "countries that have implemented faster and broader liberalization have achieved faster recovery." Are these arguments true? Liberalization as elimination of regulations may be relatively easy.

The World Development Report (1996) translated liberalization of domestic trade, liberalization of foreign trade and participation of new enterprises (privatization as an alternative indicator) into scores, used the scores to calculate degrees of liberalization for each year from 1989 to 1995, and worked out seven-year averages. It then classified economies in transition in the order of the average scores. According to the assessment, seven countries-Hungary, Poland, the Czech Republic, the Slovak Republic, Slovenia, Macedonia and Croatia-were classified as the most advanced in transition to market economies. The indices of liberalization for the six years to 1994.

However, this assessment includes clear mistakes. This is because five of the seven countries classified as the most advanced in the transition, excluding the Czech and Slovak Republics, had already promoted liberalization before 1989. The five's liberalization indices were thus higher in 1989 and remained higher until 1994 than those of others. As indicated by gaps between 1989 and 1994, however, their liberalization progress in the five countries during the five years was less than in other countries. In other words, the five never implemented faster or more positive liberalization than others during the period. As well known by those who have followed former Soviet republic and East European economies, the former Yugoslav republics of Slovenia, Croatia and Macedonia have promoted liberalization since the early 1950s, Hungary has introduced commodity markets since 1968 and Poland has implemented similar reforms since 1981. These five countries have been historically advanced in transition to market economies or in liberalization. In fact, the reason for their good economic performance is that they have been historically advanced in liberalization.

From the viewpoint as discussed earlier, this is a natural development. Subjective and objective conditions must be developed over a long time for meaningful liberalization or privatization. Hasty development of these conditions cannot be successful in achieving meaningful liberalization or privatization. This may be clear if considerations are given to enterprise managers' business senses and market economy practices that cannot be developed over any short term. Every economy in transition must promote liberalization and privatization. At the same time, each has to develop conditions for liberalization and privatization that must be implemented firmly and steadily.

5

Economic Transition in the Czech Republic

Academic Research in the Transition Economy of the Czech Republic

The Czechoslovak Academy of Sciences was founded in 1952 on the standard Soviet model. In 1969 it was comprised of 87 research institutes, and a learned society. The Academy was relatively free from state ideology during the communist regime. In 1989, it was made up of 12.500 staff, 7.854 of whom were scientists. Now the Academy is comprised of 4.780 scientists and 70 institutes, and its staff totals over 7.000. Since the velvet revolution, about 50% of all researchers and technicians have left science. Since 1989, the budget for basic research institutions has been cut dramatically, causing deterioration in research capacity. The remaining research capacity, crucial for future technological innovation, suffers from major structural problems. Academic institutions, long left in a traditional socialist, secure market are now forced to find new ways to organise management and increase their income. Most scientists agree that the Czech Republic cannot and should not support as much basic science as was supported during the communist regime.

There were two reasons for the decrease in the number of researchers in the Academy's institutes. The first is the improved efficiency and productivity of research institutes and the reduction of under-developed scientific fields. The second reason is because scientists in the private sector are much better paid and have more stable jobs. The average monthly salary in the Academy is now about 350 DM. Scientists there have always been relatively poorly paid in comparison to other occupational groups. Young scientists are generally unable to support their families on their salaries which are below the national average for state employees. This had resulted in an expansion of the practice of taking on additional private work, which is often performed in the institute on behalf of other organisations. This situation produced negative opinions in the media and the political arena, but had little impact on the prestige of the Academy in the eyes of the general public.

The current shrinking of the scientific community is random and incidental. However, the people leaving science include some of the best young talent. There has recently been considerable discussion about "human capital" and the "brain drain". Contrary to conventional thought, few scientists have left the Czech Republic. Some scientists have left their basic research institutes to work on projects for foreign business. Many more researchers have left science altogether, though they have stayed in the Czech Republic. In my opinion, this process is inevitable, and probably desirable. Hundreds of talented Czechs became scientists during the communist regime by default, as science was one of the few outlets for creative people. Presently, there are many opportunities in the private sector and some of these gifted people can, and should, move in that direction. Science's loss will be the economy's gain.

Czechoslovakia, with its centrally planned economy during the communist regime, was rigid and lacked sensitivity and adaptability towards the technological development happening outside the Soviet Block. Since socialism gave priority to science, the actual research system we have today is relatively well developed. But the typical corporate strategy was passive and conservative, relying on using accumulated data rather than introducing new, more risky, technologies. The collapse of the integrated East European "market" hit most businesses very badly, and it has been virtually impossible to replace the secure contract system of the past with the market-led new technology orientation. Clearly, such a situation, does not provide a climate for the development of new academic or industrial research. It was also responsible for reducing the prestige given science and technology by the general public. This, though, has not had serious consequences.

The former communist system was based on a linear innovation model which is understood as a technical development model, whereby centrally planned and produced technologies were developed and deployed via a chain of separate institutions unrelated to market pressures. These institutions had a clear purpose and a simple organisation, and were all separate from each other.

Many problems have been inherited along with the existing scientific research structure. The Czechoslovak Academy of Sciences was organised in 1952, with a brief to pursue basic research in discipline-based research institutes. The Academy, in fact, performed a dual function. It acted as an eminent society for the scientific elite, while also co-ordinating basic research for the state as a whole. These two overlapping roles caused confusion and even conflict. Members were selected on the basis of honour and reputation rather than on any managerial skill in policy-making. The academicians' status was guaranteed by political "nomenclature". Institutes operated under governmental accounting rules with funding from the State budget to meet costs. Funding was allocated to institutions rather than individuals or research groups, while evaluation was weak. After 1968, under central control, this system became more superficial as well as more rigid.

It is possible to identify many sources of this type of inefficiency within Czech science of the past. There was an imbalance between basic and applied research and development. As a rule, basic research was quite good, but development and application of technologies were rather poor. The balance between basic research and applied research could be improved through greater diversity in funding. In the Czech Republic, the central government still provides about 90% of the funding for basic science, whereas in Western countries much of the government funding comes from different sectors. About 80% of basic research is still carried out by the Czech Academy. The lack of diversity in funding is one of many sources of inefficiency. Others include the lack of equipment, poor communications, weak technical support and inflexible inherited structures.

Universities in the Czech Republic were developed to educate, and scientific research was not their prime responsibility. During the decades of socialist administration, higher education and research were separated, resulting in an unhealthy rivalry as they both competed for government resources. Czech universities are deeply conservative and protectionist.

For a whole generation, universities were forced to abandon their tradition of free intellectual thought, and research almost disappeared. University staffs are weary of change, and weary of the stress of constant assessment and competition.

It will probably be necessary to shift a lot of the basic and applied research back to the universities, where basic researchers can mingle with applied researchers, and influence the education of the next generation. The present lack of diversity is one of many sources of inefficiency.

There is no consensus on how much effort should be put into either preserving the Academy's elite research institutes or incorporating them in the university organisation. People from the Academy think that the elite Academy institutions must be preserved and should be given top priority. Others, from the universities, argue that our limited resources should be spent on young scholars and on applied, rather than on basic research, especially during this period of transition. I only hope that the new organisation of basic and applied research in the Academy, in the universities and in technical and development institutes, including the new system of financial support, will be completed this year. And I hope that the current competitive market conditions will bring the latent research capacity of these groups out into the open.

The most important tasks connected with developing more effective basic and applied research in the Czech Republic are:

- overcoming the historical split between universities and the Academy in the best possible way;
- clarifying the shape and character of scientific activity in the medium and long term and to establish foci and priorities and how best to meet disciplinary and interdisciplinary needs;
- determining who is best suited to undertake the very different science-based activities crucial to the future innovation system of the Czech Republic;
- preparing a new organisation for basic research and contracted R&D, and to formulate new business and management development strategies;
- improving the University-Academy link. This will depend on wider educational reforms;

- reforming academia, universities and research institutes. This will depend on the informal reorganisation of decision-making on the one hand, and the setting of clear rules for research and business management on the other.

However, we still have no concept of science policy: science policy is "about priorities". Science in the communist era was a "feudal system" and this system must now be changed. In a "market economy system" there is no other way.

Economic System of the Czech Republic

The territory of the Czech Republic was one of the most economically developed parts of Europe at the beginning of the last century. It was the most industrial part of Austria-Hungary. After the establishment of an independent state in 1918, then ranked among the top twenty developed states in the world.

After the Second World War, and as a result of the social changes related to the rise of the socialist regime, significant changes in the economy system were enforced. All industrial companies were nationalized and the economy started to be controlled centrally on the basis of a national economic plan. Within the Soviet bloc, the Czechoslovak economic system focused even more on the heavy-industry development, which was demanding in resources and energy. Traditional economical branches such as the glass industry, the food industry and the textile industry were markedly suppressed. The proportion of producing the means of production grew at the expense of consumer goods. The national collectivization was on many occasions enforced in the agricultural industry. Farmers independently managing their farms were forced to give up their land and production means for the benefit of the agricultural associations. Thereafter they became members of such associations. Chemical fertilizers and heavy technology were used to a great extent, hence the land resources were greatly degraded.

From the 1960s, animal production developed rapidly in the factory farming plants. The Czech economy's development during the socialist regime resulted in the loss of competitiveness and in a high ecological burden on the landscape.

After the fall of the Communist party in 1989, the Czech economy system was at the start again; previous competitors, who had not been affected by socialism, were far ahead. In the years right after the revolution, the Czech economic system had to absorb all changes that had occurred on world markets; the changes were often very dramatic. Within the restitution system, businesses and land were returned to their previous owners; during the coupon privatization, a large majority of state companies were privatized. Some important companies were sold to foreign investors (Skoda Auto, Plzeò Brewery); some were bought by interested Czech parties (EKD, Skoda Plzeò). Currently, the Czech Republic ranks among the fastest-developing countries in the region and compensates for the delay that resulted from the historical development.

Economy of the Czech Republic

Of the emerging democracies in central and eastern Europe, the Czech Republic has one of the most developed industrialized economies. It is one of the most stable and prosperous of the post-Communist states of Central and Eastern Europe. GDP per capita at purchasing power parity was $26,800 in 2008, which is 82% of the EU average. The principal industries are heavy and general machine-building, iron and steel production, metalworking, chemical production, electronics, transportation equipment, textiles, glass, brewing, china, ceramics, and pharmaceuticals. Its main agricultural products are sugarbeets, fodder roots, potatoes, wheat, and hops.

History

Its strong industrial tradition dates to the 19th century, when Bohemia and Moravia were the economic heartland of the Austro-Hungarian Empire. Today, this heritage is both an asset and a liability. The Czech Republic has a well-educated population and a well-developed infrastructure, but its industrial plants and much of its industrial equipment are obsolete. According to the Stalinist development policy of planned interdependence, all the economies of the socialist countries were linked tightly with that of the Soviet Union. With the disintegration of the communist economic alliance in 1991, Czech manufacturers lost their traditional markets among former communist countries to the east.

1990-1995

The "Velvet Revolution" in 1989 offered a chance for profound and sustained political and economic reform. Signs of economic resurgence began to appear in the wake of the shock therapy that the International Monetary Fund (IMF) labelled the "*big bang*" of January 1991. Since then, consistent liberalization and astute economic management has led to the removal of 95% of all price controls, low unemployment, a positive balance of payments position, a stable exchange rate, a shift of exports from former communist economic bloc markets to Western Europe, and relatively low foreign debt. Inflation has been higher than in some other countries-mostly in the 10% range-and the government has run consistent modest budget deficits.

Two government priorities have been strict fiscal policies and creating a good climate for incoming investment in the republic. Following a series of currency devaluations, the crown has remained stable in relation to the U.S. dollar. The Czech crown became fully convertible for most business purposes in late 1995.

In order to stimulate the economy and attract foreign partners, the government has revamped the legal and administrative structure governing investment. With the breakup of the Soviet Union, the country, till that point highly dependent on exports to the USSR, had to make a radical shift in economic outlook: away from the East, and towards the West. This necessitated the restructuring of existing banking and telecommunications facilities, as well as adjusting commercial laws and practices to fit Western standards. Further minimizing reliance on a single major partner, successive Czech governments have welcomed U.S. investment (amongst others) as a counter-balance to the strong economic influence of Western European partners, especially of their powerful neighbour, Germany. Although foreign direct investment (FDI) runs in uneven cycles, with a 12.9% share of total FDI between 1990 and March 1998, the U.S. was the third-largest foreign investor in the Czech economy, behind Germany and the Netherlands.

Progress toward creating a stable investment climate was recognized when the Czech Republic to become the first post-communist country to receive an investment-grade credit rating by international credit institutions.

The republic boasts a flourishing consumer production sector and has privatized most state-owned heavy industries through the voucher privatization system. Under the system, every citizen was given the opportunity to buy, for a moderate price, a book of vouchers that represents potential shares in any state-owned company.

The voucher holders could then invest their vouchers, increasing the capital base of the chosen company, and creating a nation of citizen share-holders. This is in contrast to Russian privatization, which consisted of sales of communal assets to private companies rather than share-transfer to citizens. The effect of this policy has been dramatic. Under communism, state ownership of businesses was estimated to be 97. Privatization through restitution of real estate to the former owners was largely completed in 1992. By 1998, more than 80% of enterprises were in private hands. Now completed, the program has made Czechs, who own shares of each of the Czech companies, one of the highest per-capita share owners in the world.

1995-2000

The republic's economic transformation is far from complete. A recession in 1997 revealed that the government still faces serious challenges in completing industrial restructuring, increasing transparency in capital market transactions, fully privatizing the banking sector, transforming the housing sector and solving serious environmental problems.

Political and financial crises in 1997 shattered the Czech Republic's image as one of the most stable and prosperous of post-Communist states. Delays in enterprise restructuring and failure to develop a well-functioning capital market played major roles in Czech economic troubles, which culminated in a currency crisis in May. The currency was forced out of its fluctuation band as investors worried that the current account deficit, which reached nearly 8% of GDP to introduce two austerity packages later in the spring (called vernacularly "The Packages"), which cut government spending by 2.5% of GDP.

Growth dropped to 0.3% in 1997, -2.3% in 1998, and -0.5% in 1999. The government established a restructuring agency in 1999 and launched a revitalization program-to spur the sale of firms to foreign companies. Key priorities include accelerating legislative convergence with EU norms, restructuring enterprises, and privatizing banks and utilities. The economy, fuelled by increased export growth and investment, is expected to recover in 2000.

2000-2005

Growth in 2000-05 was supported by exports to the EU, primarily to Germany, and a strong recovery of foreign and domestic investment. Domestic demand is playing an ever more important role in underpinning growth as interest rates drop and the availability of credit cards and mortgages increases.

Current account deficits of around 5% of GDP are beginning to decline as demand for Czech products in the European Union increases. Inflation is under control. Recent accession to the EU gives further impetus and direction to structural reform. In early 2004 the government passed increases in the Value Added Tax (VAT) and tightened eligibility for social benefits with the intention to bring the public finance gap down to 4% of GDP by 2006, but more difficult pension and healthcare reforms will have to wait until after the next elections. Privatization of the state-owned telecommunications firm Èeský Telecom took place in 2005. Intensified restructuring among large enterprises, improvements in the financial sector, and effective use of available EU funds should strengthen output growth.

2005-2010

Growth continued in the first years of the EU membership. The credit portion of the financial crisis of 2007–2009 did not affect the Czech Republic much, mostly due to its stable banking sector which has learned its lessons during a smaller crisis in the late 1990s and became much more cautious. As a fraction of the GDP, the Czech public debt belongs among the smallest ones in Central and Eastern Europe. Moreover, unlike many other post-communist countries, an overwhelming majority of the household debt-over 99%-is denominated in the local Czech currency. That's why the country wasn't affected by the shrunken money supply in the U.S. dollars.

However, as a large exporter, the economy was sensitive to the decrease of the demand in Germany and other trading partners. In the middle of 2009, the annual drop of the GDP for 2009 was estimated around 3% or 4.3%, a relatively modest decrease. The impact of the economic crisis may have been limited by the existence of the national currency that temporarily weakened in H1 of 2009, simplifying the life of the exporters.

Energy

The Czech Republic is reducing its dependence on highly polluting low-grade brown coal as a source of energy. Nuclear energy presently provides about 30% of total power needs, and its share is projected to increase to 40%. Natural gas is procured from Russian Gazprom (roughly three-fourths of domestic consumption) and from Norwegian companies (most of the remaining one-fourth). Russian gas is imported via Ukraine (Friendship pipeline), Norwegian gas is transported through Germany. The gas consumption (approx. 100 TWh in 2003-5) is almost two times higher than the electricity consumption. South Moravia has a small oil and gas deposits.

Statistical Indicators

- GDP (pp.): $266.3 billion (2008).
- GDP Growth: 3.9% (2008).
- GDP per capita (pp.): $26,100 (2008).
- GDP by sector: *Agriculture:* 2.9% *Industry:* 38.7% *Services:* 58.7% (2008).
- Inflation: 3.6% (2008).
- Labour Force: 5,370,000 (2008) *Unemployment:* 6% (2008).
- Industrial production growth rate: 7% (2008).
- Household income or consumption by percentage share: (1996).
    - *lowest 10%:* 4.3%
    - *highest 10%:* 22.4%
- Public Debt: 29,4% GDP (2008)

Trade and Finance

- Exports: $122 billion (2007) *Export goods:* machinery and transport goods 52%, raw materials 9%, chemicals 5%, other 34% (2003).
- Imports: $116.6 billion *Import goods:* machinery and transport goods 46%, raw materials and fuels 16%, chemicals 10%, other 28% (2003)
- Current Account balance: -$4,533,000 (2007).
- Export partners: Germany 30.8%, Slovakia 8.7%, Poland 5.9%, France 5.4%, UK 5.1%, Italy 4.9%, Austria 4.6% (2007).

- Import partners: Germany 31.4%, Netherlands 6.7%, Slovakia 6.4%, Poland 6.3%, Austria 5.1%, China 5.1%, Russia 4.5%, Italy 4.4%, France 4.1% (2007).
- Reserves: $34.59 billion (2007).
- Foreign Direct Investment: $86.75 billion (2007).
- Czech Investment Abroad: $6.058 billion (2007).
- External debt: $74.7 billion (2007).
- Value of Publicly Traded Shares: $48.6 billion (2006).
- Exchange rates: koruny (Ke) per US$1 – 18.277 (December 2007) 23.957 (2005), 25.7 (2004), 28.2 (2003), 32.7 (2002), 38.0 (2001), 38.6 (2001), 34.6 (1999), 32.3 (1998), 31.7 (1997), 27.1 (1996), 26.5 (1995).

Energy (Production and Consumption)

Electricity production: 77.38 GWh (2005) *Electricity-production by source:*

- *fossil fuel:* 75.54%.
- *hydro:* 2.55%.
- *nuclear:* 20.37%.
- *other:* 1.54% (1998):
    * Electricity-consumption: 59.72 GWh (2005).
    * Electricity-exports: 24.99 GWh (2005).
    * Electricity-imports: 12.35 GWh (2005).
    * Oil-production: 18,030 bbl/day (2005).
    * Oil-consumption: 213,000 bbl/day (2005 est.).
    * Oil-exports: 20,930 bbl/day (2004).
    * Oil-imports: 203,700 bbl/day (2004).
    * Oil-proved reserves: 15 million bbl (1 January 2006).
    * Natural gas-production: 165 million m³ (2005 est).
    * Natural gas-consumption: 9.076 billion m³ (2005 est).
    * Natural gas-exports: 81.52 million m³ (2005 est).
    * Natural gas-imports: 8.976 billion m³ (2005 est).
    * Natural gas-proved reserves: 3.802 billion m³ (1 January 2006).
    * Natural resources: coal, timber, lignite, uranium, magnesite.

Agriculture products: wheat, rye, oats, corn, barley, potatoes, sugar beets, hops, fruit; pigs, cattle, poultry, horses; forest products.

The Economic Transformation of the Czech Republic: Challenges Faced and Lessons Learned

Václav Klaus is president of the Czech Republic. He presided over economic reforms in the former Czechoslovakia as finance minister. After the Czechs and Slovaks separated on January 1, 1993, Klaus continued with his reform program as prime minister of the Czech Republic. This essay is based on a longer paper delivered at a conference sponsored by the Centre for Economics and Politics in Prague on January 10, 2006, to commemorate 15 years since the beginning of the Czech Republic's economic transition.

The collapse of communism in the Czech Republic (then Czechoslovakia) in 1989 produced an extraordinary euphoria among the Czech people. It created an unusually great unity in the whole country. As reformers, we knew then that unity was explicitly negative. The people were united "against something," not "in favour of something." Fortunately, that was enough to allow us to look for the way forward. It seems almost unimaginable today, but for the majority of people the alternative to communism in our country was not capitalism. A utopian "third way" was being sought and promoted.

Proponents of the third way opposed the establishment of political parties, defended so-called nonpolitical politics, and claimed an exceptional role for intellectual and cultural elites in the running of the country. Theirs was a neocollectivist vision of society that rejected liberal democracy. In essence, promoters of the third way advocated "postdemocracy."

The proponents of the third way did not want to change the existing economic system; they wanted merely to deepen perestroika. They wanted to realize the 1960s' idea of convergence of the economic systems of socialism and capitalism. They did not trust the market. Instead, they believed in an enlightened economic centre, which would, with the aid of the Internet and popular managerial pamphlets, wisely organize the economy. They wanted to privatize only small businesses and give the larger ones to their employees. They feared selling "the family silver" abroad, and so on.

Václav Klaus is president of the Czech Republic. He presided over economic reforms in the former Czechoslovakia as finance minister. After the Czechs and Slovaks separated on January 1, 1993, Klaus continued with his reform program as prime minister of the Czech Republic. This essay is based on a longer paper delivered at a conference sponsored by the Centre for Economics and Politics in Prague on January 10, 2006, to commemorate 15 years since the beginning of the Czech Republic's economic transition.

When it came to foreign policy, the proponents of the third way intended to make the Czech Republic a bridge between the East and the West and create a new world that would eliminate the faults of both. They wanted to abolish the Warsaw Pact and the North Atlantic Treaty Organization at the same time. They were idealists without a realpolitik understanding of foreign policy who mocked the long-term national interests of the Czech Republic.

It is necessary to remember that the conflict at that time was not between authentic reformers on the one hand and apologists for the old order or former communist officials on the other. The communists knew very well that they had lost, and for that reason they had no, or only very small, political ambitions—at least in the short run. The communists did not have any influence on the discussion at the time the Czech economic transformation began.

Those who hindered a thorough overhaul of the Czech economic system belonged to two influential groups. The first group consisted of the communist reformers of the 1960s, who were expelled from the Communist Party after the Soviet invasion in 1968. Their wish was to implement their 20-year-old reform agenda. The second group consisted of the anti-communist dissidents from the cultural and intellectual sphere. Led by Václav Havel, my predecessor as president of the Czech Republic, the group wanted to create something new—something without the faults of either liberal democracy or communism. The world, they reasoned, was supposed to be governed by a chosen few. They considered market forces demeaning. It is not an accident that Mr. Havel recently said that "the invisible hand commits various clearly visible crimes."

Promoting Democratic Capitalism

A different, relatively small, group of people was not afraid to say that the goal of transformation in the Czech Republic was capitalism and a parliamentary democracy. That group knew that it was necessary to say where they wanted to go, outline how to get there, and convince the Czech public to move in that direction. That group, of which I was a part, pushed for the adoption of the Scenario for Economic Reform by the Federal Parliament of the then-Czechoslovakia in the fall of 1990. A compromise document, the Scenario for Economic Reform, contained the main policies needed for the liquidation of the institution of the centrally planned economy, not just the partial adjustments that were advocated by others. Those policies included annulling thousands of orders and bans, allowing Czech and foreign subjects to enter the market, liberalizing prices and foreign trade, and privatizing state enterprises.

All the while, we kept in mind the two indispensable preconditions for the success of economic transformation: macroeconomic stability and gradual creation of the infrastructure needed for the functioning of the market. All of us who were thinking about economic reforms at that time knew that it was necessary to take all of those steps simultaneously. We did not consider any of them less important than the others. However unbelievable it might sound today, we had to fight hard over every sentence in the Scenario for Economic Reform.

We knew that there was nothing to wait for, because the euphoria that followed the collapse of communism would not provide us with unlimited time and room for unpopular and painful steps. We knew that it was necessary to take advantage of the temporary weakening of all the various interest groups, which, as Mancur Olson explained, would under normal circumstances obstruct change, and promote their own special interests. We knew that any fundamental change in a free democratic society is, not an exercise in applied economics, but a real social process, which cannot be designed and gradually implemented by constructivists. (Thus, the advice given by Joseph Stiglitz—that we should have made our transformation more gradual as the Chinese have done—is laughable.) Also, we had to avoid partial reform because partial reform creates new disequilibria that harm the economy as a whole. It was, therefore, essential to take a big step and create a "critical mass" of reforms that signaled that there would not be a return to the past.

We also knew that we could not destabilize the economy and with it millions of people's lives. We had to minimize inflation as well as the unavoidable losses of output—some of which, unfortunately, was irretrievably lost. We tried to achieve the best possible shape of the proverbial J-curve. If we were to create our own "Tobin's" index showing the losses suffered by the Czech economy because of transformation, I am confident that it would be the most favourable such measure among all the transforming countries.

The key to minimization of transformation losses was a cautious fiscal policy—in particular a surplus budget in 1990—and a cautious monetary policy. That allowed us to avoid the risks resulting from price and foreign trade liberalization, a price-wage spiral, and an exchange rate spiral. It can be said that we did avoid them even though—especially when we were looking for the correct rate of devaluation of the Czechoslovak crown at the end of December 1990—we did not sleep for a few nights.

The Critics and Our Accomplishments

In the end, we did only what we were allowed to do by the social and political consensus of that time. But it was far from being all that we dreamt about and that we considered correct. Other evolutionary, but not revolutionary, changes would follow, and the system would be fine-tuned in the future and within the framework of the intricate process of parliamentary democracy.

Over the years, we were criticized for price liberalization in a monopolistic economy. But we knew that monopolistic structure was the main reason for parallel liberalization of foreign trade. Essentially, we had to "import" competition. The results bore out our hypothesis, and our country had the lowest rate of inflation of all countries where prices had been liberalized.

We were also criticized for the extent of the crown's devaluation, but our rate of devaluation secured our main aim—equilibrium of the balance of payments. We also won our fight with the International Monetary Fund when we refused to accept the even greater devaluation that the IMF advocated. The exchange rate survived at the level chosen by us in December 1990 for six long years.

We accepted the dominant doctrine at that time that argued in favour of a fixed exchange rate as the only possible anchor of a sharply fluctuating transformation economy—even though I feared that measure. We wanted to liberalize prices and trade and fix the exchange rate afterwards. It came out well. Unfortunately, after a couple of years, we missed the moment when we should have left the fixed exchange rate. That mistake was partly responsible for the exchange rate problems of 1997.

Moreover, we pushed for privatization of businesses as we found them and not, as some of our critics wanted, after first bailing them out financially. If we were to wait for the financial bailouts to happen, transformation would be stopped. Calls to postpone the beginning of transformation until the economic institutions and the rule of law were perfect (and they never are) were similarly wrongheaded. We knew that institutions and legislation are endogenous rather than exogenous. We knew, therefore, that they would have to evolve gradually. We recognized that the faster that happened, the better, but we also recognized that institutions and the rule of law cannot be created in the offices of a few reformers.

Economic and Financial Data for the Czech Republic

Unless Other Wise Indicated, Data are not Seasonally Adjusted.

A comma (,) represents a decimal point delimiter; a blank between figures or a point (.) within one number represent a thousand group delimiter; x sign shows that the figure is not applicable.

Czech Republic Economy

Czech Republic is an Upper middle-income country comes under the Europe and the Central Asian region, according to the classification made by the World Bank on the basis of Region and Income for the year 2005. The country has a total surface area of 78,870.0 square kilometre as of the year 2004 with a forest area of 26,370.0 square kilometre in 2000.

Demography and Social Indicators

The total population of the country as of the year 2004 has reached at 10.2 millions with an annual percentage growth rate of 0.1. The following graph gives a clear picture upon the annual percentage growth rate of the population of the country.

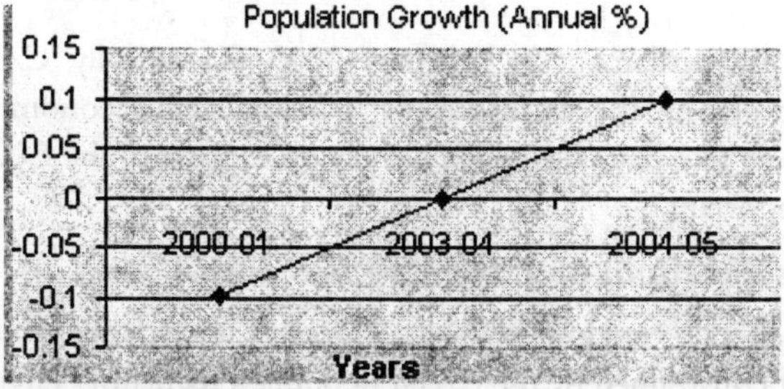

The Czech Republic's economic freedom score is 69.4, making its economy the 37th freest in the 2009 *Index*. Its overall score is 1.2 points higher than last year, primarily reflecting improvement in fiscal freedom and freedom from corruption. The Czech Republic is ranked 21st out of 43 countries in the Europe region, and its overall score is higher than the regional and global averages.

The Czech Republic's transition to a market-driven economy has been successful. The private sector accounts for more than 85 percent of GDP. As reflected in relatively high scores for fiscal and investment freedom, low taxation and openness to foreign investment have contributed to a strong economy. A reduced flat personal income tax of 15 percent became effective in January 2008. Trade freedom is relatively strong, and inflation is moderate, though the government maintains some price supports. The extensive banking sector includes significant foreign ownership, and financial services are highly developed.

There is room for improvement, however. The regulatory environment is generally consistent with a market economy, but bureaucracy and red tape retard entrepreneurial dynamism. Corruption is still perceived as significant. In January 2008, the government implemented a fiscal reform package that targeted tax policy and entitlement spending, but a fractured political environment has slowed needed health care and pension reforms.

Background Back to the Top

The Velvet Revolution of 1989 peacefully overthrew the Communist dictatorship and led to the election of dissident playwright Vaclav Havel as president of a democratic Czechoslovakia. The Czech Republic separated from Slovakia and became an independent nation in 1993 and joined the European Union in 2004. President Vaclav Klaus of the conservative Civic Democratic Party was elected in 2003 and narrowly re-elected by Parliament in February 2008. Historically, Czech lands have been among the world's most industrialized. Economic growth over the past five years has relied heavily on exports to the EU. Tourism is also important.

Business Freedom 65.1 *Back to the Top*

The overall freedom to start, operate, and close a business is somewhat constrained by the Czech Republic's regulatory environment. Starting a business takes an average of 15 days, compared to the world average of 38 days. Obtaining a business license requires twice the world average of 18 procedures. Closing a business is burdensome.

Trade Freedom 85.8 *Back to the Top*

The Czech Republic's trade policy is the same as that of other members of the European Union. The common EU weighted average tariff rate was 2.1 percent in 2005. Non-tariff barriers reflected in EU policy include agricultural and manufacturing subsidies, import restrictions for some goods and services, market access restrictions in some service sectors, non-transparent and restrictive regulations and standards, and inconsistent customs administration across EU members.

Non-transparent government procurement regulation exceeds general EU policy, and the enforcement of intellectual property rights remains problematic. Consequently, 10 points were deducted from the Czech Republic's trade freedom score.

Fiscal Freedom 80.2 *Back to the Top*

The Czech Republic has a low income tax rate and a moderate corporate tax rate. In 2008, the top income tax rate was reduced to 15 percent, and the top corporate tax rate was reduced to 21 percent. Other taxes include a value-added tax (VAT), a property transfer tax, and a tax on dividends. In the most recent year, overall tax revenue as a percentage of GDP was 36.3 percent.

Government Size 43.0 Back to the Top

Total government expenditures, including consumption and transfer payments, are high. In the most recent year, government spending equaled 43.6 percent of GDP. The government has sold its remaining stakes in a telecommunications company and a petrochemicals refiner.

Monetary Freedom 79.7 Back to the Top

Inflation is low, averaging 2.6 percent between 2005 and 2007. As a participant in the EU's Common Agricultural Policy, the government subsidizes agricultural production, distorting the prices of agricultural products. The Ministry of Finance can fix prices, set minimum or maximum commercial transaction prices, and establish periods when prices may not change. Energy, some raw materials, domestic rents, and rail and bus transport are subject to controls. Maximum prices apply to mail and telecommunications tariffs. Ten points were deducted from the Czech Republic's monetary freedom score to account for these policies.

Investment Freedom 70.0 Back to the Top

The law treats foreign and domestic capital equally. Foreign investors can establish joint ventures and participate in existing enterprises, with 100 percent foreign ownership allowed in both cases. Licensing is required for sectors, such as insurance, media, and energy, where the state is a partner. There are no restrictions on payments or current transfers, and residents and non-residents may hold foreign exchange accounts. Non-transparent procurement discourages foreign tenders for government contracts. Foreigners may not purchase land, but branches or offices of foreign companies may buy local real estate, except for farmland or woodland.

Financial Freedom 80.0 Back to the Top

The Czech Republic's financial sector is one of Central and Eastern Europe's most advanced, and intermediation has become even deeper since 2006. As of June 2007, there were 37 banks. The state is a controlling shareholder in two banks. There are few or no restrictions on foreign banks, and foreign-controlled banks accounted for over 90 percent of assets in 2007. Insurance companies and pension funds are competitive, with significant foreign and EU participation. By mid-2007, there were 52 insurance companies. Capital markets are small and lack transparency, but regulatory bodies have been merged to streamline oversight.

Property Rights 70.0 Back to the Top

All forms of property rights are protected by law. Contracts are generally secure. The judiciary is independent, although decisions may vary from court to court. Commercial disputes can take years to resolve. Company registration is in the hands of the courts and can be slow and complicated.

Freedom From Corruption 52.0 Back to the Top

Corruption is perceived as significant. The Czech Republic ranks 41st out of 179 countries in Transparency International's Corruption Perceptions Index for 2007. Convictions for bribery result in long prison terms. Allegations of corruption most often involve the court-controlled company registration system and the police. The Czech Republic has ratified the OECD's anti-bribery convention and has signed (but not ratified) the U.N. Convention Against Corruption.

Labour Freedom 67.8 Back to the Top

Further reform of relatively flexible labour regulations would create more employment opportunities and productivity growth. The non-salary cost of employing a worker can be high, but dismissing a redundant employee is relatively inexpensive.

Czech Republic's Top Imports & Exports 2008

The Czech Republic's Gross Domestic Product (GDP) was an estimated US$217.1 billion in 2008, making the Czech Republic the world's 40th richest country. With a population of 10.2 million Czechs who enjoyed an average GDP of $26,100 per person last year, The Czech Republic placed 50th among other nations in terms of GDP per capita. As the world's 30th biggest exporting nation, the Czech Republic shipped $145.7 billion worth of exports in 2008. About half of Czech exports were machinery and transport equipment while other Czech exports include raw materials, fuels and chemicals. Based on 2008 statistics, top customers for the Czech Republic's exports are Germany (30.6%), Slovakia (9.2%), Poland (6.5%), France (5.3%), the United Kingdom (4.8%), Austria (4.7%) and Italy (4.6%).

According to the CIA World Factbook, the Czech Republic imported $139.4 billion worth of foreign goods last year. Major commodities imported into the Czech Republic mirror that country's exports: machinery and transport equipment, raw materials, fuels and chemicals. Leading suppliers to The Czech Republic were Germany (30.3%), Slovakia (6.6%), Poland (6.4%), Russia (6.2%), Netherlands (5.6%), Austria (5.2%), China 4.9% and Italy (4.1%). In total, the Czech Republic's international trade amounted to $285.1 billion or 131.3% in relation to its overall GDP. This compares with roughly 25% for the U.S. and 60% for Canada.

Gross Domestic Product (GDP) of Czech Republic

Gross Domestic Product (GDP) is a useful economic indicator of the performance of the economy in a given country or economic area. Is allows not only for a yearly comparison of the country's economic situation but also facilitates comparisons with other countries or regions.

The indicator shows domestic production including the service sector, imports and exports, general consumption and public expenses. The entry of a large investor or a willingness on the part of consumers to spend is positive economic stimuli.

Between 1993 and 2006 the Czech economy as a whole underwent some significant structural changes. Generally, a decrease in the proportion of agriculture and industry in the country's GDP decreased to that of service sector was seen. This phenomenon occurred, with varying degrees of intensity, in all regions of the country. One of the basic economic indicators used to gauge a given country's economic performance is GDP per capita. During the last several years, GDP in the Czech Republic has been very satisfactory and this trend looks likely to continue in the future.

2005 Evaluation

2005 was an exceptionally favourable year for the Czech Republic. GDP reached CZK 2,931.1 billion, which was an increase of 6.0% over the previous year. In addition to the increased tempo of growth, significant changes to the structure of the country's GDP also occurred, while inflation was kept at low levels. Expenditures for gross capital formation were slower than household spending, while exports outweighed imports.

Key GDP indicators

GDP growth for 2005	+ 6%
Expenditures for gross capital creation	+ 0%
Expenditures for household consumption	+ 2.6%
Expenditures for gross fixed capital creation	+ 3.7%
Total exports	+ 11.1%

Other positive developments influencing GDP in 2005 was an increase in the work force and a decrease in unemployment, a sharp drop in the budget deficit in relation to GDP, an incline in domestic supply and demand, growth in gross national savings and a decrease gross capital financing from external sources. A decrease in the balance of payment deficit in relation to GDP and in foreign borrowing also contributed to the overall improvement of the Czech Republic's international investment position.

While higher oil and gas prices in 2005 did have an effect on the Czech economy in 2005, these external factors did now lower industry performance for the year.

GDP growth through 2005 was marked by a faster tempo of growth that ranged from 5.3% in the first quarter to 6.9% in the fourth quarter. This was due to significant structural reforms. Net exports had the largest influence on year-on-year growth of GDP. This was thanks to expanded foreign trade and a reduction in imports. Net exports accounted for three-quarters of GDP growth while total exports increased by 11.1% year-on-year.

This favourable economic situation appears likely to continue. Year-on-year growth in the second quarter of 2006 was calculated at 6.2% while the average of the EU 25 was 2.8%. This increase was due in large part to industrial manufacturing and building. As a result, the Czech Republic currently has the fastest growing economy in the European Union and has further established its economic position on the international stage.

GDP per Capita-Czech Republic Compared to Continent

The gross domestic product (GDP) per capita is the national output, divided by the population, expressed in U.S dollars per person, for the latest year for which data is published.

The Czech Republic publishes annual house price statistics in the Statistical Yearbook of the Czech Statistical Office (CSO). General economics statistics are also available from CSO. The Czech National Bank has money and banking statistics

Czech Republic GDP Growth Rate

Czech Republic Gross Domestic Product (GDP) contracted 5.80% over the last 4 quarters. The Czech Republic Gross Domestic Product is worth 216 billion dollars or 0.35% of the world economy, according to the World Bank. Czech Republic has one of the most developed industrialized economies among the emerging democracies in central and eastern Europe. It is one of the most stable and prosperous of the post-Communist states of Central and Eastern Europe. The Czech Republic has a well-educated population and a well-developed infrastructure. The country's strategic location in Europe, low-cost structure, and skilled work force have attracted strong inflows of foreign direct investment (FDI). This page includes: Czech Republic GDP Growth Rate chart, historical data, forecast and news.

Year	*Mar*	*Jun*	*Sep*	*Dec*	*Average*
2009	-4.40	-5.80			-5.10
2008	2.70	4.20	3.90	0.00	2.70
2007	6.20	5.90	6.00	5.70	5.95
2006	6.60	6.40	6.30	6.70	6.50

Czech Republic: Inflation to Rise

Growth peaked at the end of 2005 and is expected to level out over the projection period with annual GDP growth averaging 5.25% over 2006-08. While export and investment growth are expected to remain strong and household consumption growth to increase, these will be accompanied by stronger import growth. Headline inflation will be pushed up, largely due to increases in excise duty and price deregulation.

Political stalemate following the general election in June has meant delay in the structural reforms needed for sustainable deficit reduction. No concrete progress is being made in either pensions or healthcare and weaknesses in the Medium-term Expenditure Framework are not being addressed.

Population (000s), 2005	10 221
Area (000 sq km)	79
Currency	Koruna
GDP (Billion USD), 2005	206.5
Life expectancy at birth (Women, Men), 2004	79.0, 72.6
Total labour force (000s), 2005	5 174
Government type	Parliamentary Democracy

Indicators	% change unless otherwise indicated		
	2006	2007	2008
GDP growth	6.2	4.8	4.6
Consumer price index	2.8	3.4	3.1
Unemployment rate (%)	7.3	6.8	6.3
General government financial balance(% GDP)	-3.7	-4.1	-4.3
Current account balance (% GDP)	-2.9	-2.0	-2.0

Czech Republic Inflation Rate (Consumer Prices)

Inflation Rate down to 0.3% yoy in July

Czech consumer prices dropped by 0.4% compared to one months ago and the inflation rate was down to 0.3% yoy in July from 1.2% in June. According to the consensus the market expected only a 0.1% mom decline, while our estimate of-0.3% mom was closer to the actual outcome. On the one hand the prices of packaged holidays showed the expected seasonal rise. Rents and fuel prices increased slightly as well. On the other hand this was more then offset by the decline of food prices (-2.4% mom), the price of natural gas (-6.3% mom) and clothing (-3.0% mom). The weak demand by consumers and a base effect are likely to push the inflation rate even lower in coming months. In autumn year-on-year inflation could be close to zero and even a negative figure would hardly be a surprise. In light of the July inflation data last week's interest rate cut by the Czech National Bank seems logical. However, a further rate cut is regarded as rather unlikely. From the market point of view July inflation surprised to the downside and, thus, some further gains of CZK bonds are likely. We maintain our buy recommendation for Czech government bonds with maturities over 5 years.

Czech Republic: Czech Inflation Surprises on the Downside

Inflation for July stood at 0.3% y/y – a significant drop from 1.2% y/y in June. We look for lower rates and yields as this still keeps the door open for more rate cuts from the Czech central bank. Unemployment for July was 8.4%, up from 8.0% in June.

The Czech Statistical Office has this morning published inflation for July. Inflation of 0.3% y/y surprised significantly on the downside and was much lower than our forecast of 0.7% y/y and the consensus expectation of 0.6% y/y. The Czech central bank (CNB) had also been expecting higher inflation in July – at 0.5% y/y. The main culprit behind the lower-than-expected inflation figure for July was lower food prices. Base effects also played a role in such the dramatic decline. Today's significantly lower-than-expected number will reignite speculation about whether the Czech central bank has finished with monetary easing following last week's 25bp rate cut, which brought the key policy rate to an all-time low of 1.25%. At this moment in time, we believe that the monetary easing has come to an end. Our main scenario assumes stable Czech interest rates and a key policy rate of 1.25%. However, taking into account our revised inflation outlook, which confirms very low inflation for the rest of the year and inflation close to zero next year, we believe scope for further monetary easing does exist.

Annual Inflation Rate (CPI)-Czech Republic (%)

Year	*Inflation rate (consumer prices)*	*Rank*		*Percent*
Change	*Date of Information*			
2003	.60 %	198		2002
2004	.10 %	206	-83.33 %	2003 est.
2005	3.20 %	109	3,100.00 %	2004 est.
2006	1.90 %	45	-40.63 %	2005 est.
2007	2.70 %	66	42.11 %	2006 est.
2008	2.90 %	79	7.41 %	2007 est.
2009	6.30 %	106	117.24 %	2008

Definition: This entry furnishes the annual percent change in consumer prices compared with the previous year's consumer prices.

Impacts of the Adoption of Euro in the Czech Republic

Discussion material for the IPE conference in Bratislava, 11. November 2006 Petr Gocev My aim in this document is to assess some effects of the expected adoption of euro in the Czech Republic. I am focusing only on effects of joining the euro currency union as such, not on the consequences of fulfilling the Maastricht criteria. I think that it is useful to differentiate between these two sets of issues. Effects of fulfilling the Maastricht criteria may change substantially in case these criteria themselves are reviewed, while the effects of joining the monetary union are inescapable. However it is necessary to keep in mind the limited scope of this article.

Effects of Adopting the Euro on the Official and Perceived Rate of Inflation

It is a generally accepted fact that switching to euro will cause an inflationary "jump", mainly in a consequence of "rounding-up" the prices and charging the transition costs on customers. However, according to the European Central Bank this inflationary jump in individual countries was quite negligible in the range of 0,12 to 0,29 %. This finding is in a sharp contrast with the substantial increase of perceived inflation. Various hypotheses to explain the wide discrepancy between the official inflation rate as measured by the Eurostat methodology and inflation rate perceived by the public were offered. Some authors argue that the high rates of perceived inflation shall be attributed to „inflationary illusion" or even „inflationary masochism". Wolfgang Brachinger (2005) argued, that the higher rate of the perceived inflation is caused by the fact that the inflation rate was relatively higher for goods and services that are purchased with a relatively high frequency. This is an explanation of how the „inflationary illusion" may occur. Price increases within goods and services purchased with relatively high frequency have higher subjective weight in formation of the inflationary perceptions, while their effect on the real income is in line with the official rate of CPI change. While the psychological effects explain part of the discrepancy between official and perceived rate of inflation, I believe it is vital to focus on the „real" effects hypotheses: A. The official rate of inflation measures the rate of inflation for an average household. However, adopting the euro caused higher price increase for goods and services which are to 1 Staff training, accounting software upgrades, dual pricing, dual cash reserves and so on. a greater extent represented in consumption baskets of households with under average income. And because at least 2/3 of households have an under average income, it follows that the inflation rate for an median income household (which is measured by the perceived inflation surveys) is higher than the official rate of inflation for an average income household (which is measured by the Eurostat).

As early as in 1958 Kenneth Arrow noted that "there should be a separate cost-of-living index number for each income level," because lower income households are likely to have consumption patterns that differ from those of higher income households. Congress of the United

States discussed a proposal to construct a special CPI for elderly for the purpose of adjusting the Social Security benefits. Several researches were undertaken, leading to a conclusion that although there are differences between inflation rates for different types of households, these differences are not substantial and/or persisting. Therefore, these papers concluded, it is possible to continue using the Consumer Price Index for All Urban Consumers as a proxy for inflation rate for all types of households. Recently there was a similar discussion in the Czech Parliament. In the Czech Republic, the situation is different than in the United States. Here the CPI rates of change are consistently higher for poorer households and households of elderly. This is a consequence of relatively very high inflation rates for categories as apartment rent, public transport, energies, health care and so on, which were during the previous regime heavily subsidized and since then there is a continuing process of their „narrowing". Needles to say, these groups of services have a lion's share in the consumption baskets of households of poorer households. And the Czech Parliament declined the proposal to adjust or valorize the Social Security payments according to the specially constructed CPI for elderly or poorer households precisely because these indices are consistently higher than the average household CPI and therefore it would require higher payments to be made.

B. It is possible that the real living standard of the below-median income households in the Eurozone countries declines. And in the history the declines of the living standard were by the workers usually attributed rather to "dearness" than to stagnation of the nominal wages. Therefore, whenever there was a decline of the living standard in the Middle Ages, workers demanded that the maximum price of bread should be fixed, instead of demanding the minimal nominal wage to be fixed or increased. This bias may explain to some extent the recent increase of the perceived inflation rate. Although the official rate of inflation may change (presumably) only little over time, it may be perceived as low during the period when the nominal wages are increasing sufficiently to offset the rate of inflation, while it may be perceived as high during the period when the nominal wages stagnate. But then it is just a coincidence that the period of switching to euro is the period of stagnation of the nominal wages at the same time. Nominal wages of workers stagnate not only in the Eurozone area, but as well in other EU countries and in the US. In the specific situation of the Czech

Republic, the "inflationary jump" will be accentuated due to the fact that the current price level is approximately 60 % of the EU15 average price level. Convergence of the Czech Republic price level to the average price level in the EU is currently mediated through the ongoing appreciation of the CZK to EUR. The Czech National Banks aims to keep the rate of this appreciation at approximately 3 % p. a. However, in case of an immediate adoption of euro, this appreciation mechanism would be ruled out and the whole rate of appreciation would transform into an increase of the rate of inflation. Currently the inflation targeting of the CNB is 1 percentage point above the inflation targeting of the ECB. It follows that an immediate switching to euro would cause the official rate of inflation in the Czech Republic to be 4 percentage points above the inflation rate in the EU15. However, this huge „inflationary jump" will constantly decrease over time, as the rate of CZK appreciation will decrease with narrowing of the price level gap.

Effects of the Impossibility to Realize an Independent Monetary Policy

Although the monetary independence of the CNB is currently limited to setting the key interest rates for CZK, the lost of this possibility may have serious consequences. Impossibility to maintain different nominal interest rates in different EU countries causes serious problems as long as these countries experience different phases of the business cycle or different rates of inflation at the same time. In 2002 the there was a higher rate of inflation in Spain than in Germany. Spain needed to reduce its rate of inflation by restricting the money supply, while Germany needed to expand the money supply. But the effect of constant nominal ECB interest rate was exactly the opposite: the real interest rate in Spain was 0,15 %, while in Germany it was 2,15 %. Single ECB interest rate for EUR causes that countries which need a relatively higher real interest rate have relatively lower real interest rate instead, and vice versa. The only solution to this problem is the alignment of the business cycles and substantial reduction of currently divergent rates of inflation differentials within the Eurozone countries. But in a monetary union the reduction of rates of inflation differentials is only possible after the price level gaps are substantially reduced, which in turn requires a higher level of the realconvergence between EU countries.

6

Economic Development and Loss of Biodiversity

Reversing the Loss of Biodiversity: An Overview of International Measures

Our generation has the singular misfortune of living during—and helping to create—a period of biological simplification. Generations from now it will be hard for people to appreciate what has been lost, but we have ringside seats for the event. It is happening during our watch, a fact that will not soon be forgotten by our descendants.

There is virtually no place on Earth where biodiversity is not under siege from the combined pressures of human population growth, excessive resource demands, exotic species introductions, and atmospheric pollutants. Although we often dwell on biodiversity loss in the tropics, major problems exist in the temperate, arid, and semiarid zones as well. Worldwide, an estimated 2 to 5 percent of species will be committed to extinction per decade in the near future and habitats and genetic resources are disappearing at least as rapid a rate. With growing populations and growing demands on resources, the magnitude of the problem is overwhelming.

Even the United States, which has the resources to tackle the problem and the benefit of a declining rural population, is at best only slowing the rate of loss of biodiversity; more likely, we are only slowing the rate *of increase* in the loss of biodiversity. If the resource-rich United States is losing the battle, how are countries without abundant resources and with growing rural populations to meet the challenge?

Even if we stopped cutting forests, filling wetlands, and damming rivers worldwide today, species extinctions caused by historic habitat destruction would continue for centuries. Yet it is unrealistic, given a global human population that is growing by nearly a billion people every ten years, to think of halting habitat loss anytime in the near future. If we were to halt the loss of biodiversity at a level somewhere near today's, we would need not only to stop habitat loss immediately but also to restore a substantial fraction of the habitat that already has been lost.

So, what will it take to stop biodiversity loss? Although population growth and resource consumption are the proximate threats to biodiversity today, over the long run biodiversity's fate will in fact lie with social and economic progress around the world. The steps countries take to improve literacy, empower women, invest in health and child survival, and stimulate sustainable economic development will in the end determine the level where human populations stabilize and what demands those populations place on natural resources. And that is what ultimately will define the amount of the planet's biodiversity that survives to pass through the bottleneck we are entering.

Categories of International Action for Biodiversity

We can influence both the rate of loss of biodiversity and the final levels of diversity that survive through actions we take today to protect species, genetic resources, and critical habitats and to use them sustainably to meet social and economic needs. International action can help the conservation and sustainable use of biodiversity to the extent that it helps nations (1) anticipate and prevent threats to biodiversity, and (2) align the goals of biodiversity conservation with local and national development goals. The four major types of international action that influence biodiversity conservation today are:

International Resource Management Coordination. A long history of treaties and agreements seeks to promote coordinated and complementary actions among countries that share resource management goals or concerns. For example, Mexico's efforts to maintain its shorebird populations would fail if the U.S. and Canada did not protect habitats for the birds during migration. Similarly, U.S. efforts to protect sea turtle populations would fail if other countries did not ban the import of turtle shells. Thus, nations have reached such agreements as the

Convention on the Conservation of Migratory Species of Wild Animals, the Convention on International Trade in Endangered Species of Wild Fauna and Flora (CITES), the Convention on the Conservation of Antarctic Marine Living Resources (CCAMLR), and the International Undertaking on Plant Genetic Resources, and have established numerous regional and species-specific councils and agreements addressing transboundary resources or migratory species, such as UNEP Regional Seas programs.

"Bargains" Among Nations. Another set of international mechanisms seeks not only the coordination of action, but also the establishment of reciprocity among nations. In a sense, these treaties or agreements strike "bargains" among countries with different needs and different resource pressures. For example, the Ramsar Convention on Wetlands of International Importance obliges countries to take steps to conserve their wetland resources and provides funding from relatively wealthy countries to support the conservation activities in poorer nations. The pilot phase of the Global Environmental Facility provided financial support for conservation in developing countries; in return, those countries took steps to protect their biodiversity, actions that result in both national and global benefits. The recently negotiated Convention on Biological Diversity establishes obligations for parties to undertake conservation activities and ensures that wealthy countries will support conservation with financial and technical resources in return for maintaining their access to these resources. And a number of bilateral development assistance programs provide financial resources to countries to assist their conservation efforts.

International Financial and Trade Agreements. Although we don't typically think of their influence on biodiversity, international agreements that influence economic development and trade policies can have important conservation consequences, both positive and negative. Such agreements include structural adjustment programs, regional and global trade agreements, and commodity agreements such as the International Tropical Timber Agreement (ITTA). It is already standard for such agreements to address economic issues related to resource use, but increasingly the argument is being made to address conservation concerns as well. Because of their major influence on patterns of development, these agreements may offer a far more valuable opportunity to promote the conservation and sustainable use of biodiversity than more narrowly focused conservation agreements.

For example, Bob Repetto at World Resources Institute (WRI) has proposed a mechanism for making commodity agreements such as ITTA instruments for promoting the sustainable use of resources. For decades, Southern producers have sought to improve their commodity terms of trade through commodity agreements designed to "stabilize" (i.e., reduce) supply, efforts that have been resisted by consuming Northern countries such as the U.S. However, producers could improve export prices and revenues if they jointly agreed to adopt more sustainable production practices and to internalize the full environmental costs of production in their pricing structure. Northern countries could not complain about agreements among producers to reduce logging to sustainable levels or to protect biodiversity, and Southern producers could pass on the costs of these measures to Northern importers.

International Science. Finally, much of the basis for both the concern over the loss of biodiversity and for knowledge of what steps need to be taken to protect biodiversity stems from the results of the international scientific community's research in systematics, ecology, and conservation biology. Although we often don't think of this as an international "measure," international scientific cooperation provides a model for the type of cooperation needed in such areas as technology and capacity building.

The Biodiversity Convention

Although economic and trade agreements provide significant opportunities to imbed concerns for sustainability in development plans and despite the potential for other treaties to help coordinate resource management among nations, all attention is now focused on The Convention on Biological Diversity, one of the notable achievements of the United Nations Conference on Environment and Development (UNCED) held in Rio de Janeiro in June 1992. The 157 countries signing the Convention believed that it struck a balance among the interests of nations differing widely in development needs, biodiversity endowments, and environmental threats.

The Convention is a framework agreement, meaning that it establishes an international legal structure for a coordinated response to the loss of biological diversity. It establishes general obligations for the parties to the Convention rather than legally binding targets for specific actions.

But even as a framework agreement, its impact will be significant. The Convention increases the economic incentives for conservation, a key element of the long-term strategy to slow the loss of biodiversity. It also establishes short-term obligations to meet pressing conservation needs. Signatories have already begun to develop the required biodiversity action plans, which detail how they will meet obligations to identify, monitor, and conserve biodiversity and identify their priorities for training, education, and capacity-building. The Convention establishes a multilateral mechanism to provide financial support for these conservation needs in developing countries and sets up a scientific panel to help governments guide limited resources to the highest priorities.

The Convention marks a basic change in the international status of genetic resources. Before it, these resources were considered to be the "common heritage of mankind." This principle is a central tenet of the International Undertaking on Plant Genetic Resources and the FAO Commission on Plant Genetic Resources, both of which were established in the 1980s and together involve some 135 countries. Under this regime, countries that violated the common heritage principle and restricted access to unimproved germplasm (such as Ethiopia, which placed an embargo on the export of its coffee germplasm in 1977) were soundly criticized.

Though the intent of the open access regime was to ensure the widespread availability of genetic resources for agriculture and industry, it had one major flaw: by allowing free exchange of genetic resources, the source country received no direct benefit from their use. As a result, commercial use of these resources provided no additional economic incentive for conservation.

The Convention on Biological Diversity corrects this policy failure by establishing that states have sovereign rights over their genetic resources, although it affirms that the *conservation* of biodiversity is a "common concern of humankind." It thus enables market incentives to be used to complement the various multilateral mechanisms that might directly fund biodiversity conservation. The Convention adopted the principle that a portion of the benefits stemming from the productive use of genetic resources should flow back to the nations that act to conserve and provide access to these resources.

Not surprisingly, the negotiators envisioned that the flow of benefits would include both financial resources (i.e., royalties) and technologies. Given the central role of new technologies in addressing many environmental concerns, the inclusion of technology transfer articles is now commonplace in international agreements—including, for example, the Montreal Protocol on Substances that Deplete the Ozone Layer, Agenda 21 (another product of UNCED), and the United Nations Framework Convention on Climate Change. Such provisions aid biodiversity conservation in two ways: (1) technologies like seedbanks, tissue culture, and data management systems help meet conservation objectives directly, and (2) technologies enabling countries to make greater use of biodiversity in agriculture and industry add even greater economic incentives for conservation.

The technology transfer envisioned under the Convention is not a hand-out to poor countries but a recognition that simple cash payments for access to resources are rarely the most effective mechanism to support their conservation.

Indeed, the first country to take action to ensure technology transfer consistent with the convention was not even a developing country. After the U.S. National Cancer Institute extracted a chemical showing promise against HIV from an Australian shrub, Western Australia aggressively pursued its right to benefit from the resource. Australian scientists will now be involved in the research and Australia will receive a share of any potential commercial benefits.

There is no dispute that countries that obtain genetic resources from other countries assume the obligation under the Convention to compensate those countries, both financially and by facilitating technology transfer. Because developed countries successfully negotiated for language in the agreement to ensure that compulsory licensing is not authorized to meet these objectives, the burden falls squarely on the developed countries to take the actions needed to facilitate technology transfer.

An array of policy tools, including tax incentives and cooperative research programs, can meet the Convention's objectives without infringing on property rights. Rather than continuing to stress what actions developing countries *can't* take to meet the Convention's objectives, it is essential that developed countries quickly demonstrate what actions developed countries *will* take.

Next Steps

A scaffolding for international action to support the conservation and sustainable use of biodiversity now exists. But what are the greatest needs for further international institutional evolution to support biodiversity conservation?

Build Capacity in Developing Countries. International institutional development in the area of biodiversity conservation has far outpaced the growth of local and national expertise and institutions in many countries. Faced with new obligations under the Convention to survey and protect species, new awareness of the need to control the transboundary flow of genetic resources, a clear need for legal and technical expertise related to intellectual property rights and technology transfer, and new opportunities to benefit from biodiversity as more information about biodiversity is obtained, most countries—with the exception of a handful of industrialized countries—confront a major shortage of expertise and capacity.

So long as many developing countries lack the expertise needed to deal with these issues, not only will progress toward goals of conservation and sustainable use suffer, but so too will these countries be placed at a disadvantage in the further elaboration of international institutional mechanisms. If we are not careful, our scaffolding of international measures will turn into a house of cards. We need to screen every protocol, every project, and every new agreement to ensure that first priority is given to building local expertise and capacity in such areas as resource management, technology transfer, biological inventory, data management, environmental policy research, legal expertise, conservation biology, participatory methods, and biotechnology.

Control Genetic and Biochemical Transfers. Although the economic value associated with the transfer of genetic and biochemical materials often is exaggerated, effective mechanisms for dealing with these transfers and for ensuring equity in the distribution of benefits should nevertheless be a priority. Equity in the distribution of the benefits from these resources will be the standard against which international measures are judged.

Several problems confront any such mechanism. First, the pharmaceutical industry, which receives the most attention today in relation to the Biodiversity Convention, is involved increasingly in the transfer of chemical extracts rather than of samples of plants or animals. Because these are not strictly "genetic resources," they are not governed by the requirement in Article 15 for the prior informed consent of the donor country. On the other hand, Article 8 of the Convention enables countries to establish policies for the regulation and management of their biological "resources." Thus it is within the rights of countries to require collectors to obtain a permit before exporting chemical extracts.

Second, mechanisms that make sense for the use of *chemicals* in the pharmaceutical industry may not make sense for the use of *genetic resources* in agriculture and medicine. There is no particular difficulty associated with tracking the development of a drug from a plant or animal extract. Countries could readily establish access regulations requiring contracts that stipulate royalties, technology transfer, and conservation requirements whenever chemical extracts are exported. Although it is possible for companies to evade the terms of such contracts, most would not consider it worth the risk, given the relatively low royalty rates typical for such agreements.

On the other hand, gene transfers present major monitoring problems. A soil sample sold to a pharmaceutical company might hold hundreds or thousands of microorganisms that could easily be cultured. The supplier would have no means of knowing whether a microorganism that produced a valuable chemical came from a particular sample and would not know if the organisms were transferred to another user. Similarly, a supplier would have no way of knowing whether a particular gene from a plant sample provided to a seedbank or to a seed company eventually was patented. Thus, in the case of agriculture, the only "winner" from a scheme that would require the return of royalties to countries of origin of genetic material is likely to be the legal profession. Modern crop varieties are built from genes derived from dozens of countries. The cost associated with parceling out royalties among those countries and litigating the identify of various genes could quickly exceed the profits of the seed industry, which makes most of its profits from agrochemicals, not seeds, to begin with.

Third, the Biodiversity Convention grandfathers seed collections that already exist when the Convention comes into force. Thus, we face the prospects of an extraordinarily burdensome two-tiered system of gene regulation and monitoring that would keep track not only of country of origin but also of whether the material was collected before or after 1994.

There is a possible solution to these problems. An international fund could be established that obtained its resources from a small tax on the seed, pharmaceutical, and biotechnology industries. Such a mechanism was specified in the International Undertaking on Plant Genetic Resources, but contributions were voluntary and companies never contributed. Faced with the specter of a Byzantine regulatory system, companies may now look more kindly on such a fund.

Extend Rights Under the Biodiversity Convention to Local Communities. The Convention is premised on the notion that unless countries receive benefits from the use of their resources they will have insufficient incentive to conserve them. Governments were quick to accept this principle; shouldn't they then be equally quick to accept the notion that local communities within the country also should receive benefits from the use of their resources if they are to have an incentive to conserve them? If the convention is to achieve its goals, the key elements of the Convention (informed consent prior to collecting material and sharing of benefits on mutually agreed terms) should apply to private landowners, local communities, and indigenous groups with territorial claims.

A case in point may be taxol, a chemical derived from the Pacific yew in the United States. If we want to maintain our public forests for such values as biodiversity rather than for timber alone, shouldn't we ensure that benefits from the use of biodiversity flow back to the region where it was found? Even though we now accept internationally that both equity and the need for incentives for resource conservation require far more than traditional spot payments and sourcing contracts, we fail to apply this standard domestically. We will not shift regional economies from exploitative uses of biological resources if those are *the only* economically viable uses.

Bury the Concept of Global Incremental Costs. Are there benefits that accrue globally from the conservation of biodiversity that exceed the national benefits from conservation? Of course. Should we then premise international financial support only on international benefits? Of course not. In the abstract this might make sense, but in reality we are so far away from protecting even that biodiversity which is in the long-term interest of the nation itself that it is meaningless to define a conservation "increment" of this nature. (The incremental cost defined in the Convention is something different; it refers to the added costs to developing countries of implementing the Convention.)

Owing to inclusion of the concept of incremental costs in the Global Environmental Facility, countries are approaching biodiversity conservation not as something that is in their self interest, but rather as something to be bought with international funds.

Deal With Biosafety. A protocol on biosafety is likely to be one of the first protocols negotiated under the Convention on Biological Diversity. The continued opposition of the U.S. to the need for such a protocol is misguided, but the protocol currently being discussed is equally off-target.

There is substantial concern in developing countries about the risks of release of genetically modified organisms. This concern is justified. Developing countries do not have the regulatory mechanisms in place to monitor or enforce testing guidelines, and there already is documented evidence that scientists have taken advantage of the lax rules in developing countries to test organisms that could not be tested in the U.S. Given this legitimate concern, it is hard to justify the U.S. position in opposition to a biosafety protocol. However, this position is remarkably parallel to the long-standing efforts of the U.S. nuclear industry and the Nuclear Regulatory Commission to ignore public fears and doubts about the risks of nuclear power. As historians are quick to note, we seem fated to repeat the mistakes of history. Because the concern exists, we should accept it as legitimate and deal with it through a protocol.

The more pressing problem from the standpoint of biodiversity and biosafety, however, is not genetically modified organisms but common, garden variety, genetically unmodified "weeds." The most rapidly growing threat to biodiversity is the introduction of exotic species. Already, for example, the U.S. has some 4,500 introduced species—accounting for some 2 to 8 percent of such groups as insects, vertebrates, and mollusks—and more frequent and rapid international travel is resulting in ever more frequent introductions. Not only are exotic species often serious threats to native biodiversity and extremely difficult to control, they can have substantial negative economic impacts. Between 1906 and 1991, 79 introduced species caused a documented $97 billion in losses in the U.S. It is estimated that a recently introduced species, the zebra mussel, will cause more than US$3 billion in losses in the coming years.

If we do negotiate a biosafety protocol, therefore, it should not be restricted to genetically modified organisms but also should address the broader issue of introduction of exotic species and their social and ecological impacts.

Fundamental changes in society are needed if we are to significantly slow the loss of biodiversity. We can invest in parks and protected areas today, but these will prove to be only stop-gap measures if broader changes are not made. The current framework of international measures provides hope because it is premised on the need to integrate the concern for biodiversity conservation with development needs. But an urgent need exists for further international action to give flesh to that skeleton. The greatest current obstacle to surer progress toward the intertwined goals of biodiversity conservation and sustainable use is the shortage of capacity in developing countries. We must ensure that in our haste to elaborate the international framework we do not outpace the growth of this capacity.

Mourning the Increasing Loss of Bio-diversity

Our planet's essential goods and services depend on the variety and variability of genes, species, populations, and ecosystems. Biological resources feed and clothe us and provide housing, medicine and spiritual nourishment. The natural ecosystems of forests, pastures, range lands, deserts, rivers, lakes and seas contain most of the Earth's biodiversity. Farmers fields and gardens are also of great importance as repositories, while gene banks, botanical gardens, zoos and germ plasma repositories make small but significant contributions. The current decline in biodiversity is largely the result of human activity and causes serious threats to human development. At the advent of the 21st century, its being loudly proclaimed by many influential entities that genetic engineering will deliver 'designer' food crops capable of greatly improving contemporary agricultural systems. The biotechnology industry and its supporters are holding out the promise of plants that can be engineered to our precise specifications, creating a future of environmentally sustainable agriculture, more flexible crops, and an abundance of food with which to finally bring an end to world hunger. Life science corporations proclaim, with great fanfare, that their new products will make agriculture sustainable, eliminate world hunger, cure disease, and vastly improve public health.

The reality, however, is that through their business practices and political lobbying, the gene engineers have made it clear that they intend to use biotechnology to dominate and monopolize the global market for seeds, foods, fiber, and medical products. It is also true that the genetic engineering of food crops represents a continuation-indeed an intensification-of the techno-industrial approach to agricultural production, and will intensify the social inequalities, concentrations of power and wealth, and ecological problems it has produced. Genetic engineering also creates new avenues for the corporate domination of agriculture, and poses new kinds of environmental threats, introducing an entirely novel form of industrial pollution into our vocabulary and into the world: genetic pollution.

Biodiversity

"Biodiversity" describes the variety of living organisms of all kinds— animals, plants, fungi, and microorganisms — that inhabit a particular area. The general public is acquainted with only a small proportion of the 1.7 million species that science has identified. Far more species in the world remain unknown to anyone; most of these in tropical forests and other poorly studied ecosystems. Thousands of different and genetically distinct varieties of our major food crops owe their existence to centuries of evolution and to careful selection and improvement by our farmer ancestors. This diversity protects the crop and helps it adapt to different environments and human needs. Today, much of this diversity is being lost. Many unique varieties are disappearing and becoming extinct. The FAO estimates that since the beginning of this century, about seventy five percent of the genetic diversity of agricultural crops has been lost. Beyond conserving species, it is also important to conserve genetic diversity within individual species. Genetic diversity within species is particularly important in domesticated plants and animals and their wild relatives. The breeding of new strains of pest-resistant crops and livestock is critically dependent on the continued supply of new genetic varieties.

Humans benefit from biodiversity in many ways. Besides the animals and plants that we use for food, shelter, raw materials, and companionship, there are thousands of species whose natural products are literally life-saving — nearly 25 percent of the drugs used in the United States originally came from plants. There is strong scientific evidence that we are now in the opening phase of a massive extinction. In almost all cases, humans are the ultimate cause. The most frequent reason for this loss of biodiversity is loss of habitat: species become extinct when the places they live are destroyed. Preserving natural ecosystems is an important way to protect the endangered species within them. But preserving ecosystems has other important benefits. The quality of the water we drink, the air we breathe, and the soil in which we grow our food all depend on the integrity of natural ecosystems. People have long recognized the role of healthy forests, for example, in reducing erosion, preventing flooding, maintaining the purity of the water, and tempering climatic fluctuations. In recent years scientists have come to see that many other ecosystems provide similar benefits.

Genetic Engineering and the Threat to the Widespread

Eradication of Biodiversity: There are currently more than four dozen genetically engineered foods and crops being grown or sold in the U.S. These foods and crops are widely dispersed into the food chain and the environment. Over 70 million acres of GE crops are presently under cultivation in the U.S., while up to 500,000 dairy cows are being injected regularly with Monsanto's recombinant Bovine Growth Hormone (rBGH). Most supermarket processed food items now "test positive" for the presence of GE ingredients. In addition several dozen more GE crops are in the final stages of development and will soon be released into the environment and sold in the marketplace. According to the biotechnology industry almost 100% of U.S. food and fiber will be genetically engineered within the next five to ten years.

The widespread commercial release of genetically engineered plants will continue the process of eroding the diversity of plant varieties that still exist in the world. This is a process begun many decades ago, as the few new industrial seed varieties that were supplied by seed companies began to replace the enormous diversity of varieties within each crop that have been developed by traditional farmers over thousands of years. Much of this plant diversity has already been lost. The industrial manufacture and supply of seeds is creating a level of uniformity of crop varieties that may threaten future food security.

The new biotechnologies further heighten this biological uniformity through the new tissue culture techniques that have been developed for reproducing seeds in factories. These new techniques for the first time allow millions of genetically identical copies of a particular seed variety to be reproduced. But in mass-producing these perfect copies, they introduce an even higher level of uniformity into plant varieties and into farmers' fields. As noted earlier, such highly uniform plant varieties create ever more serious pest problems. There is also another type of uniformity made possible by genetic engineering. By allowing the transfer of genes across all species boundaries, genetic engineering begins to erase the distinctions and boundaries between species. The genetic structure of all life forms, and the parts that make it up, become interchangeable with every other. One consequence of this erosion of species boundaries will be that we will hardly know any more what it is that we're eating. What looks, feels, smells, and even tastes like an apple or an orange may also contain genes from a capsicum or a pig or a human.

In developing new products, scientists take plant samples from the field to the laboratory, where the simple act of moving a single gene from one spot to another within a cell-whether or not it causes an actual variation in the next generation, creates a "plant variety" deemed sufficiently "new" to qualify as a patentable invention. In most cases, such genetic engineering experiments produce nothing worthwhile. In a few cases, the variations have desirable traits that can be reproduced and marketed. The emphasis on finding and isolating plants with the most marketable traits leads to the decline of other plant species, as only those required to create the new techno-varieties are cultivated. In the U.S. alone, the focus on commercial varieties has already led to the loss of many varieties of plants in seed bank storage. A survey of U.S. seed banks showed that some varieties of non-commercial crops such as chufas, martynia and rampion have been lost entirely.

Biodiversity as a Must: Diversity within each crop is essential to agriculture, as is the diversity between crops and the genetic diversity among all species on earth. Diversity within crops refers to the multitude of ancestral and domesticated forms. This diversity has two components. First are the close relatives of cultivated crops, such as the many species of wheat— einkorn, emmer, durum, spelt, goatgrass, and common wheat. Second are the different cultivated varieties of each crop, including the breeding lines that are the source of new varieties. Many of the varieties are landraces, which are locally used varieties of the crop developed by farmers for their own use. These landraces harbour most of the crop's genetic diversity. The world wheat collection, stored in dozens of national and international seed banks, includes 125,000 accessions (strains) that are held as an international service by the United States Department of Agriculture (USDA). Most of these strains are landraces. It is genetic diversity that has allowed wheat to be grown successfully around the world, allowing breeders to find varieties with genes that can overcome local problems such as novel diseases, insects, and climate. Genetic diversity has also been essential for maximizing and stabilizing the productivity of a crop in a given region. About half of the year-to-year increases in crop productivity result directly from genetic improvements— superior new crop varieties. The genes that make these varieties unique come from the existing genetic variability of crops, but genetic biotechnology now potentially allows genes to be transferred to crops from any other living species.

Maintaining distinct strains of agricultural crops is important because these strains may contain genes useful in the continuing fight against pests and diseases, even those strains with overall characteristics that may not be attractive economically. Crop genetic diversity is not just a raw material for industrial agriculture; it is the key to food security and sustainable agriculture because it enables farmers to adapt crops suited to their own ecological needs and cultural traditions. Without this diversity, options for long-term sustainability and agricultural self-reliance are lost. The type of seed sown to a large extent determines the farmers's need for fertilizers, pesticides and irrigation. Communities that lose community-bred varieties and indigenous knowledge about them risk losing control of their farming systems and becoming dependent on outside sources of seeds and the inputs needed to grow and protect them. Without an agricultural system adapted to a community and its environment, self-reliance in agriculture is impossible. Diversity may help to decrease risk by decreasing the year-to-year variability of yields. For instance, landraces of wheat often have lower yield variances than many modern varieties. This lower variation in yields likely occurs because individual plants within a genetically variable population differ from each other. The ones favoured by particular climatic and soil conditions in a given year can grow well and thus compensate for those that do poorly under those conditions. Similarly, farmers often will grow mixtures of two or more varieties as a hedge against the risk of disease or environmental stress.

These effects of diversity illustrate two general. First, greater diversity leads, on average, to greater productivity. This effect of diversity on productivity should occur whether the diversity comes from growing many different plant species together in a pasture or forest; from growing a mixture of genotypes (a landrace) as a crop; from growing different crops in sequence, as in crop rotation; or from maximizing the genetic diversity within each individual plant, as it occurs in high-yielding crop varieties and commercial hybrids.

The level at which diversity is most important, and the kind of diversity that is needed, varies with the situation. For example, genetically diverse landraces are essential for farmers who must grow their crops in marginal, variable environments and who have no access to outside sources of diversity. These farmers must have plentiful diversity in their crops in the field. In contrast, commercial farmers are highly dependent on diversity in the foundation breeding pools of plant breeders who continually supply diverse new varieties to the commercial farmers, providing them with a kind of sequential diversity that has been called 'diversity in time.' The more heterogeneous the habitat and the more the environmental condition fluctuation during the growing season, the greater the beneficial effects of diversity. Conversely, in a spatially uniform, unchanging habitat in which a single factor always limits growth, a single strain is hypothesized to provide as great a yield as a mixture of several different strains grown together.6

Agricultural conditions, especially climate and disease and other pests, rarely are stable and predictable. Perhaps because of this, study of maize yields and years of practical experience lead to the recommendation that a farmer's best policy is to grow several unrelated single cross hybrids with good records for stability of performance as well as high yield. Second, greater diversity leads, on average, to lower year-to-year variability in productivity; that is, to greater stability. The ability of diversity to decrease year-to-year variability in yield means that diversity can act as crop risk insurance. Farmers may plant several different crop varieties as an additional way to decrease risk. Planting several kinds of crops, several varieties of a given crop, or a mixture of varieties as one crop increase the chance that some plants will be resistant to a disease or insect, or will perform well under existing climatic conditions. Greater crop diversity would thus decrease the odds of crop failure and may increase average yields. These features of biodiversity are greatly under utilized and merit further study and application.

Evidence from the Green Revolution leaves no doubt that the spread of modern varieties has been an important cause of genetic erosion, as massive government campaigns encouraged farmers to adopt genetically engineered varieties and to abandon many local varieties. The uniformity caused by increasing areas sown to a smaller number of varieties is a source of increased risk for farmers, as the varieties may be more vulnerable to disease and pest attack and most of them perform poorly in marginal environments.

Field performance of some recently released transgenic crops has shown that increased endeavors in this area may not necessarily lead to success:

1. Bt transgenic cotton-Additional insecticide sprays needed due to Bt cotton failing to control bollworms in 20,000 acres in eastern Texas.
2. Cotton inserted with Roundup Readgo gene-Bolls deformed and falling off in 4-5 thousand acres in Mississippi Delta.
3. Bt corn-27% yield reduction and lower Cu foliar levels in Beltsville trial.
4. Herbicide resistant oilseed rape-Pollen escaped and fertilized botanically related plants 2.5 km away in Scotland.
5. Virus resistant squash-Vertical resistance to two viruses and not to others transmitted by aphids.
6. Early FLAVR-SAVR tomato varieties-Did not exhibit acceptable yields and disease resistance performance.
7. Roundup Ready Canola-Pulled off the market due to

contamination with a gene that does not have regulatory approval.

8. Bt potatoes-Aphids sequestered the Bt toxin apparently affecting coccinellid predators in negative ways.
9. Herbicide tolerant crops-Development of resistance by annual ryegrass to Roundup.

Conclusions and Suggestions

Most scientists agree that the earth's biodiversity is threatened and that steps should be taken to preserve it. Thus the public debate has focused on the costs versus the benefits of such preservation. In addition, groups and individuals supporting unfettered property rights have increasingly viewed government acts to preserve habitat as efforts by an overly powerful federal bureaucracy to restrict individual freedom. Consequently, biodiversity protection has become increasingly controversial. The Convention on Biological Diversity's objectives are "the conservation of biological diversity, the sustainable use of its components and the fair and equitable sharing of the benefits arising out of the utilization of genetic resources." The Convention is thus the first global, comprehensive agreement to address all aspects of biological diversity: genetic resources, species, and ecosystems. It recognizes-for the first time-that the conservation of biological diversity is "a common concern of humankind" and an integral part of the development process. To achieve its objectives, the Convention-in accordance with the spirit of the Rio Declaration on Environment and Development-promotes a renewed partnership among countries. Its provisions on scientific and technical cooperation, access to genetic resources, and the transfer of environmentally sound technologies form the foundations of this partnership.

The Endangered Species Act19, the programs of the former National Biological Service (now part of the U.S. Geological Survey)20, and the Convention on Biological Diversity are vehicles for slowing the massive extinction of species currently under way. But resistance from property rights groups has made biodiversity legislation controversial in the United States, and many people continue to focus on the cost instead of the benefits of maintaining the habitats and ecosystems of endangered species. Widespread recognition and acceptance of the importance and value of conservation and sustainable use of biodiversity is indispensable in order to secure sustainable economic development and to meet public desire for a better environment. The following are some of the many steps we could take to achieve conservation and the sustainable development of biodiversity:

1. Develop a national strategy for biodiversity conservation,
2. Carrying out a national research project for biodiversity,
3. Implementation of a Nationwide Green Network Plan;
4. Strengthening conservation capacity;
5. Effective environmental impact assessments;
6. Establishment of an information management system for biological diversity.

Biodiversity Loss and Economic Growth: A Cross-country Analysis

Biodiversity loss is among the most serious environmental problems facing the world today. Natural habitats in the moist tropical regions, which harbour the majority of the world's flora and fauna, are being lost at an alarming rate. It is estimated that in tropical rain forests alone the rate of loss of entire species (not merely genetic varieties or subspecies) is now a minimum of about 27,000 per year, or 3 per hour, and the rate is increasing. This rate of decline is believed to be at least 1000 times the "ordinary" (i.e., background) rate of extinction. There are many who believe that we are facing a biodiversity crisis, and others have gone as far as to suggest that we are slipping into a rate of extinction that may well rival that which resulted in the demise of the dinosaurs some 65 million years ago.

Within the past decade, there has been a resurgence of the debate about the effects of economic growth on environmental quality. This particular debate has been fuelled by studies carried out in the early 1990s that showed that there is an inverted U-shaped relationship between certain indicators of environmental degradation and economic growth. This relationship is now widely known as the environmental Kuznets curve (EKC). The EKC hypothesis suggests that environmental effects are initially low at low levels of economic growth. However, as development proceeds, the rate of pollution increases. At higher levels of economic development, countries are able (through structural change) to substitute toward industrial and agricultural technologies that are less harmful to the environment. A typical feature of the EKC is the inverted U shape, which suggests that the level of pollution reach es a maximum level with respect to income, after which it begins to decline.

The EKC debate is of considerable national and international importance. The existence of such a relationship would lend support to the view that as countries develop they will experience a cleaner environment. A corollary of this view is that pollution is a necessary evil for countries at an early stage of development and that economic growth is the key to solving environmental problems.

This article considers the issue of biodiversity loss in the context of the current debate on economic growth and environmental quality. The EKC debate has given rise to a rapidly expanding literature, part of which is reviewed in the next section. (1) However, the majority of these studies focus on aspects of environmental degradation such as air and water pollution and deforestation. The basic premise here is that biodiversity belongs to a special class of environmental degradation because it involves complex ecosystems, the loss of which cannot be recovered by technological advances. As such they differ from other types of environmental degradation, such as pollution and deforestation, for which improvements are possible to some extent. Furthermore, biodiversity levels are not related to energy use, unlike pollutants commonly used in EKC studies. Thus at the global level, there cannot be a turning point in the relationship as income increases. Rather than estimating an EKC relationship, here the article en deavors to investigate the determinants of biodiversity loss and offer suggestions for policy. The main finding of the study is that although economic growth has an expected adverse effect on biodiversity, the composition of output can be important, particularly in low-income countries. For some aspects of biodiversity (such as mammal and bird species), the results indicate that there is some scope for using appropriate institutional and macroeconomic policies to reduce the rate of species decline.

7

Economic Growth in Asia

Economic Growth in East Asia

Over the past three decades remarkable economic growth has occured in East Asia. This policy forum will examine key features of economic growth in eight East Asian economies: Japan, Singapore, Hong Kong, the Republic of Korea, Taiwan/China, Malaysia, Thailand, and Indonesia. This forum will also focus on some central ideas of growth theory. Tools and concepts from growth theory provide important insights into the East Asian experience. This experience, in turn, also provides new insights into the process of economic growth. One goal of this forum is to confront growth theory with an important example of economic growth, and in doing so promote understanding of both growth theory and an outstanding growth experience.

Fundamental Aspects of East Asian Growth

- Macroeconomic Stability.
- Rapid Economic Growth.
- Broad Sharing of Growth's Benefits.

Macroeconomic Policy in East Asia

World experience suggests that macroeconomic stability is a key factor for facilitating economic growth. Macroeconomic stability means that inflation is kept low and that the real exchange is stable at a competitive level. Moreover, the government budget deficit and foreign debt are kept within limits consistent with price and exchange rate stability. When the economy is struck by external shocks, such as an export price shock or a large rise in world interest rates, fiscal and monetary policy are adjusted quickly to avoid inflation or exchange rate volatility..

The high-performance East Asian economies have been very successful in creating macroeconomic stability. During the past three decades they have experienced:

- Inflation stabilized around 6% per year.
- Relatively small government budget deficits.
- Relatively stable real exchange rates.

Maintaining macroeconomic stability is less costly than regaining it once it has slipped. The high performance East Asian economies' prudent and consistent pursuit of macroeconomic stability has helped contribute to their high growth. Even more importantly, they have avoided major macroeconomic crises that cause sharp reductions in aggregate demand and investment.

Macroeconomic crises are very costly in terms of years of economic growth. For developing countries, the standard deviation of growth rates is four times the mean growth rate. Thus a single-year crisis (growth two standard deviations below mean growth) costs the equivalent of eight years of accumulated growth. Chile, for example, had on average from 1963 to 1988 zero growth in GDP per worker, largely because GDP per worker fell 16% between 1973 and 1975, and 19% between 1981 and 1983. Such dramatic shocks have been absent in the macroeconomic record of the high-performance East Asian economies over the past three decades.

Rapid Economic Growth in East Asia

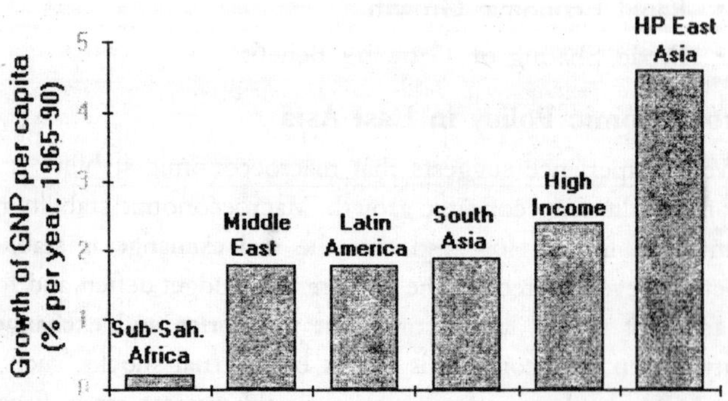

East Asia has a remarkable record of high and sustained economic growth over the past three decades. Growth in East Asia during this period has been concentrated in eight economies that have formed three waves of growth. The first wave was growth in Japan, followed by a wave of growth in the "Four Tigers" — Hong Kong, the Republic of Korea, Singapore, and Taiwan/China. Another wave of growth is apparent in Indonesia, Malaysia, and Thailand. Since 1960 these eight economies together have grown about twice as fast as the rest of East Asia and the industrial economies, about three times as fast as Latin America and South Asia, and about five times as fast as Sub-Saharan Africa. Between 1960 and 1985, real income per capita increased more than four times in Japan and the Four Tigers and more than doubled in Indonesia, Malaysia, and Thailand.

Recent growth in the transition economies of China and Vietnam presents the latest wave of growth in East Asia. Given their economic history as state-dominated economies, these transition economies have rather different starting points than those of the East Asian economies in the previous three waves of growth. Nonetheless, their rapid growth re-enforces the importance of studying the East Asian experience for understanding the factors that promote economic growth.

The high-performance economies of East Asia have several common characteristics:

- Dynamic agricultural sector.
- Rapid growth of exports.
- Rapid demographic transition.
- High investment and saving rates.
- High investments in human capital.

There are important interactions between these characteristics. For example, the export orientation of these economies created a demand for skilled workers that helped to support the value of investments in education. The dynamic agricultural sector allowed labour to be shifted into export industries. The rapid demographic transition improved the focus of investments in education and allowed a larger amount of savings to be invested in physical capital. Fostering beneficial interactions between growth processes in an economy is a key to development.

More generally, an important feature of the East Asia economies is the transfer of general ideas and models among countries. Japan started the process and other countries followed in what has been termed the "flying geese" effect. Successive waves copied effective institutions, policies, and technologies of previous waves of growing economies. While learning from the experience of successful economies in the region, followers changed and adapted the approaches of the leaders. For example, the first and second waves of growth in East Asia employed a considerable amount of government intervention during industrialization. In contrast, the third wave — Indonesia, Malaysia, and Thailand — placed much more emphasis on liberalization of the private sector. While there may not exist a single East Asian model, a central characteristic of these highly successful economies is an ability to learn from other economies' experiences.

Broad Sharing of Growth's Benefits

A fundamental aspect of economic policy in the high-performance East Asian economies is the principle of shared growth. In Malaysia, economic policy addressed income imbalances between different ethnic groups, with particular focus on the welfare of Bumiputera, the largest but poorest ethnic group. The concept of "economic democracy" espoused in Indonesia includes the idea that everyone shares in economic opportunity. Leaders in Taiwan/China recognized equity considerations needed attention to avoid repeating previous political failures. Japan and Singapore, both benefiting from the absence of a landlord elite, also put significant emphasis on equity. Attention to distributional considerations in Korea developed more gradually. Leaders in all these countries, while often authoritarian or paternalistic, recognized that their political viability and legitimacy depended on their ability to deliver gains in economic welfare to everyone rather than just to a narrow elite.

Several types of policies helped to promote the broad sharing of economic growth's benefits. Investments in education promoted social mobility and enhanced workers' economic opportunities. Land reform was carried in Japan, Korea, and Taiwan/China in order to distribute landholdings more equally and to foster the incentives of workers in agriculture to be productive. Economic policy, particularly in Japan and Taiwan/China, and in the 1980s in Korea, also fostered the development of small and medium-size enterprises. Hong Kong and Singapore provided low-cost housing for a majority of residents. While governments in the high-performance East Asian economies tended to surpress radical labour activity in the name of political stability, they have also stressed labour-management cooperation, consultation, and commitments to raise wages in line with economic growth.

The success of policies of shared economic growth are evident:

- Relatively equal income distributions.
- Relatively good health indicators.

Another important poverty indicator shows scope for improvement:

- Share of population with access to safe water.

Growth in East Asia what we can and what we cannot Infer

The spectacular growth of many economies in East Asia over the past 30 years has amazed the economics profession and has evoked a torrent of books and articles attempting to explain the phenomenon. Articles on why the most successful economies of the region Hong Kong, Korea, Singapore, and Taiwan Province of China have grown, to say the least, robustly invariably refer to the phenomenon as "miraculous." When practitioners of the Dismal Science have recourse to a Higher Power, the reader knows that he is in trouble. Confusion is compounded when he discovers that ideological debate has multiplied even further the analyses of this phenomenon. Rather than swelling the torrent of interpretations, this paper sets for itself the modest agenda of reviewing the weightiest arguments in the literature that attempt to identify the reasons for the extraordinary economic growth in East Asia and trying to decide which arguments make sense. The exercise has value because finding the right explanation might suggest how to replicate this success elsewhere and, as a bonus, might also satisfy the reader's urge to solve an engaging intellectual puzzle. It is best if we start with the facts.

Since 1960 Asia, the largest and most populous of the continents, has become richer faster than any other region of the world. Of course, this growth has not occurred at the same pace all over the continent. The western part of Asia grew during this period at about the same rate as the rest of the world, but, as a whole, the eastern half (ten countries: China, Hong Kong, Indonesia, Japan, Korea, Malaysia, the Philippines, Singapore, Taiwan Province of China, and Thailand) turned in a superior performance, although variations in achievement can be observed here too. The worst performer was the Philippines, which grew at about 2 percent a year (in per capita terms), about equal to the average of non-Asian countries. China, Indonesia, Japan, Malaysia, and Thailand did better, achieving growth rates of 3-5 percent. This impressive achievement is, however, still modest compared with the phenomenal growth of Hong Kong, Korea, Singapore, and Taiwan Province of China, known as the "Four Tigers" because of their powerful and intimidating economic performance. The Tigers have had annual growth rates of output per person well in excess of 6 percent. These growth rates, sustained over a 30-year period, are simply amazing. While the average resident of a non-Asian country in 1990 was 72 percent richer than his parents were in 1960, the corresponding figure for the average Korean is no less than 638 percent.

This paper begins by looking at the long-running debate over the nature of growth. Is growth the result for the most part of an accumulation of manpower and machinery, or is it the result of employing the latest technology? The paper then looks at the growth record of the four countries from three other angles: the influence of government intervention, the extent to which investments and exports can be considered the main engines of growth, and the significance for sustained growth of the economic conditions prevailing at the very beginning of the countries' period of extended growth. The paper concludes with a few minimalist observations on possible areas for future study.

The Nature of Growth: Factor Accumulation or Technological Progress

Everyone agrees that the economies of East Asia, and particularly the Four Tigers, have grown spectacularly over the past generation, but nobody seems to agree on why. The debate over why they have grown so well in the past raises difficult questions about regional growth in the future and about the aspiration of countries elsewhere to replicate the East Asian success. The arguments at the centre of the debate are based on theoretical notions of growth accounting.

This accounting method deals with three elements that contribute to the production of goods and services: labour, capital, and technology. Labour and capital, known collectively as the "factors of production," refer in this context to the work force and to the capital goods (buildings, machines, vehicles) that the work force uses in manufacturing some product or providing some service. Technology refers to all the methods employed by labour and capital to produce a good and depends on the development or acquisition of practical skills to get the job done more quickly and more efficiently. No one denies that all three elements must be present to some degree if an economy is to grow. What is subject to debate is the contribution of the factors of production relative to that of technology. Some believe that increased use of labour and capital explain all growth; others are persuaded that the answer to growth lies in the use of more efficient technology.

Within the growth accounting framework it is possible to describe mathematically, using a simple equation, the contributions of these three elements to the overall production of an economy. By dividing the equation by the number of people in the work force, one can derive a dynamic equation that shows how output per person increases over time. Such an equation mathematically describes the contribution to higher output of the growth rate of labour participation, of capital employed per person, and of technology (the latter also known as the growth of "total factor productivity"). If applied empirically to specific economies this equation can give a good idea of what proportion of increased output is a result of higher labour participation and better use of capital and what proportion is the result of technological progress.

The traditional formulation of this equation suggests that a significant and sustained rate of technological progress is the only possible way, over the long run, for an economy to achieve a sustained rate of growth in output per person. Why? The labour participation rate can be increased for a while and will increase production, but obviously it cannot increase indefinitely (everybody will ultimately be employed). And more growth in capital than in labour ultimately leads to diminishing returns to capital, resulting in a fall in the growth of output even if capital continues to grow at a constant rate. Therefore, in order to achieve permanent growth, an economy must continuously improve its technology. This kind of growth is called "intensive growth." In contrast to intensive growth, increasing output by increasing inputs of labour and capital (extensive growth) can work only for a limited period, but it cannot last too long.

In a famous study, Solow (1956) conducted a growth accounting exercise such as the one described above. He found that accumulation of capital and an increase in the labour participation rate had a relatively minor effect, while technological progress accounted for most of the growth in output per person. Further studies have reconfirmed the validity of these conclusions. Accordingly, the standard view about the success of the East Asian countries emphasizes the role of technology in their high growth rates and focuses on the fast technological catch-up in these economies. In this view, these economies have succeeded because they learned to use technology faster and more efficiently than their competitors did.

A Contrarian view

The collapse of the Soviet Union in about 1990, after years of apparent economic success, caught most people by surprise. This collapse seemed to lend credence to the "extensive growth hypothesis," which argues that the Soviet Union, after many decades of extensive growth, ran into the inevitable diminishing returns effect, just as predicted in the growth accounting framework, because it had relied for its economic growth on a massive accumulation of capital and labour and had been slow to accept innovative technology. These developments in the economy of the Soviet Union served to raise concerns about other economies, including some East Asian countries, that have invested primarily in labour and capital rather than in technology over the past few decades. Krugman (1994) makes the comparison specific:

> The newly industrializing countries of Asia, like the Soviet Union of the 1950s, have achieved rapid growth in large part through an astonishing mobilization of resources. Once one accounts for the role of rapidly growing inputs in these countries' growth, one finds little left to explain. Asian growth, like that of the Soviet Union in its high-growth era, seems to be driven by extraordinary growth in inputs like labour and capital rather than by gains in efficiency.

Likewise, in explaining the extraordinary postwar growth of the Four Tigers, Young (1994b) concludes that one arrives at total factor productivity growth rates, both for the nonagricultural economy and for manufacturing in particular, which are well within the bounds of those experienced by the OECD and Latin American economies over equally long periods of time. While the growth of output and manufacturing exports in the newly industrializing countries of East

Asia is virtually unprecedented, the growth of total factor productivity in these countries is not.

In the same vein, Kim and Lau (1994), comparing the sources of economic growth in these countries with those of Germany, France, Japan, the United Kingdom, and the United States, found that by far the most important source of economic growth in these countries [the Four Tigers] is capital accumulation, accounting for between 48 and 72 percent of their economic growth, in contrast to the case of the Group of Five industrialized countries, in which technical progress has played the most important role, accounting for between 46 and 71 percent of their economic growth.

The results of these studies are not only strikingly different from the view presented earlier of the primacy of technological progress, but they also convey a very pessimistic message. First, economic growth in the Four Tigers is hardly miraculous: it is just the expected outcome of a massive accumulation of labour and capital. Second, the progress of these economies along this growth path for the past 30 years cannot continue. Sooner or later they will experience a dramatic decrease in growth. Third, the societies in these countries made enormous sacrifices of consumption and leisure to achieve these growth rates. Therefore, even if their so-called success can be replicated in other countries, it is probably not wise to do so. But how conclusive are these results? In fact, conclusions based on these studies are not very robust in that they are sensitive to the specific assumptions of each study.

The main reason for this sensitivity is the difficulty of estimating the rate of growth of capital stock in the East Asian countries during the period under study. Especially in the case of the Four Tigers, for which there are no good data before 1960, it is extremely difficult to estimate the capital stock at that time. To estimate how much capital was available in 1960, dubious assumptions have to be made about the depreciation rate of capital stock and about how much investment flowed in during the years of explosive growth beginning in 1960. What, for example, are the depreciation rates of different types of capital (buildings, industrial machinery, computers)? Are they equal for all countries and for all industries, or are they higher in faster-growing economies? What method is being used to estimate investment flows in the past?

Additional interpretational problems come from trying to estimate the share of national income attributable to capital and the share attributable to labour. Does the same amount of capital produce equal income in all countries and in all industries? Can statistics about the labour participation rate be trusted? Is the amount of effective work proportional to the hours that people work, or does working extra hours lead to diminishing returns? Should different types of labour (factory, office) be summed together? How should human capital be treated? Because of these unanswered and perhaps unanswerable questions, the results of studies that emphasize the contribution to growth of capital and labour and depreciate that of technology should not be regarded as definitive. They should be viewed as interesting, but only suggestive.

Some Counter-Contrarian Evidence

Using conventional parameters and a conventional method of extrapolation, we have conducted a growth accounting exercise for the Four Tigers during 1960-90 along the lines suggested by Young (1994a). The capital stock in these economies is assumed to be 0 in 1900 and subsequently to increase by investment flows less depreciation. The intention of this exercise is to demonstrate the general fragility of conclusions about the nature of the growth process in East Asia.

Figures 1-4 describe the results of this growth accounting exercise. Figure 1 compares the growth rates of output per person of the Four Tigers with those of the rest of the world during 1960-75 and 1975-90. The first four bars in this figure describe the growth rates of the individual Tigers. The fifth bar describes the simple average growth rate of 100 countries, representing the rest of the world (row). The sixth bar represents the mean of the growth rate of the rest of the world plus a 1.96 standard deviation (row + 1.96sd).

Growth rates can be regarded as "high" if they are above the row but below row + 1.96sd, "very high" if they are around row + 1.96sd, and "outstanding" if they exceed this value. Figure 1 shows that in this comparison the growth rates of output per person of Hong Kong, Korea, and Taiwan Province of China were very high in the 1960-75 period and outstanding in 1975-90, while the growth rate of Singapore was outstanding during the first period and very high during the second.

Figure 1. The Four Tigers: Growth of Output Per Person (Annual percentage change)

Figure 2. The Four Tigers: Growth of Labor Participation (Annual percentage change)

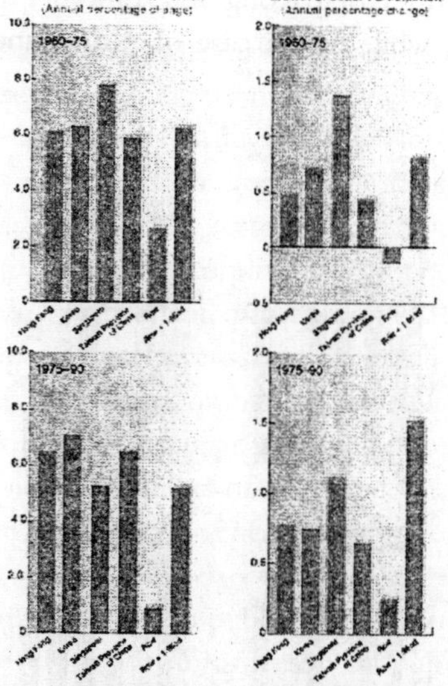

Figure 2 describes, in the same manner, the growth rate of labour participation, which was generally high for the Four Tigers and outstanding in the case of Singapore during 1960-75. The first panel in Figure 3 describes the growth rate of capital per person during 1975-90. The rate of capital accumulation was high in Hong Kong, very high in Singapore and Taiwan Province of China, and outstanding in Korea.

The second panel of Figure 3 describes the estimated rate of productivity growth during 1975-90: outstanding for Hong Kong, very high for Taiwan Province of China, somewhere between high and very high for Korea, and high for Singapore.

Finally, Figure 4 compares the rates of technological progress (total factor productivity) in the Four Tigers during 1975-90 with those achieved by Japan and the United States during the same period. The first panel of Figure 4 shows that the growth in productivity in all Four Tigers exceeded by far productivity growth in the United States.

Three of the four (except Singapore) also exceeded productivity growth in Japan. The second panel of Figure 4 describes the proportion of growth of output per person that is explained by productivity growth. It demonstrates that in the case of the Four Tigers this proportion was not systematically different from those of Japan and the United States: for Hong Kong and Taiwan Province of China it was slightly higher, while in the case of Korea and Singapore it was slightly lower.

Figure 3. The Four Tigers: Capital Accumulation and Total Factor Productivity Growth (Annual percentage change)

Figure 4. The Four Tigers, Japan, and United States (Annual percentage change)

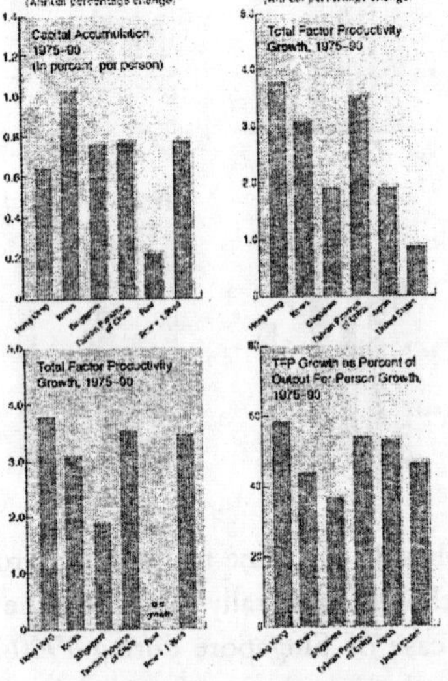

What conclusion emerges from this exercise? Although the Four Tigers accumulated capital and increased labour participation at a much faster rate than other economies, the increase in these two factors far from fully explains their exceptional growth rates; growth in productivity attributable to innovative technology also accounts for a significant fraction. In the case of Hong Kong, Korea, and Taiwan Province of China, their growth rates of total factor productivity are as outstanding as their output growth rates. Productivity growth in Singapore is less spectacular, but is still much above the world average. As a percentage of the growth rates of output per person, the productivity growth rates in these four economies are roughly similar to those in Japan and the United States.

A final note on the debate. Just when one seems to have arrived at the above unambiguous and intellectually satisfying conclusions, a nagging doubt recommends checking on how sensitive these findings are to changes in the main parameters of the growth accounting exercise, such as the *a* parameter (usually at 0.3333) indicating the relative contribution of labour and capital, the depreciation rate, the reference period for extrapolation, the chosen estimation period, and the date for the beginning of capital accumulation. A sensitivity analysis shows that most parameters do not affect the results in any significant way, but that the *a* parameter and the choice of a specific estimation period are all-important. Small, simultaneous changes in both *a* and the estimation period give results opposite to the neat conclusions presented above. The findings reported by Young (1994a) regarding the low productivity growth in the Four Tigers were obtained by using a relatively high value for *a* (0.45) and a specific estimation period (1970-85). These choices, though only slightly different from those in the baseline calculation, together yield an estimate of productivity growth significantly lower than the baseline result. In other words, the debate over the relative contribution to economic growth of factor accumulation versus more efficient technology is still very much alive. Stay tuned.

Role of Public Policy

As the foregoing consideration suggests, the labour and capital accumulation versus total factor productivity debate remains inconclusive. Can other factors shed light on the mystery of growth? One suggestion is to look at the role of government.

Lucas (1988) asked, "Is there some action a government of India could take that would lead the Indian economy to grow like Indonesia's or Egypt's? If so, what, exactly?" The importance of this question can hardly be exaggerated. A usable answer would be the academic equivalent of alchemy, turning the dross of everyday economics into pure gold. Accordingly, the highest ambition of economists who examine the East Asian success is to identify a set of public policies that has promoted economic growth there and gives promise of doing so elsewhere.

It should come as no surprise that opinions vary considerably about the effect of public policy and selective government interventions on stimulating economic growth. Exponents of these opinions fall into three schools. The first emphasizes the primacy of free markets. This school requires only that the government "get the basics right" and opposes any other kind of government intervention. (Getting the basics right means creating an environment in which the economy will thrive by, for example, making sure that the exchange rate reflects the economic fundamentals, that interest rates yield a positive return, that inflation is kept under control, and that taxes are not so burdensome as to discourage economic activity.) The second also embraces the view that the government get the basics right, but in addition advocates selective interventionist policies, particularly in developing countries. The third, somewhat agnostic, school denies the possibility of coming to any conclusion about the effects of public policy or of selective interventions on economic growth. The whole debate, according to this school, gets you nowhere.

Free Markets

The first school, basing its views on what is known as the neoclassical approach to economics in general and to economic growth in particular, espouses an underlying belief in classical liberalism. The production possibilities of any economy at any time are determined, according to this view, by the availability of physical resources and of innovative technology. The rate of economic growth in the long run is determined by the rate of technological progress, which is itself a natural outcome of fierce competition in the laissez-faire economic system. Since it regards markets as efficient, this school maintains that government should confine itself to providing public goods (roads and bridges, police protection) and to getting the basics right and should abstain from any further intervention in the market.

This school wishes to restrict the role of government in the economy, but it is not anarchistic. It would assign to government both a microeconomic and a macroeconomic function. In its microeconomic aspect, government should ensure property rights, law and order, and adequate provision of public goods. It should avoid high tax rates, price controls, and other distortions of relative prices. On the macroeconomic side, government should ensure stable and low inflation, avoid excessive budget deficits, promote the integrity of the financial and banking system, provide for open markets, and strive for stable and realistic exchange rates. Advocates of this view see the success of East Asia as the natural outcome of these cautious policies.

Selective Intervention

The revisionist view does not share the neoclassical belief in the efficiency of markets. It asserts that, especially in the poorer countries, markets work imperfectly. In poor countries, production creates externalities (unintended undesirable effects, such as pollution), credit is limited, and the market is a melée in which foreign and domestic firms savage one another and the public through unfair trade practices. Accordingly, the revisionists recommend an activist government that will moderate the excesses of the market and assist the orderly development of the economy by acquiring technology and by allocating funds for useful projects that promise a good rate of return. De Long and Summers (1991) sum up this view: "The government should jump-start the industrialization process by transforming economic structure faster than private entrepreneurs would." Advocates of this view see the success of East Asia as confirming their conviction.

The revisionist view recognizes that the government must often choose firm-specific, highly complex, and nonuniform interventions. In extreme contradiction to the neoclassical doctrine, it allows, and even recommends, the active use of tax policy to manipulate relative prices in the economy. Even the World Bank (1993) report, after emphasizing the necessity of neoclassical "getting the basics right" policies in East Asia, concedes that these fundamental policies do not tell the entire story. In each of these economies the government also intervened to foster development, often systematically and through multiple channels. Policy interventions took many forms: targeted and subsidized credit to selected industries, low deposit rates and ceilings on borrowing rates to increase profits and retained earnings, protection of domestic import substitutes, subsidies to declining industries, the establishment and financial support of government banks, public investment in applied research, firm-and industry-specific export targets, development of export marketing institutions, and wide sharing of information between public and private sectors.

Agnosticism

A third school, rejecting the claims of both the neoclassicists and the revisionists, claims that we can say nothing meaningful about selective interventions because we cannot properly identify how such policies spur economic growth. There are four reasons for this skepticism.

First, in analysing "successful" policies, there is clear selection bias. Success has a thousand fathers; failure is an orphan. We know from the outset that the East Asian economies have been successful and that therefore government intervention did not inhibit growth. Consequently interventions in these economies are widely studied. On the other hand, since economists find unsuccessful economies much less attractive to study, they rarely look at government intervention in economies of this type. The selection of interventions to be analysed is therefore skewed and is not scientifically neutral.

Second, in most cases it is impossible to offer a realistic counterfactual scenario. Would the Hawaiians have invented innovative igloos if it snowed a lot in Honolulu? Would the U.S. economy have grown faster if, like the Soviet Union, its government had turned Communist in 1917? In other words, in analysing specific interventions, we cannot address the most (and perhaps the only) relevant question, "How fast would these economies have grown if these policies had not been in place?"

Third, public policy in the successful East Asian economies is far from homogeneous. Variation is large in the specific sectors and industries targeted for selective intervention in different countries. The more one examines the policies individual East Asian economies have pursued, the more evident it becomes how different, and indeed contradictory, these policies have been. Rodrik (1994), for example, remarks that the East Asian model encompasses highly interventionist strategies (Japan and Korea), as well as noninterventionist ones (Hong Kong and Thailand); explicitly redistributive policies (Malaysia), as well as distributionally neutral ones (most of the rest); clientelism (Indonesia and Thailand), as well as strong, autonomous states (Japan, Korea, Singapore); emphasis on large conglomerates (Korea), as well as on small, entrepreneurial firms (Taiwan). This range of strategies, all followed more or less successfully, suggests that the search for a simple explanation of the East Asian miracle may well be futile.

Fourth, determining the correct direction of causality is tricky. For instance, in successful economies one usually finds policies that encourage low fiscal deficits and good educational systems. Are these policies responsible for the success of the economy, or is the success of the economy responsible for the policies? Observing that a specific variable is present along with growth does not necessarily constitute proof that the policy generates growth. It might be the other way around. For example, it is much easier for a government to maintain a healthy fiscal position when the economy is growing and tax revenues are on the increase than when the economy is stagnant and demand is strong for deficit-creating social expenditures, such as unemployment compensation. Is a small deficit a result or is it a cause of economic growth? Conventional wisdom relates education to wealth. But which causes which? When an economy is booming, a government can afford generous subsidies for education. Moreover, the demand for education increases when an economy is growing and the population is becoming richer (it is unnecessary for children to start working at age 12). Furthermore, when an economy experiences rapid technological change, the advantage of educated over uneducated workers will be greater than when the economy is stagnant. Therefore there will be an increase in the demand for education by individuals who want a better job in the dynamic economy. In this case, by the way, further education constitutes an advantage for the specific individual relative to other individuals but does not necessarily improve the macroeconomic prospects of the economy.

These examples are presented not to prove that government policies are unimportant, but to make the modest point that we still understand very little about the relationship between public policy and the extraordinary growth rates of the East Asian economies. Other countries should be careful in trying to imitate the East Asian policies. Not understanding the causality between growth and industrialization, in particular, has proved to be a costly mistake for many poor countries that pushed for rapid industrialization in a futile effort to boost economic growth.

Investment and Exports: The Engines of Growth?

Among the many reasons suggested to account for the East Asian success, the investment rate and the export orientation of these economies enjoy enthusiastic support. These are often called "engines of growth" because their strength seems to be pulling the whole economy forward. Moreover, they appear to generate beneficial spillover effects for the rest of the economy. The policy implication of this view is obvious. If the hypothesis is valid, the government should jump start the engines of growth, and if certain sectors continue to contribute to economic progress, while others do not, then government should assist the economy's forward motion by promoting the "good" sectors. Therefore, it should encourage investments and exports, using such policy instruments as direct subsidies or preferential allocation of credit to promote these activities.

Main Arguments

The view that investments and exports are engines of growth is based on one empirical and one theoretical argument. The empirical argument is that most East Asian countries that experience phenomenal growth rates also enjoy impressive rates of investment and are successful exporters. The theoretical argument as regards investment is that a high investment rate increases the capital stock (things used to create wealth) and that this can permanently increase the growth rate through economies of scale (e.g., bigger, more efficient factories, larger markets) and other beneficial side effects. In the case of exports, the theoretical argument is that export orientation increases the openness of the economy and, by exposing it to foreign technology and foreign competition, provokes a rapid rate of technological progress.

What is the Direction of Causality?

As stated above, a positive correlation between two variables (where one is found, the other is found) does not prove that one causes the other. In all the East Asian economies one can find export orientation and rapid technological progress. How are export orientation and technological progress related? The theoretical argument suggests that because a country is oriented to exporting, it becomes exposed to foreign technology: export orientation is the cause of technological advance. But the opposite might also be true, that technological advances cause export orientation. Suppose that some industries improve their technology and others do not. It is natural that industries with more advanced technology can compete in international markets and increase the quantity of their exports. In this case, the data will reveal a strong correlation between export performance and the rate of technological progress across industries. Likewise, developing countries that are better in learning and applying advanced foreign technology will enjoy an advantage in world markets and be able to sell their products abroad.

Investment rates (or equivalently, saving rates) appear to have a causal relationship to growth rates (i.e., saving causes growth). Nevertheless, a strong argument of reversed causality can be made even in this case. A study by Carroll and Weil (1994), examining data on savings and investment within households in various countries, found, in fact, that growth causes saving, but saving does not cause growth. Using these data, they discovered that households whose income is on the rise save more than households that experience little or no growth in income, a finding that represents a powerful reinterpretation of the growth-saving relationship. The study also offers from its findings a theoretical explanation that recognizes savers as creatures of habit. Although their incomes may be growing, households will respond slowly to their expanding wealth and will increase their consumption only gradually, with the effect that they save more. In this case, increased saving rates are caused by increased growth rates, and not vice versa.

Initial Conditions

The main empirical argument that a high rate of investment and a concentration on exporting have caused economic growth is the strong positive correlation between these two variables and the rates of growth found in the East Asian economies. In particular, the Four Tigers, the best performing economies in the region, display exceptional investment rates and an extremely high degree of openness (that is, they have a lot of exports and imports relative to the size of the economy). The section above stressed the problem of possible reverse causality between growth and these variables. A further problem is that of averages. Most studies observe a correlation between investment and exporting that are averaged over a period and a rate of growth that is averaged over the same period. Using averages over a period obscures the relation between the variables. A simple partial solution to disentangling the skein of causality is to observe the values of the explanatory variables at the beginning of the period rather than to take their average values over the period. Finding, for example, that economies with high growth rates during the 1960-90 period had very high investment rates or a significant export orientation around 1960 would go a long way toward solving the problem of reverse causality.

An examination of the dynamics of the investment rate and the openness of the economies of Hong Kong, Korea, Singapore, and Taiwan Province of China that compares the 1960 levels of these variables in the Four Tigers with those in other countries does not offer much support for the view that export orientation and investment have been engines of growth. The comparison of the 1960 investment rates of the four economies with the investment rates of 100 other economies clearly rejects the view that investment rates were high in the Four Tigers in 1960. Not only were the investment rates in these economies low in absolute values, but they were very modest even when compared with rates in other countries with a comparable level of income.

The same comparative exercise can be performed to test for openness (imports and exports as a percentage of GDP), taking into consideration such factors as the geographical size of the country, an important variable in determining the degree of openness of an economy. Small countries need to trade more than large countries with big internal markets. Reflecting this, Hong Kong and Singapore show a high degree of openness both during 1960-90 and at the beginning of the same period. On the other hand, Korea and Taiwan Province of China, which are geographically much larger, were not particularly open in 1960, either in absolute terms or relative to other countries of comparable size.

This analysis demonstrates that high investment rates and a large degree of openness were certainly not a general feature of the Four Tigers in 1960. The high investment rates (Korea, Singapore, and Taiwan Province of China) and the high degree of openness (Korea and Taiwan Province of China) were economic features that evolved in these economies only gradually, accompanying rather than preceding the process of economic growth. The conclusion is that the view of these activities as engines of growth does not find much support in the data.

Some Positive Evidence Regarding Initial Conditions

Were there other variables that characterized the initial conditions in the East Asian countries and, if so, what contribution might they have made to the subsequent growth of these economies? A study by Rodrik in 1994 examined precisely this question. It was inspired by the view that "In searching for the secrets of the East Asian miracle, the obvious place to look is the set of initial conditions that precede economic takeoff." Examining the initial conditions, the study finds that, in certain important respects, they were very different from what one would expect, given the income level of these economies.

Tracing average growth of income per person in 41 countries during 1960-85 back to initial conditions in 1960, Rodrik shows that countries that were poorer, but that had good primary education systems and less inequality of income and land distribution around 1960, grew faster than the others during the following period. The study compares actual data on education and demographics (fertility rate and mortality rate) in eight East Asian countries with the predicted values we would expect, given their initial income, and compared inequality of income and land ownership around 1960 with the same characteristics of other developing countries at a comparable income level. The results show strong evidence that in terms of initial conditions (equality of land and income, school enrolment, high life expectancy and low fertility rates), the eight East Asian countries were significantly better off than countries with similar levels of income. These findings raise the possibility (but do not prove) that these initial conditions may help explain the phenomenal growth rates we observed in East Asia after 1960.

The empirical evidence presented by Rodrik regarding the possible influence of initial conditions in explaining the East Asian miracle is impressive but should be accepted with caution because of the small number of observations. Data on initial conditions in 1960, especially for developing countries, are rare and are of questionable quality. While Rodrik's results suggest a possible explanation for the East Asian success, they are not robust enough to rule out other possibilities. Furthermore, it is not clear what the normative implications of these findings are. For example, suppose that land equality is indeed beneficial for economic growth. Does that mean that land redistribution is a good policy to promote growth? Not necessarily. The redistribution may be extremely damaging by weakening property rights or disrupting political stability, which are obviously essential to growth. Likewise, lowering fertility rates by government decree may be bad for growth, even if low fertility rates are found to be good for growth.

Concluding Remarks

The recent literature on the East Asian growth experience has sparked an intense intellectual debate. This study has attempted to review critically the main arguments in this debate, covering some of its most important dimensions. Inevitably, other important dimensions did not receive fair representation, such as theories about nonmonotonic dynamics of growth (in which middle-income countries can take off and grow faster than either rich or poor countries) and about the importance of the geographical concentration of growth successes (why is East Asia the habitat of all Four Tigers?).

The study does not offer clear and conclusive results nor does it makc clear policy recommendations. Its main judgment is that, from a positive point of view, a promising avenue for the explanation of growth performance is the examination of initial conditions. Nevertheless, from a normative point of view, it is far from clear what specific policies governments should pursue, beyond the standard set of policies aimed at getting the basics right.

Cross-Country Patterns of Economic Growth

The countries of East and Southeast Asia grew extremely rapidly during the last quarter century. The eight best performers — Hong Kong, Singapore, Taiwan, Korea, China, Malaysia, Thailand, and Indonesia — grew at an average of over 5.5% per year in per capita terms between 1965 and 1990. With the exception of several European countries in the immediate post World War II period, growth rates of this magnitude and duration are unprecedented in human history. But as remarkable as was the growth performance of these eight core economies, not all Asian developing countries were able to follow their lead. South Asia, the Philippines, Burma, Central Asia, and many of the Pacific Island nations all recorded average or below average growth in comparison with developing countries in other regions of the world.

In this section we explore the Asian growth patterns by quantifying the empirical relationships between long-term growth and various structural and policy variables. We base the analysis on a general framework of cross-country regression analysis that allows us to put the Asian experience in a global context. Our objective is to understand the critical dimensions in which the East Asian countries differed from other countries that allowed them to achieve rapid growth, and to explore the extent to which those dimensions are unique to these fast-growing economies.

Our approach does not identify all of the specific factors associated with economic growth across countries, nor does it in every case clarify the precise channels through which certain variables affect growth. Rather, it is an attempt to distill the vast amounts of information available on dozens of countries into a tractable, parsimonious framework that identifies a small set of variables that stand out as the most important factors influencing rates of growth around the world. This approach allows us to discern broad trends across countries that illuminate some of the key differences between fast and slow growing economies.

Most importantly, this exercise provides strong clues to what lies ahead for Asian countries during the next thirty years. It provides a foundation to understand the likelihood of continued rapid growth in the "tiger" economies, as well as insights to the most appropriate steps that other countries in Asia can take to accelerate growth.

The Basic Growth Framework

The basic empirical framework is based on an extended version of the neoclassical growth model, as described by Barro (1991), Barro and Lee (1994), and Sachs and Warner (1995a and 1995b). This model predicts conditional convergence of income: a country with a low initial income relative to its own long-run (or steady-state) potential level of income will grow faster than a country that is already closer to its long-run potential level of income. The basic idea is that the farther an economy is located from its steady-state income level, the greater is the gap of reproducible (physical and human) capital and technical efficiency from their long-run levels. The gap of existing capital and technology from steady-state levels offers the chance for rapid "catching up," via high rates of capital accumulation as well as the diffusion of technology from more technically advanced economies. Hence, the lower is the initial level of per capita income relative to steady state, the higher will tend to be the subsequent growth.

This framework presumably helps to explain why wealthier countries, with relatively large capital stocks and already operating near the world's technological frontier, tend to grow more slowly than some lower-income countries that are catching up with the leaders. If we could presume that all countries have the same steady-state income levels, then the neoclassical approach would imply, simply, that poorer countries would grow faster than richer countries. In fact, such a pattern is not generally observed. Over the period 1965-90, poorer countries did not, on average, narrow the income gap with the richer economies. The crosscountry growth framework therefore builds in a crucial assumption, that countries have *distinctive* long-term levels of per capita income to which each is converging. Crucially, the long-term levels depend on two main kinds of variables: economic policies and economic structure. Countries with favourable economic policies (as identified below) tend to have a higher steady-state level of income, and therefore faster growth at any given initial level of income. Similarly, countries with a favourable economic structure (also identified below) tend to experience faster growth, on a path of convergence to a higher long-term level of income.

We should stress the precise meaning of "long-term" or "steady-state" as used in this analysis. In our interpretation, the steady state to which an economy is converging at any time t is conditional on the actual policies in place at time t.

For example, an economy that is closed to international trade at time t is found to have a lower "steady-state" income level than an open economy. Strictly speaking, we are measuring the "steady state" on the assumption of *no future changes* in the explanatory (policy and structural) variables. If a closed economy subsequently opens to trade, then we interpret this as raising the steady-state level of income to which the country tends to converge.

A variety of policy and structural variables Zi will affect growth rates by changing the long-run potential level of income. With regard to policy variables, considerable research and experience has shown that trade and financial policies, macroeconomic management, and maintenance of the rule of law (including property rights) all affect the climate for business activity, and thus the long-term potential level of income. Improving these policies increases the level of potential income, thus increasing the growth rate for any given initial level of income.

With regard to structural variables, a country's geography, resource base, and ecology can affect long-term income levels. For example, the extent of endemic disease in the population — which tends to be much higher in the tropics than in temperate climates — can influence the long-term productivity of the labour force, and therefore the rate of growth at any given income level. In order to account for cross-country difference in growth rates, we consider a wide variety of explanatory variables that have been proposed by earlier studies as important determinants of long-run income, and therefore current economic growth. We categorize these explanatory variables into four broad dimensions: (1) initial conditions (initial per capita GDP and initial human capital stock); (2) natural resources and geography, including natural resource intensity, landlockedness, location in the tropics, and the ratio of coastline distance to land area; (3) policy variables (government savings, quality of institutions, and openness); and (4) demographic variables (growth of the working age population, growth of the total population, and initial life expectancy at birth).

Initial Conditions

In the basic framework, for given values of the other explanatory variables, the model predicts a negative relationship between initial income and subsequent growth — that is, a country with a lower initial per capita GDP is in a more favourable position for future growth. It is wellknown that, without controlling for other factors, poor countries do not generally grow faster than rich countries. However, a considerable body of empirical evidence has shown that once important structural and policy variables are taken into account, poor countries indeed grow faster than rich countries. This outcome has become known as conditional convergence.

Sachs and Warner (1995a), for example, found that poor but open economies tend to grow faster than rich open countries. Countries that isolate themselves from the global economy are in a much weaker position to take advantage of new technologies, or to develop as extensive a division of labour, and therefore show less tendency to catch up. Figure 1 shows the basic relationship between the initial level of income and the subsequent rate of economic growth for the group of thirty countries that have been most open to the global economy during the last 25 years (specifically, where the Sachs/Warner openness variable has a value of 0.8 or higher, on a scale of 0-1, with 1 being the most open). In this set of open countries, the poorest countries exhibit the highest growth rates, and the richer countries record slower growth rates. In all but one of these open economies, the level of income relative to the U.S. in 1990 was higher than it was in 1965. Switzerland, the one exception, was the country closest to the U.S. average in 1965, and thus the one with the weakest tendency towards further catching up.

The tendency for poor countries to grow faster than rich countries has two important implications in the Asian context. First, it provides one piece to the puzzle of explaining East Asia's rapid growth during the last thirty years. Low levels of income in the 1960s provided the *potential* for rapid growth. Importantly, this reasoning also implies that some of the other, slowgrowing Asian countries have the capacity for more rapid growth in the future. Second, as East Asian countries become wealthier, their growth rates are likely to slow. Japan is a clear example of this pattern; its expansion slowed considerably during the 1980s as it narrowed the gap in per capita income with Europe and the United States. When income per capita in Japan was less than 50% of the U.S. average in the 1960s, annual growth exceeded 9%. By the time Japan had reached 70% of U.S. income, its annual growth rate had slowed to 4%, and now that its income is about 90% of the U.S. level, its growth rate is closer to 2%.

The data on 1965 income, indicate that all three groups of Asian countries were well placed for rapid growth, based on their relatively low levels of income. But obviously there is more to the story — sub-Saharan Africa and South Asia had the lowest initial income levels, and therefore had the potential, all other things equal, to grow more rapidly than the East Asian countries. Clearly, differences in long-term potential income, as conditioned by policies, structure, and demography, have played a role in the differences in growth within Asia and between East Asia and the rest of the world.

Human capital, measured in terms of levels of education and health, is often suggested as a possible source of growth. A better educated, more skilled work force is likely to be able to produce more from a given resource base than less-skilled workers. Following Barro and Lee (1996), we use the average years of secondary schooling for the working-age population at the start of the period of observation (1965) as our primary measure of the initial skill level of the population (we explore several other measures as well). The Four Tigers' average of 1.5 years of secondary schooling was the highest of the developing country regions in our sample.

Natural Resources and Geography

We examine four kinds of structural variables that may represent natural barriers to economic growth. The first variable measures natural resource abundance, and is calculated as the ratio of primary-product exports to GDP in 1971 (the earliest year in which data are available for all countries). Sachs and Warner (1995b) observe that natural resource-abundant economies have tended to grow *more slowly* than resource-rich economies during the past twenty years. For example, countries with primary product exports valued at between 0 and 5 percent of GDP recorded growth per person of over 3.2 percent between 1965 and

1990, whereas countries with primary product exports equivalent to over 20 percent of GDP grew just 0.8 percent per person per year. This pattern continues to hold once other variables, including initial income, geography, government policies, are taken into account. We note here that the Four Tigers recorded primary exports equivalent to an average of just 1 percent of GDP in 1971, far less than the average for other regions.

The reasons for this negative relationship remain unclear. After all, natural resource exports can provide foreign exchange earnings and finance investments in infrastructure, health, and education. Indonesia and Malaysia are examples of how governments can use the revenues earned from natural resource exports to boost incomes and improve welfare. During the last century, exports of natural resources also played a critical role in supporting sustained growth and development in several countries, including the United States and Argentina.

Over the last thirty years, however, many countries with abundant natural resources have performed poorly. In Mexico, Venezuela, Nigeria, Zambia, and a host of other countries, the 3 For summaries of these studies, see Sapsford and Balasubramanyam (1994) and Balassa (1989). initial fillip to income from natural resource exports was followed by long periods of stagnation or even decline. There are several possible explanations for this poor performance. One hypothesis is that natural resource abundance produces a "Dutch Disease" phenomenon, in which a strong resource base causes an appreciation of the real exchange rate, and thereby renders unprofitable an export-oriented or import-competing manufacturing sector. In this way, the natural resource abundant economies may have found themselves priced out of world markets in the production of labour-intensive goods — such as apparel, footwear, toys, and electronics assembly — which have been the first steps on the ladder towards rapid industrialization in East Asia. This impoverishment of resources may have contributed to their success by forcing the NICs to compete in manufactured exports. We also note, however, that South Asia, the region with the next smallest share of primary exports, achieved much less success in manufactured exports than in the Four Tigers, while much of Southeast Asia has recorded rapid growth in manufactured exports despite the relative natural resource abundance in Malaysia, Indonesia, and the Philippines.

Another possible reason why we observe slower growth in resource abundant economies is that profitable investments in the resource sector itself tend to be limited in scope, so that after the resource sector is developed, it usually does not generate continuing marked improvements in technology and job growth. Workers in resource abundant economies may initially receive higher wages, but without the impetus to productivity gains that comes from competing on world markets for manufactured goods, wages tend to stagnate, a pattern observed in recent decades in resource-based Latin American economies.

In addition, resource-abundant economies may provide greater opportunity and incentive for rent seeking and corruption, particularly if the resources are government owned, or heavily taxed. In these situations, entrepreneurial energies are likely to be focused on obtaining a larger piece of the existing economic pie, rather than on efforts to enlarge the pie. Additionally, resource abundant countries tend to follow boom-and-bust cycles in line with sharply fluctuating prices of their export commodities. Export receipts and government revenues are subject to sharp increases and declines, complicating macroeconomic management, creating uncertainty, and undermining long-term investment.

Finally, long-term structural trends in commodity markets may have put primary producers at a disadvantage. Raul Prebisch (1950, 1959) argued long ago that secular declines in commodity prices would doom the exporters of primary products to slow growth. Ragnar Nurske (1961) concluded that because of technological innovations, world demand for primary products would grow slowly at best. Although there is much debate on these trends, the evidence appears to support both a gradual decline in commodity prices and slower growth in demand for primary products, especially since 19703.

The second structural variable we examine is access to the sea, as indicated by whether or not a country is landlocked. Landlocked countries have enormous cost and risk disadvantages that they must overcome to compete on world markets. Shipping costs for all imported goods are much higher, as landlocked countries must pay for transport by road and rail, as well as the costs associated with crossing at least one additional international border. The cost of extra shipping is magnified by the uncertainty of inland road conditions and customs clearance, which lead to higher insurance costs for each shipment. Their only alternative is to ship by air, which can be prohibitively expensive for many goods. Thus, it is much more difficult for manufacturing firms located in landlocked countries such as Nepal, Mongolia, Uzbekistan, Kazakhstan, and the Kyrgyz Republic to be competitive in world markets, unless they are processing domestic natural resources.

A third, and closely related structural variable is the ratio of a country's coastline distance to its total land area. This indicator gives a rough measure of the share of the population with relatively easy access to the sea. In countries where this ratio is relatively high (such as island economies), a larger share of the population is likely to be engaged in activities grounded in international trade. Adam Smith, who pointed out in *The Wealth of Nations* the difficulties facing landlocked countries, also discussed the importance of access to the sea *within* countries. He predicted that an extensive division of labour would develop mainly where sea-based trade was feasible. "[S]o it is upon the sea-coast, and along the banks of navigable rivers, that industry of every kind naturally begins to sub-divide and improve itself, and it is frequently not till a long time after that those improvements extend themselves to the inland part of the country." China represents an excellent example of this phenomena, with basically all of its fast-growing economy activity located along the Southeast coastline, and little dynamism in its more inland regions.

Smith's example was England, where he attributed the economy's relatively high productivity to, in part, its access to the sea. "England, on account of the natural fertility of the soil, of the great extent of the sea-coast in proportion to that of the whole country, and of the many navigable rivers which run through it, and afford the conveniency of water carriage to some of the most inland parts of it, is perhaps as well fitted by nature as any large country in Europe, to be the seat of foreign commerce, of manufactures for distant sale, and of all of the improvements which these can occasion." Our variable, the ratio of coastline distance to total land area, is Smith's suggested specification. In the terminology of the neoclassical model, we expect higher values of this indicator to be associated with higher steady state levels of GDP, and therefore higher growth rates. The Four Tigers' ratio of coastline to land area was by far the highest of any region in the world, with

Southeast Asia's the second highest. Our fourth structural variable is location in the tropics. Very few countries located in the tropics have achieved sustained economic success. Tropical countries face several important disadvantages.

The prevalence and burden of infectious diseases in much higher in the tropics than in more temperate climates. Malaria, schistosomiasis, and many other debilitating maladies are most prominent in tropic climates. These diseases reduce worker productivity and add to the cost of health care. In additional, tropical agriculture is hindered by warmer temperatures and torrential rains (which tend to leech soils of important nutrients). There are some exceptions — such as the richly fertile volcanic soils of Java — but such cases are relatively rare. As a result of these influences, tropical climates tend to support much lower population densities and thereby a less extensive division of labour than more temperate climates. Singapore and Hong Kong have been much less affected by their location in the tropics, probably because as city states, they have always had a relatively large share of manufacturing and small share of agriculture in GDP. The tropics are likely to have a far smaller deleterious impact on manufacturing firms in the tropics than on agriculture. In the closed space of a factory, air conditioning can compensate for hot, humid weather, putting tropical manufacturing on a par with factories in more temperate climes.

This reasoning suggests the possibility of a tropical poverty trap. Agricultural-based economies will have great difficultly in generating sustained growth and affecting the transformation to a manufacturing-base economy. The few economies that are able to make the jump to manufacturing — like Singapore and Hong Kong — are in a much better position for rapid growth and catching-up with the world economic leaders.

Policy Variables

The first policy variable we consider is openness to international trade. Open countries have greater access to new technologies, larger markets, and improved management techniques.

They also tend to have fewer distortions and better resource allocation, and their firms are more likely to be competitive on world markets. We use the openness measure constructed by Sachs and Warner (1995a). This index is the fraction of years between 1965 and 1990 that the country was considered to be open to trade. The judgement on the country's openness is made on the basis of four policy dimensions: (i) average tariff rates, (ii) extent of imports governed by quotas and licensing, (iii) average export taxes, and (iv) the size of the black market premium on the exchange rate. A country is considered to be open if it meets minimum criteria on all four aspects of trade policy: average tariffs must be lower than 40 percent; quotas and licensing must cover less than 40 percent of total imports; the black market premium must be less than 20 percent; and export taxes should be moderate.

Second, neoclassical growth theory suggests that an increase in the national saving rate will raise the growth rate associated with any level of income. However, there is a strong simultaneous relationship between aggregate saving and growth — growth may influence saving as much or more than saving affects growth. The precise nature of the saving-growth relationship remains unclear. As an alternative, we explore the relationship between government saving (defined as the difference between current government revenues and current government expenditures) and economic growth. There are two distinct channels through which government budget policies are likely to influence growth. First, the more governments save, the more the nation as a whole saves (though the relationship is not one to one). This adds to the pool of finances available for investment. Second, higher government saving tends to be indicative of sounder overall macroeconomic management, including lower rates of inflation, prudent exchange rate policies, and capable monetary management. Stable economies, in turn, lower the risks for investors and therefore lower the cost of capital for long-term investments. Government savings in the Four Tigers were far higher than any other region of the world between 1965-90, averaging 5.6 percent of GDP, whereas governments in the four Southeast Asian countries saved 3.5 percent of GDP. By comparison, government savings in South Asia averaged just 1 percent of GDP during the period. A third policy indicator is a measure of the quality of public-sector institutions and their relationship to the functioning of markets. We use the index from Knack and Keefer (1995), which is based on data compiled in the International Country Risk Guide (1995). The overall index is itself an average of five indicators of the quality of public institutions, including: (i) the perceived efficiency of the government bureaucracy; (ii) the extent of governmental corruption; (iii) efficacy of the rule of law; (iv) the presence or absence of expropriation risk; and (v) the perceived risk of repudiation of contracts by the government. Each country is scored on these five dimensions on the basis of surveys of business attitudes within the countries. The sub-indexes on the five measures are then averaged to produce a single, overall index that is scaled between 0 and 10. The overall index therefore aims to measure the security of property and contractual rights, the efficiency of the government's intervention in markets, and the allocation of public goods. A lower index indicates poorer quality institutions, and thus higher investment risks and production costs. The Four Tigers' institutions score very high, registering 7.8 on a scale of 1 to 10. For all the other developing regions, the average index ranges between 4.3-4.9. Malaysia and Thailand both score above 6.0, and India records 5.8. The lowest institutional scores in Asia were recorded by Bangladesh (2.7), the Philippines (3.0), and Indonesia (3.7). These scores compare with an average score of 4.5 for both Latin American and sub-Saharan African countries included in the International Country Risk Guide data.

Demographic Variables

Economists have generally given scant attention to the relationship between demographic change and economic growth. Explorations of the role of demography are usually limited to aggregate population growth, which has yielded mixed results. In this paper, we explore the role of changes in the structure of the population, as well as its size, in economic growth. We do so by including the growth rates of both the working-age population (aged 15-64) and the total population in the growth equation. For a given population growth rate, faster growth in the working-age population increases the size of the work force, which should be positively related to output growth. At the same time, for a given growth rate of the working-age population, faster overall population growth implies an increase in the relative size of the dependent population.

Therefore, the growth of GDP per capita is favoured when the growth of the working-age population outpaces overall population growth; and GDP growth per capita is reduced in the opposite case, when population growth outpaces the growth of the working-age population. Our basic growth specification in equation (6) stipulates a precise relationship between income growth, population growth, and labour force growth. It predicts that for a given population growth rate, a one percentage point increase in the growth rate of the labour force should lead to a one percentage point *increase* in the growth rate of per capita income. Similarly, for a given growth rate of the labour force, a one percentage point increase in the growth rate of the total population should lead to a one percentage point *decrease* in the growth rate of per capita income. In the four fast-growing East Asian economies, between 1965-90 the working age population grew one percentage point faster than the total population. In Southeast and South Asia, the differences were 0.55 and 0.25 percentage points, respectively. This suggests that the Four Tigers were given an important demographic boost which raised growth rates.

Our final demographic variable is Life Expectancy at Birth (LEB), measured in the initial year of the growth period. LEB can be viewed as a broad measure of the overall health of the population, encompassing the prevalence of disease and illness of the work force. A higher life expectancy would tend to indicate a healthier, more productive work force. LEB also measures changes in population structure, with a higher LEB associated with lower mortality rates and a longer life span for older workers and retirees. In the data, East Asia recorded a much higher level of life expectancy than the other developing countries in 1965. Life expectancy at birth was already 63 years in the Four Tigers in 1965, whereas it was only 49 years and 52 years, respectively in South and Southeast Asia. These lower levels presumably reflect both inherent geographic deficits (i.e. a tropic climate, prone to microparasitism) and lags in public health as of 1965.

Taken together, reveal stark differences across regions of developing countries. The Four Tigers recorded the most favourable conditions on every single variable, except for the initial level of income and location in the tropics. They were initially well endowed with human capital stock, measured by average years of secondary schooling (1.5 years). They had the *smallest* natural resource endowment, and therefore presumably the least Dutch disease pressures, and had the highest ratio of coastline distance to land area. The region recorded the most favourable stance on all three of the policy variables (openness, government saving, and quality of government institutions). It received the largest boost from the demographic composition of the population, and recorded the highest life expectancy at birth.

South Asia, by comparison, was disadvantaged by its lower levels of education and in particular by a relatively weak policy stance. The region scored particularly low on the openness index. Its demographic shift was much less favourable than East Asia's and it recorded a very low initial life expectancy, suggesting an environment particularly sensitive to microparasitism.

Southeast Asia, by contrast, had a very favourable policy stance, especially on openness and the savings rate. These policies helped to compensate for average or below average initial conditions and structural characteristics. Sub-Saharan Africa has the most adverse natural conditions — high transportation cost, high natural resource intensity, and high disease endemicity (as proxied by LEB) — and it was further disadvantaged by below average scores on each of the policy variables. It also recorded the smallest difference between the growth of the working age population and the total population. Latin America is close to the average on most of the variables, but was well below the mean for both openness and institutional quality, suggesting that policy deficiencies are the main source of Latin America's poor growth performance in recent decades.

Basic Results

The results shows strong evidence for conditional convergence. For the basic set of results in column 1, the coefficient on the log value of initial GDP is highly significant, and the estimated coefficient is -1.98 (t = -9.42). Countries with lower incomes in 1965 grew faster than countries that began with higher incomes, after controlling for the other variables that influence the steady-state level of income. Specifically, a country at half the income level of another country tends to grow by 1.4 percentage points (= 1.98 x ln(2)) faster than the richer country, assuming the same level of long-term income. Much of the variation in cross-country growth is the result of poorer countries catching up with richer countries. For example, since average income in the Four Tigers was one-sixth the U.S. level in 1965, the catch-up factor boosted their growth rates by 3.5 percentage points a year relative to the U.S. between 1965 and 1990.

The estimated coefficient on the initial educational attainment variable (the log value of mean years of secondary schooling) is positive, but is not statistically significant. This result is consistent with other studies that have found a weak direct link between education and growth. One possible explanation is measurement problems. For example, available data do not make any adjustment for the quality of schooling, which arguably is a key determinant of human capital accumulation. It is also possible that low levels of schooling in 1965 implied faster increases in schooling after 1965, and therefore a faster improvement in human capital in the subsequent 25 years.

The estimated coefficient for the natural resource abundance variable is -2.43 (t=-2.36), indicating that during the period 1965-90, countries with abundant natural resources grew more slowly than other countries. This result is consistent with that of Sachs and Warner (1995). The finding suggests that one reason the Four Tigers grew rapidly was that they were resource poor, which may have induced them to turn to manufacturing more quickly and vigorously than other countries. Of course, there were exceptions to the general correlation of natural resource abundance and slow growth: resource-poor India grew slowly while resource-rich Malaysia and Indonesia both recorded strong growth rates. The negative relationship between resource abundance and growth is a tendency, not a straightjacket. Natural resource abundance is not necessarily an impediment to growth, but it creates challenges in economic management with which many countries have had difficulty coping. As a result, resource abundant countries have tended to grow more slowly than others.

The regression results confirm our hypotheses about geography: countries that were landlocked, or whose populations had relatively little access to the sea, or that were located in the tropics all recorded lower growth rates between 1965-90. Landlocked countries grew on average six-tenths of a percentage point more slowly than other countries between 1965 and 1990, accounting for a cumulative 14 percent lower level of income by the end of the period. Similarly, countries with less coastline relative to their total area grew significantly more slowly than other countries, after controlling for other variables. Location in the tropics had a very strong, negative impact on growth. We find that countries located in the tropics grew 1.26 (t=-4.29) percentage points slower than countries located in more temperate zones. These results, together with the estimated coefficient on initial income, imply that the long-run level of income in countries in the tropics is only 53% (1/e (1.26/1.98)) of the long-run level for countries outside of the tropics. Only eight countries in the tropics (out of sixty tropical countries for which we have data) recorded growth rates in per capita GDP in excess of 3 percent between 1965-90. Five were in East Asia (Singapore, Hong Kong, Malaysia, Indonesia, and Thailand), and the other three were very small island economies (Cape Verde, Barbados, and the Seychelles), which because of their geographic separation may have been spared some of the worst effects of endemic tropical diseases.

The regression results forcefully point to the role of policy variables in determining the rate of economic growth. We find that openness to international trade is very strongly and positively associated with long-term growth, as much theory and previous evidence has indicated.

We find that an economy open to trade during the entire period 1965-90 grew 1.97 percentage points faster per year (t=6.20) compared with an economy that was completely closed throughout the period. This result is consistent with Sachs and Warner (1995), and indeed a long tradition of studies of growth and trade, which have shown that integration with the global economy is associated with faster growth. The East Asian countries were among the most open of all developing countries between 1965 and 1990, a fact that helps to account for their better growth performance. Following an initial stage of modest import substitution, most of the fast-growing Asian countries lowered import tariffs and export taxes, removed quantity restrictions on trade, and reduced the barriers to international flows of capital. Although import barriers remained high in some sectors in certain countries, each of the successful East Asian countries ensured high profitability for manufactured exporters. They gave exporters easy access to inputs at world market prices by following prudent exchange rate policies, and by developing new institutions, such as export processing zones and duty drawback systems, to support export-led growth.

The PRC provides a clear and dramatic example. The PRC transformed itself from one of the most closed economies in the world in the 1960s to a moderately open one in the mid-1990s. When it began its program of economic reforms in the late 1970s, total trade was the equivalent of an astonishingly low 1 percent of GNP. Even today, the economy is far from fully open. However, like the East and Southeast Asian countries, the PRC introduced facilities to help exporters circumvent these distortions and to compete on world markets. Other Asian countries have remained more closed to trade. South Asian countries generally isolated themselves from the global economy by imposing high tariff rates and a plethora of controls on imports in order to protect domestic industries. Only very recently have these countries, led by India, begun to open themselves to the global economy. Government saving has a positive and statistically significant impact on growth. The estimated coefficient implies that a 10 percentage point increase in the government saving-GDP ratio is associated with higher growth of 1.2 percentage points per year. Countries in which governments kept spending programs under control and realized larger surpluses on their current budget grew substantially faster than those with smaller surpluses or deficits. Such surpluses financed government investment programs, and had a net positive impact on total national saving, as we discuss in more depth later in the paper. Our third policy related variable is the quality of government institutions vis-a-vis market regulation. As expected, countries with more constructive interactions between the government and the market tended to record faster economic growth. According to our estimation results, each increment of 1.0 in this index (which is measured on a scale from a low of 0 to a high of 10) is associated with an increase in the growth rate of 0.25 percentage points. Thus, the difference between the Philippines' relatively poor score on institutional quality (2.97) and Singapore's high rating (8.56) accounts for a 1.4 percentage point difference in their average annual growth rates.

Finally, demographic variables are strongly associated with differences in growth rates. Both of the population change variables are of the expected sign and approximately the expected magnitude. As we discussed previously, in theory, the estimated coefficients for the growth rates of the working-age population and the total population should be 1 and -1, respectively. The empirical results do not permit rejection of these hypotheses, since the estimated coefficients (1.13 and -0.77) are not significantly different from 1 and -1, respectively. Bloom and Williamson (1997) explore these issues in much more depth. The important, and usually unrecognized point, is that part of East Asia's rapid growth in income is simply due to the rising share of the working age population among the total population between 1965-90. In South Asia, the share of the working age population increased much more slowly, partly accounting for that region's slower growth performance. These patterns are likely to change in the near future.

We find evidence for a non-linear relationship between life expectancy at birth and economic growth. At low levels of life expectancy, further increases are strongly associated with more rapid economic growth. In this range, higher life expectancy probably boosts growth by increasing the supply of working-age labour (as a result of lower morbidity); by raising labour productivity (as a healthier population is also a more productive one); by raising the rates of human capital accumulation (as people are more likely to invest in skills and education if they live longer); and by promoting more saving for retirement.

Higher life expectancy in East Asia in 1965 (63 years) gave the sub-region a higher growth potential than South Asia, where life expectancy was just 49 years. But the positive effect on growth diminishes as life expectancy increases, and once it passes 68 years, further increases actually have a *negative* effect on growth. The most plausible explanation for this shift is that after 68 years, further increases in life expectancy indicate that the retired age population is living longer and consuming out of their lifetime savings, with a negative impact on aggregate growth.

Columns 2 and 3 show the results after adding regional dummy variables for East and Southeast Asia (combined), South Asia, Latin America, and sub-Saharan Africa. In each case, these regional variables are insignificant, and there is little change in the estimated coefficients of the other explanatory variables. This result indicates that the basic set of explanatory variables account for most of the differences in growth rates between these regions and the full sample. Of course, these results represent the "average" relationships across countries, rather than a precise recipe applicable to all countries across time. Some individual countries undoubtedly differ in terms of the magnitude of the relationships, and in terms of the list of the most important variables affecting growth. Nevertheless, the basic specification captures the broad relationships influencing economic growth across countries very well. The adjusted R for our base specification is 0.87, indicating that this set of variables explain about 87 percent of the variation in growth rates across the sample, a strong result for this kind of analysis.

In particular, the basic specification tracks the actual growth performance of Asian countries very well. The "fitted" growth rates for each country (calculated by multiplying the estimated coefficients by the actual value for each variable for each country, and adding these terms together) correspond closely with the actual growth rates in most cases. For example, the fitted growth rate for India for 1965-90 is 2.16 percent, compared to the actual rate of 2.03 percent. China's fitted growth rate is 5.30 percent, compared to the actual rate of 5.09 percent.

The largest Asian outlier is Malaysia, for which the fitted growth rate (3.53 percent) fell below the actual rate (4.49 percent) by about one percentage point. Indonesia was also a relatively large outlier. These differences are most likely due to Malaysia's and Indonesia's ability to deftly manage the challenges that accompany natural resource abundance. As we discussed earlier, natural resource abundance has been associated with relatively slow economic growth during the last several decades. Malaysia and Indonesia managed to avoid the most deleterious effects of the Dutch disease and disruptive terms of trade shocks by diversifying their economies (exploiting a wide range of natural resources as well as encouraging manufactured exports) and reacting quickly to changing international circumstances.

On a regional basis, the basic regression accounts for 6.6 percent growth for the "Four Tigers," very close to the actual rate of 6.7 percent during the period. Similarly, the fitted growth rates are close to the actuals for Southeast Asia (3.4 percent fitted versus 3.8 actual), South Asia (2.1 percent fitted versus 1.7 actual), and almost exactly the same for sub-Saharan Africa (0.7 percent fitted versus 0.6 actual) and Latin America (0.8 percent fitted versus 0.8 actual). Variations in Sample Size and Specification To test the robustness of these results, we re-estimated the equation with two subsets of countries. First, one-fourth of the countries in the sample were randomly dropped (by eliminating every fourth country in alphabetical order). The estimation results were broadly similar to those from the full sample. We then used these new results to estimate fitted values for the one-fourth of the countries that we omitted. The fitted values matched the actual values with a correlation of 92 percent, a very satisfactory result. Second, we dropped the Asian countries from the sample to check the extent to which the Asian countries may have been influencing the overall results. Once again, the results were broadly similar to our base results. In this case, the fitted values for the omitted Asian countries matched the actual values with a correlation of 93 percent.

The results from several alternative specifications. We tried many alternative measures of education and human capital accumulation, with little success. For example, column 1 shows the results using primary school enrolment rates rather than average years of education, with slightly weaker results than with our base specification. Column 2 uses adult literacy rates as the education indicator. The results are similar and perhaps a bit stronger than in the base specification, but data on literacy rates in 1965 are available for only 60 countries. Columns 3 and 4 show the results after substituting government consumption and total government expenditures, respectively, for the government saving rate.

The results are similar to, but weaker than, our basic results. The results using the national saving rate as a regressor instead of the government saving rate. Conceptually, this specification is preferable to our base specification, since national savings is more consistent with underlying neoclassical theory as a determinant of economic growth. However, economic growth also affects savings rates, and this simultaneous relationship makes interpretation of the results problematic. Another problem bedeviling such an approach is that national saving rates, and in particular private saving rates, tend to be measured with substantial error, as they are calculated as a residual from the national accounts.

Similar problems affect the results using the investment rate. One way to treat the simultaneity issue is to employ a two-stage estimation procedure using instruments for the national saving variable. Column 3 shows the results when national savings is instrumented by the 1965-90 average of the young-age and old-age dependency ratios, the government saving rate, and government social security expenditures as a share of GDP. Column 4 adds three additional instruments: bank credit outstanding to the public sector, the ratio of broad money to GDP, and the inflation rate. This more complete list is consistent with our base specification for the determination of national saving rates, discussed in Section IV. The results from the instrumental variables approach are very similar to our basic growth results.

They suggest that a 10 percentage point increase in the national saving rate is associated with a 0.6 percentage point increase in the per capita growth rate. The estimated coefficient for the other variables remain close to their original values, with two exceptions. First, the estimated coefficient on the natural resource variable is a much larger negative. Second, life expectancy no longer displays a quadratic shape, and is better estimated by a simple logarithmic function. The negative impact on growth from life expectancy after the latter reaches 68 years disappears in this specification, reinforcing the idea that this trend indeed arises through the impact of longer life expectancy on private saving rates. Overall, the results with the instrumental variables approach are consistent with, albeit somewhat weaker than in our base specification.

In addition, we considered several other possible explanatory variables for economic growth. We explored the impact of inflation, the initial distribution of income, political stability, and political rights. Each of these variables turned out to have a statistically insignificant impact on growth in our sample once all the other explanatory variables are included. The same was true of levels of foreign debt, financial depth, prevalence of malaria, components of government spending, and so on (results not shown). Note that these results do not necessarily mean that these variables are unimportant, especially in some countries.

In some cases, it indicates that some of the effects of these variables on growth are captured by the variables already included in the regressions. For instance, inflation rates are closely related to openness and government saving, and the effects of political instability are at least partially captured by the index of institutional quality and the government saving rate.

The results when income levels and growth rates are converted by official exchange rates and expressed in constant U.S. dollars (from the World Bank data base), rather than in international (PPP) dollars. Although there are some modest changes to the estimated coefficients, the main results hold firmly — there is strong evidence for conditional convergence, and the policy variables remain strongly and positively associated with economic growth. The overall fit is much weaker with these data, which is not surprising given that they are conceptually inferior to the PPP-adjusted data for international comparisons of per capita income.

Economic Growth of the Asian Countries in Comparative Perspective

These results also allow us to undertake a simple "growth accounting" exercise that explores the relative contribution of each of the explanatory variables in the basic regression to differences in growth rates across regions. The results. For ease of presentation, and because of the strong interest in explaining the very rapid growth of most of the countries of East and Southeast Asia, we use the ten countries in this geographic region6 as the benchmark, and account for the differences in growth rates between this group of countries and the other regions. Average per capita growth for the four South Asian countries was 2.9 percentage points lower than the average for East/Southeast Asia, and the basic regression can account for a difference of 2.5 percentage points. South Asia started with a lower per capita income in 1965, which, all else being equal, should have led to a growth rate 0.5 percentage points *higher* than in East Asia. However, the positive effect on growth from low initial income was partially offset by the negative effect from low secondary school attainment. Similarly, natural resources and geography had little net effect on South Asia's performance. South Asian countries have fewer natural resources and are located in more temperate climates, on average, than the nine East/Southeast Asian countries, giving them additional potential for faster growth. The net effects of initial income, education, geography and natural resources are relatively small, and suggest the potential for *faster* growth in South Asia by 0.5 percentage points relative to East/Southeast Asia.

By contrast, policy choices had a relatively large effect on differences in growth rates. *The* combined effect of differences in government saving, openness, and the quality of institutions reduced South Asia's growth rate by 2.1 percentage points relative to its East/Southeast Asian *neighbours*. Openness was by far the most important variable: South Asia's inward-oriented trade strategy accounted for slower growth of 1.2 percentage points. Finally, South Asia received less of a boost from demographic change than did East/Southeast Asia. South Asia had lower life expectancy, slower growth in its working age population, and faster overall population growth. These three factors accounted for 0.9 percentage points slower growth in South Asia relative to East/Southeast Asia.

The strong relationship between policies and economic growth is also visible in the comparison between East/Southeast Asia and sub-Saharan Africa (SSA). Between these regions, 1.7 percentage points of the predicted difference in growth rates is due to policy variables, with differences in openness again explaining the bulk of the difference. The demographic variables also explain much of the difference in growth rates. SSA's lower life expectancy and more rapid population growth (relative to growth of the working-age population) accounted for slower growth of 1.9 percentage points. In addition, all of the geography and natural resource variables worked against countries in SSA. There are more landlocked countries in SSA than any other region in the world, and countries in the region, on average, have more natural resources, are more tropical, and have less coastline relative to their area than the countries of East/Southeast Asia. These four variables combined accounted for 1.0 slower growth in SSA relative to East/Southeast Asia.

With respect to Latin America, initial conditions play a more prominent role, mainly because Latin America started with higher income per capita, which reduced its relative growth potential. However, the largest difference between Latin America and East/Southeast Asia lies with the policy variables, which together account for 1.8 percentage points slower annual growth in per capita incomes.

The key lesson from the growth accounting exercise is that initial and resource conditions account for only moderate differences in growth rates. The major role is played by policy variables: high rates of government saving, trade openness, and maintenance of good institutions have been the most important factors behind East Asia's rapid growth during the last three decades.

The cross-country growth regressions provide a useful starting point for exploring the past and future of Asian developing economies by furnishing a framework which identifies many of the most critical factors that distinguish growth performances across regions and countries.

However, this framework, by itself, obviously does not fully explain the process of economic growth. It does not wholly capture the relationships between policy choices, institutional settings, and economic outcomes, nor does it shed light on the important role of economic leadership and skilful policymaking. To complement this simple framework, we must further explore the ways in which the fast growing Asian economies were either similar to or different from other developing economies, and how these factors might have affected Asia's economic performance.

More Evidence on How East and Southeast Asia were Different

Another way to gauge Asia's distinctiveness in an international perspective is to analyse how much Asia's sub-regions differ from other countries on a broad range of economic indicators, such as trade ratios, industrial shares, and government spending. One approach would be to simply compare average values of these variables in Asia with averages for other regions of the world. However, simple averages can be misleading, because differences across regions might themselves be due to other factors, such as levels of income or geography. For example, Korea and Taipei,China's relatively high trade ratios may simply be due to the fact that they have smaller populations and higher incomes than most developing countries.

Controlled Averages Across Countries

A more informative approach would be to examine differences across regions after controlling for structural and geographic variables. We examine controlled averages by estimating the following relationship for a group of 77 countries from all over the world: X is the variable under consideration in country i, y is per capita income, and N is population. i LD is land density (area of land per person), a measure of resource abundance; SD is the shipping distance to a major industrial port,7 DR1 is the young-age dependency ratio, and DR2 is the oldage dependency ratio.

The main focus of our attention is *A*, which is a dummy variable for sub-groups of Asian countries. The sign and significance of the estimated coefficient for this variable will tell us to what extent Asian countries differed from other countries in the world for each of the dependent variables under consideration, after controlling for the other right-hand-side variables. The relationship is estimated three times, once each with three separate Asian sub-regional dummies for the Four

Tigers, Southeast Asia, and South Asia. The explore how these differences may have changed over time, we estimated these relationships in 1970 (actually, using average values for each variable for 1969 through 1971) and again for 1990 (using averages for 1989-91). In each cell of the table, a "+" sign indicates that the coefficient on the Asian sub-regional variable was positive and significant, a negative sign indicates that the coefficient was negative and significant, and a blank indicates the coefficient was insignificant. The number of asterisks indicates the level of significance.

The results show that the Four Tigers differed from other countries in several important respects. First, exports and imports accounted for a significantly larger share of GDP in 1970 than other countries of the same size, income level, resource abundance, and demographic structure. Manufactured exports, in particular, were substantially larger in these four economies than elsewhere in the world. By contrast, primary product exports were significantly smaller.

The same basic pattern held in 1990, except that primary product exports were no longer lower in East Asia (predominately because of Singapore's large petroleum product exports). The second area in which the Four Tigers stand out is savings and investment. In 1970, savings rates in these economies were not significantly different from the rest of the world, and investment rates only marginally so. By 1990, however, both savings and investment rates were well above the average for other countries. Third, and related, the Four Tigers had slightly larger central government budget balances, and slightly lower rates of spending on social security, compared to other countries at similar income levels. Fourth, these economies recorded an unusually high level of average years of secondary schooling. As we saw earlier in examining the data for the cross country growth regressions, the Four Tigers' average of 1.5 years of secondary schooling was the highest of the developing country regions in our sample. Finally, theses countries were more urbanized than other developing countries, reflecting the presence of the city-states of Hong Kong and Singapore in the group. However, the difference was no longer statistically significant in 1990. Note that the Four Tigers did *not* stand out from the other countries in the structure of its production: the share in GDP of agriculture, industry, total manufacturing, and services was not significantly different in these economies. *An important result, then, is that while the Four Tigers'* share of manufacturing in GDP was not significantly different from other countries, its share of *manufactured exports was highly significantly larger than other countries.* What set the Four Tigers apart was not manufacturing per se, but manufactured exports. Southeast Asia differed from other countries in only a few dimensions in 1970 (higher exports and years of schooling, lower social security expenditures, and higher literacy rates and years of schooling). By 1990, however, they were following a pattern strikingly similar to the Four Tigers. Southeast Asia in 1990 recorded higher shares of imports, total exports and manufactured exports (but not manufacturing production), they saved and invested more than other countries, and they recorded a slightly larger central government budget balance. They also recorded slightly lower levels of urbanization. South Asia, by contrast, followed a very different pattern. They did not record unusually high or low trade shares or investment and savings ratios. By 1990, their savings and investment rates were significantly *lower* than for other countries of the same size and income. The structure of South Asia's production was also different. They recorded unusually high levels of agriculture, and lower shares of industry and manufacturing. The one dimension in which they were similar to the East and Southeast Asian countries was schooling: they recorded significantly higher levels of average secondary schooling in both 1970 and 1990. However, their literacy rates were marginally below average in 1990.

Different Paths to Development Within East Asia We should point out that in searching for these common traits across successful economies, we are not suggesting that there has been only one path to sustained development. The East and Southeast Asian countries differ widely in their resource endowments, human capital accumulation, population densities and structures, and political systems. They have faced different opportunities and challenges during the last thirty years, and chosen different economic strategies to achieve their goals. Among the eight rapidly growing economies, at least four different paths to development are apparent.

Hong Kong and Singapore are small, urban, very open economies that have relied heavily on commerce and a free port service as the foundation for growth. They have few natural resources, but have well-educated work forces. Their basic strategy was to rely on free and open markets, backed by a competent civil service and a strong legal system. Both governments consistently welcomed and encouraged foreign direct investment. Of course, there are important differences between the two— Singapore features many more state owned enterprises (generally operating profitably in competitive markets), and the government has been more active in encouraging the development of new technologies and promoting manufactured exports.

Korea and Taipei, China are also relatively small economies with few natural resources and a well educated work force. Agricultural growth, spurred in part by land reform and green revolution technologies, contributed significantly to aggregate growth in the early stages of the takeoff period. Both countries initially followed a strategy of import substitution for consumer goods. They kept the level of protection low and the duration of protection relatively brief, and did not extend protection to capital goods sectors. Both countries switched course to aggressively promote export production, with governments at times intervening forcefully in the market with subsidies, special lines of credit, and controls on international capital flows. Both countries discouraged foreign direct investment. Again, there are important differences in their strategies — Taipei, China encouraged small and medium enterprise development, while Korea relied on a small number of large conglomerates to meet its export goals. Indonesia, Malaysia, and Thailand are larger countries with abundant natural resources and a smaller human capital base. As with Korea and Taipei, China, agriculture has played a critical role in reducing poverty and contributing to aggregate economic growth. These countries adopted much more protectionist industrial policies than the Four Tigers, with more extensive and longer lasting import substitution policies. Many sectors have remained under the control of state enterprises or heavily protected from competition for long periods of time, even when they have performed poorly. Nevertheless, each of these countries established mechanisms through which exporters could avoid the high costs associated with protection and become competitive on international markets. Once again, there are important differences: Malaysia welcomed foreign direct investment more than the other two countries, and concentrated more on exports of consumer electronics rather than textiles and apparel. China's path to development has differed dramatically from other developing countries.

The period of total state control and near autarky prior to 1978 was followed by a dramatic decollectivization of agriculture and gradual privatization and opening of the economy. The majority of the population continues to live in rural areas and depends on agricultural production. The government maintains a heavy hand in the economy through extensive state ownership of enterprises and widespread price and quantity controls. Nevertheless, the government has actively encouraged the development of privately owned export oriented firms by establishing facilities to allow exporters to avoid the most serious price distortions in the economy. Foreign direct investment, once completely banned, is now encouraged along the coastal areas.

These differences suggest that the road to sustained growth and development has differed in important ways across the region, with each country facing different obstacles, complications, and opportunities. Yet, despite these differences, there are several striking similarities in each country's economic strategy. This analysis of controlled averages in this section, combined with the earlier cross country growth regressions point to four key areas that are associated with rapid growth across all countries, and in which East and Southeast Asia differed from other countries:

- C openness and manufactured exports;
- C higher savings and investment;
- C strong macroeconomic management, especially government fiscal policy; and
- C education.

In our view, these common elements are the key to understanding rapid growth in East and Southeast Asia, and slower growth elsewhere in the region. We proceed by turning our attention to the first three areas. Education is treated more fully in the companion papers by Don Snodgrass et. al., and Keith Lewin.

Exports of Manufactures

There is strong evidence indicating that the countries that have been most successful in expanding manufactured exports are, with very few exceptions, the same countries that have achieved the highest rates of economic growth during the past thirty years. This relationship is especially strong for non-resource-based manufactured exports (that is, excluding manufactured exports derived from natural resources, such as diamonds, plywood, and mineral manufactures). For example, consider the group of 78 developing countries (with GNP per capita of less than $15,000, or PPP-adjusted income of less than 16,000 in 1994 international prices) with 1994 population greater than 1 million. The division of these countries into fast and slow growers in both GDP per capita and weighted growth of non-resource based exports. The results are revealing. Only 12 countries recorded average annual growth in nonresource based manufactured exports equivalent to 1 percent or more of GDP during the period 1970-90.9 Almost all of these countries were also in the group of fast growers: eleven of the twelve recorded growth in GDP per capita of 3 percent or greater during the period. The relationship between rapid non-resource based manufactured export growth and GDP growth is highly statistically significant: a chi-squared test easily rejects (at the 1 percent level) the null hypothesis that the distribution of the number of countries in each cell.

There were only two countries — Indonesia and Jordan — that were able to record rapid GDP per capita growth without also achieving rapid growth in non-resource based manufactured exports. Indonesia attained high rates of economic growth without a large manufacturing base because of its unusually effective management of its natural resource base. Moreover, in the mid-1980s, Indonesia began to shift towards manufactured exports, and its growth rate accelerated. Jordan's growth rate has slowed considerably in recent years, so with more complete data it would shift to the bottom right box. Israel is the only country that achieved rapid manufacturing export growth without also recording 3 percent GDP per capita growth, and its growth rate was a very respectable 2.2 percent per annum. Israel's GDP growth also rose in the 1990s.

Export Growth, Global Integration, and Technological Development

One of the lessons of recent history-highlighted by the analysis above-is that even very poor countries without an abundance of skilled labour can achieve international competitiveness in manufactures. This was widely doubted fifty years ago. Prebisch (1950, 1959), Singer (1950) and others argued that reliance on *primary* product exports would not lead to rapid economic development and industrialization. They may have been correct in the broad sense, as indicated by the negative relationship between primary product exports and economic growth. It seems, at a minimum, that primary export led development creates difficult challenges for economic policy makers. Prebisch and Singer erred, however, in their conclusion that the only alternative for industrialization was import substitution through protection of domestic firms and withdrawal from the global marketplace. Their analyses seems to have not seriously considered the possibility of exports of manufactures, perhaps because the production of manufactures was so dominated by industrialized countries at that time. They were not alone: few economists at that time dreamed that poor developing countries could achieve rapid export growth in manufactures.

What is it about manufactured exports that supports overall economic growth? First, manufacturing export-led growth allows countries to specialize their production to a far greater degree than under import substitution. Developing country exporters can join in global production and distribution systems and use their comparative advantage in labour-intensive operations. For example, Malaysia was able to build up an electronics sector in the early 1970s almost from scratch, because U.S. manufacturers moved the labour-intensive parts of their production process there. Even though Malaysia could not design or produce computer chips, it was able to assemble and test them, both labour-intensive operations. When Intel invested in Malaysia in 1972, the country was quickly brought into a world-class production system that drew on its comparative advantage.

Second, a strategy of manufactured exports fosters technological progress. Rapid growth in manufacturing exports requires close links with multinational firms that provide intermediate inputs, technology, capital goods, and export markets. These linkages provide a powerful means through which firms can "learn by doing." There is no realistic chance of this occurring if a country is cut off from world markets through severe restrictions on trade and capital flows. No country can generate all the sophisticated capital goods and technology needed for high-quality investment projects by itself.

From an early stage, East and Southeast Asian firms bought most of their machinery and equipment abroad. For example, in 1970, capital goods imports accounted for about 50 percent of total investment in

East and South East Asia, compared to 17 percent in South Asia, and about 35 percent in Latin America and sub-Saharan Africa. These imports of capital goods were an important conduit for bringing new technologies into the region. *Although several East Asian* countries went through a moderate phase of import substitution for consumer goods, they did not *attempt to provide protection for domestic producers of capital goods.* Even today in Korea-which produces more capital-intensive exports than any other Asian country-these exports are chemicals, ships, and automobiles, not machinery. For example, between 1991 and 1994, imported capital goods accounted for 73 percent of all equipment investment in Korea (IMF, 1994). This indicates the country's continued heavily reliance on imported foreign technology.

Third, manufactured exports provide the foreign exchange necessary to pay for imported raw materials and capital goods. One of the great ironies of import substitution is that even though the strategy is designed to save on imports, the vast majority of countries that followed this strategy eventually ran into balance of payments problems because they could not generate the foreign exchange earnings necessary to pay for the raw materials and capital goods they so desperately needed. By contrast, exporters of manufacturers are better able to pay for imported capital goods, and are therefore in a better position to tap into world-class technologies.

Manufacturing export growth confers a range of other benefits on an economy. In particular, success in exporting has important spillover and demonstration effects on other sectors of the economy. Exporters compete with other firms for resources and in particular labour. Labour practices in internationally competitive export firms often serve as a model for others to follow. Exports also allow a country to generate high corporate profits which contributed to rising national saving rates; and to absorb a growing labour force in labour-intensive products, thereby ameliorating the distribution of income. Pack (1989) and others have pointed out that export markets allow labour and capital to move rapidly from low-to high-productivity sectors without encountering diminishing returns. Exporters are also more likely to demand high standards of service from their suppliers and to exert pressure for improved infrastructure provision, maintenance, and management. Positive "externalities" such as these have helped to modernize the economies of East Asia and sustain their growth. The critical element in manufactured exports, then, is the linkages between domestic firms, their foreign affiliates, and global markets. In Asia, these linkages took different forms. Foreign direct investment (FDI) was the primary connection for Hong Kong and Singapore.

However, FDI initially played a limited role in Korea and Taipei, China. Both countries actively discouraged and even prohibited some types of foreign investments until the 1980s. They chose instead to import technology under licensing agreements and as part of original equipment manufacturing (OEM) arrangements. These allowed Asian exporters to produce goods under the brand names of U.S. and Japanese firms. Southeast Asian countries, especially Indonesia and Thailand, also limited foreign investment in manufacturing (although they were more welcoming in minerals) until the 1980s or even the 1990s. South Asia, too, severely limited foreign investment until recent years. Notably, where foreign investment has taken place, it has been heavily exportoriented. Despite the modest flows of foreign direct investment, at least in earlier years, East Asian firms developed strong links with multinational firms. For example, most finished consumer goods exports were produced to precise specifications from overseas buyers' orders. In most cases, the buyers were either importer-wholesalers, or overseas manufacturers subcontracting to local firms. The first buyers to operate in the developing countries of East and Southeast Asia were from big Japanese trading houses, such as Mitsubishi and Mitsui. They in turn often sold in North American markets. Major U.S. trading firms followed, led by Sears, Roebuck, J.C. Penny, and others.

In order to establish relationships with reliable, stable suppliers, these overseas buyers often provided instruction and advice to exporting firms on virtually all aspects of business. The successful Asian firms learned quickly, and developed the flexibility and acumen to manufacture a variety of constantly-changing designs. Some firms gained specialized knowledge of particular markets, others became skilled at quickly producing "knock-off" copies of samples, and still others specialized in producing higher-quality niche products. Successful firms also often took the initiative to travel to major developed country markets and visit actual and potential buyers, thus enriching their knowledge of business practices in industrialized countries. In each of these ways, exporting firms were better positioned than domestic-oriented firms to enhance their skills, adapt new technologies, and expand their production.

Determinants of non-resource-based manufactured export growth Why have some countries been more successful than others at generating manufactured export growth? What factors determine a country's ability to compete in manufactured exports? Our earlier discussion suggest that a key condition must be openness to the world economy. Low tariff rates, the absence of trade quotas, and ease of international financial transactions are all likely to support competitiveness of exporters in international markets. Open economies will have greater access to new technologies, and are less likely to misallocate labour and capital to inefficient industries. *The key form of opening, most likely, is ready access to capital goods and intermediate inputs from world markets at world prices (i.e. without trade barriers).* Taxes on capital inputs and tariffs or quotas on intermediate inputs can impose a very high negative effective rate of protection on would-be exporters. This is especially true since in various labour intensive processes (such as electronics assembly), the intermediate input content of final output can easily rise above 80 percent. Tariffs on intermediate inputs, therefore, can easily wipe out the profitability of labour-intensive assembly operations in a low wage country, since wage costs are less than 20 percent of total output. We discuss this particular issue in greater detail later in this section.

In addition, we would expect that *resource-poor countries* would be more likely to be successful manufactured exporters. As discussed earlier in the context of income growth, resource poor countries have fewer foreign-exchange earning options than do resource rich countries, and therefore may be more likely to focus on manufactured exports as a foundation for sustained development. Moreover, resource rich countries may have a higher reservation wage, making it more difficult for them to compete on world markets in labour intensive products. A third factor is likely to be *geographical location* relative to major world markets.

Countries that are located far from major commercial centres — for example, in southern Africa or South Asia — will have to pay more in transport costs for the imported inputs required for most manufactured products. In competitive world markets, higher shipping costs would have to be offset by even lower wages to allow a firm to compete. When profit margins are relatively small-such as in many labour intensive activities — a small difference in shipping cost can spell the difference between success and failure. Finally, *the size of the domestic market* may also influence non-resource based manufactured exports. In larger countries, a greater share of manufactured products is likely to be sold on the domestic market, with a corresponding smaller share sold as exports.

To measure the relationship between these variables and non-resource based manufactured export growth, we estimated the following relationship: x is the annual growth rate of non-resource based manufactured exports in country *i* between i 1965-90, where growth is measured as a share of the preceding year's GDP. I is a vector of i initial conditions, including the size of the domestic market (real gross domestic product) in 1970. We also explore the possible influence of education (mean years of secondary schooling) and life expectancy at birth, both measured in 1970. N is a vector of natural resource and geographic conditions, including the logarithm of land per person, a measure of resource abundance. Countries with more land per person are likely to have greater abundance of natural resources, and thus slower growth in manufactured exports. We use this measure of natural resource abundance rather than primary exports as a share of GDP to avoid possible spurious correlation between the latter and non-resource based manufactured export growth. We also include the log of shipping cost, estimated by the sea distance from each country to the closest of either Tokyo, Rotterdam, or New York. An extra 1,500 miles of sea distance is added for land-locked countries. P represents government policy variables, including openness and the quality of government institutions. Countries with weaker institutions (e.g., more corruption, weaker legal standards) would be expected to recorded slower growth in manufactured exports. We also examine two additional policy variables — investment and government consumption — that may influence manufactured exports.

Estimation Results

The results of estimating the export equation for a sample of 65 countries. Note that we excluded Taiwan from the sample because of incomplete trade data. In addition, we eliminated Singapore and Hong Kong from the sample because their recorded growth rates for non-resource based manufactured exports were large outliers from the remainder of the sample, and we did not want these two economies to unduly affect the overall regression results. (Our conclusions, however, apply with great force to these two economies, so that they are not outliers in terms of key results). The basic set of results are in column 1, in which all of the estimated coefficients are of the expected sign, and significant at the 5 percent level or better.

Openness is strongly associated with more rapid growth of non-resource based manufactured exports. Open economies, on average, recorded a manufactured export growth rate 0.70 percentage points higher than closed economies. To give some idea of the magnitude of this result, recall that only 12 countries recorded weighted non-resource based manufactured export growth greater than 1 percent (and only five recorded growth rates greater than 3 percent) between 1970-90. The mean value was 0.87. The estimated coefficient on openness is highly significant and robust across specifications.

Resource-abundant economies were less successful in expanding manufactured exports, as indicated by the negative coefficient on land per person. A one standard deviation increase in the log of the amount of land available per person (st. dev. = 1.29) is associated with a decline in the non-resource based manufactured export growth rate of 0.25 percentage points per year. Similarly, more distant countries have a natural barrier to overcome that has made success in manufactured exports harder to achieve. The estimated coefficient on sea distance (-0.31) implies that a one standard deviation increase in the log of the distance (st. dev. = 1.09, or about 3,000 miles) decreases the manufactured export growth rate by 0.34 percentage points per year. Countries with higher quality government institutions have recorded faster growth in manufactured exports. This results indicates that secure contractual and property rights, as well as lower levels of corruption, help facilitate manufactured export growth. For every one unit increase in the index of government institutions (on a scale of 1-10), non-resource based manufactured exports expand 0.1 percentage point. Finally, larger countries have had less success in expanding non-resource based manufactured exports. The negative coefficient on total GDP suggests that larger countries are more likely to divert manufactured products to the home market, reducing exports. Equation 2 includes government consumption (as a share of GDP) and life expectancy at birth as additional explanatory variables. Although the estimated coefficients are of the expected sign, both are insignificant. Equation 3 includes mean years of secondary schooling and investment as a share of GDP. Again, both variables are insignificant. The last column shows the results including regional dummy variables (The Four Tigers are not included as a separate group because Taiwan, Hong Kong, and Singapore are not included in the sample). Each of the regional dummies is insignificant, indicating that the other explanatory variables fully explain the variation in growth rates across these regions. Including the regional dummies weakens the significance of the land and institution variables, reflecting the high correlation between these variables and the regions.

The Composition of Asia's Exports

The countries of East and Southeast Asia dominate the group of countries that have achieved rapid growth in non-resource-based exports and GDP per capita. As exports have grown in these countries, the composition of the products produced has changed markedly. These changes have broadly followed changes in comparative advantage. In general, exports in most countries were initially dominated by primary products, and later shifted to labour intensive manufactured products such as apparel. Some countries have further shifted their export base to skill and technology-intensive products, especially electronics. Primary products (and primary-based manufactures) accounted for over 90 percent of exports in nine of the fifteen Asian developing countries for which disaggregated trade data are available for 1970. These products varied across countries. Indonesia and Malaysia each exported rubber, palm oil, and petroleum; Myanmar, the Philippines, and the Solomon Islands exported wood lumber; and Thailand and Myanmar both exported rice. Coffee and rubber dominated Sri Lanka's exports, whereas the Philippines exported sugar and palm oil. Labour-intensive goods—especially textiles and clothing — accounted for 25 percent or more of exports in only five countries (Bangladesh, India, Pakistan, Hong Kong, and Korea). Hong Kong's exports were dominated by labour-intensive manufactures, which accounted for over sixty percent of all exports. Capital and technology-intensive products (including electronics, machinery, scale-intensive and other human capital-intensive exports) were much less common in most countries. Only in Singapore, Hong

Kong, India and Korea did exports of these products account for more than 10 percent of exports, and only in Hong Kong did the share reach 20 percent. Even these small shares are seriously overstated, as some of these products — especially electronics — are actually little more than labour-intensive assembly in which the final output is technology-intensive. By the 1990s, the picture had changed dramatically. Primary products accounted for more than 70 percent of exports in only three of the sixteen Asian countries for which data are available— Myanmar, Papua New Guinea, and Western Samoa. Several countries had shifted their export base towards labour intensive products, including Bangladesh, Indonesia, Fiji, Sri Lanka, and Pakistan, although the size of the structural change was smallest for the relatively closed economies of South Asia. In the most advanced Asian countries, exports evolved towards capital and technology-intensive products, including more sophisticated electronics in all of the higher income Asian countries. In Singapore and Malaysia, for example, capital and technology-intensive products accounted for more than 50 percent of exports (though labour intensive assembly operations remained important in these "high-tech" sectors). The PRC, India, and the Philippines are moving in that direction, with capital-and technology-intensive products accounting for 20-25 percent of exports by the 1990s. These newer exports continue to be based on comparative advantage, although that advantage is quickly shifting from labour-intensive to skill-intensive goods in many countries.

Textiles and Electronics

Two manufactured product sectors have dominated Asia's exports in recent decades: textiles and electronics. South Asia, of course, has been exporting textiles to the world for centuries. In East Asia, as with so many other manufactured products, textile exports have their origins in Japan. In the 19th century, Japan exported raw and spun silk, and then moved into cotton textiles. In the early years of the 20th century, Japanese entrepreneurs helped to organize and expand the textile industry in Shanghai, which then thrived for several decades. Following the 1949 Chinese revolution, much of Shanghai's textile industry moved to Taipei, China and Hong Kong. In the 1960s, direct foreign investment from Japan into Taipei, China's textile industry reinforced this trend. Since the 1970s, the textile industry, especially its ready-made garments component, progressively moved to East Asia, to Southeast Asia, and in the more recent years, to PRC and Viet Nam. These movements were driven by the search for cheaper labour by the textile producers and exporters in the first place, but received a substantial boost as a devise to overcome quota restrictions imposed under the Multi-Fiber Arrangement (MFA).

More recently, a common export across the fastest-growing Asian countries has been electronics products. Some countries, like Malaysia, started their export drive almost exclusively in electronics. Electrical machinery alone accounted for over 20 percent of total exports in Malaysia, Singapore and Korea between 1990-94, and about 15 percent in Hong Kong, Thailand, and the Philippines. China and Indonesia also boasted rapidly growing electronics exports. In the Philippines, electronics exports expanded from near zero in the late 1980s to 40 percent of all exports in 1995. World electronics production has now shifted to Asia. In each of twelve major categories of world electronics exports (at the SITC 3-digit level), at least seven out of the top ten exporting countries in the world in the early 1990s were from East and Southeast Asia (UNCTAD, 1995).

Why are electronics exports so heavily concentrated in Asia? The seeds of Asia's electronics industry germinated in the 1960s when U.S. firms began searching for offshore production locations. Although Latin America and the Caribbean basin were obvious choices, firms were repelled by political instability, inward orientation, and record of expropriation of foreign capital in many of the countries in the region. The Cuban revolution and the resulting nationalization of many private companies was, at that point, very recent history. Many Latin American countries were openly hostile to foreign investment, as clearly demonstrated during Vice President Nixon's ill-fated trip to South America in the late 1950s. Many Asian economies were equally uninviting, such as China, Vietnam, and, until the late 1960s, Indonesia. However, other Asian countries were much more open to foreign investment and new technology. Hong Kong, especially, proved to be an attractive location for U.S. firms. The Hong Kong economy was as open as any in the world, with a surfeit of low-wage workers available, many of whom has some English-speaking capabilities. Hong Kong sat astride the great sea lane between Japan and the Middle East and Europe. Perhaps most importantly, Hong Kong's status as a British territory provided some assurance of political stability and of a relatively well-functioning legal system. No other developing country could compete with this environment, so in the early 1960s the first U.S. electronics firms established themselves in Hong Kong. Once these firms became successful, it became easier for others to follow, first from the U.S. and later from Japan and Europe. It is important to recognize that in this initial success, Hong Kong did not attempt to "pick winners" — rather, it is much more accurate to say that the winners picked Hong Kong! Hong Kong established an attractive, free-trade and low-tax environment, and the electronics firms decided to locate there.

This initial success also encouraged other Asian countries to emulate Hong Kong's approach. Singapore, Taiwan, Korea, and Malaysia all made concerted efforts to establish more open trading regimes — and most critically, *free trade for exporters* — with an eye towards attracting electronics firms. They were very successful. Summary data on the location of offshore operations of major electronic component manufacturing firms in 1971 and 1974. Two features stand out. The first is the enormous concentration of these firms in Asia. 17 out of the 21 electronics offshore operations in 1971 were located in East and Southeast Asia; in 1974, 51 of 53 firms worldwide were located there. Almost all of the U.S., European, and Japanese electronics firms that invested offshore in the early 1970s located in Asia. The second is the huge expansion in the number of firms and the number of people employed by these firms in just the three years between 1971 and 1974. The number of firms in Asia tripled from 17 to 51, and the number of employees nearly quadrupled. At the same time, the four firms that were located in Mexico in 1971 had ceased operations there by 1974. These data, which are drawn from an early UNCTAD study of electronics firms, show the costs of producing radios receivers for the European market in 1974. Costs are shown for firms producing in Europe, Asia, and Africa, with the source of their materials either in Europe or Asia. Asian firms could produce 1,000 receivers for $12,849, below the cost of European producers and far below the costs of African producers. Asia's advantage over Europe was its access to cheaper material (from Japan) and its lower wages. As a result, Asian firms could produce less expensively than European firms, even after paying 14% duty to sell the product in Europe. In comparing Asian firms with the least expensive African firms, two key differences stand out. First, handling/freight/

insurance charges for imported inputs were far cheaper for Asian firms, presumably because they were located so close to Japan, the source of materials. Second, African countries charged their firms an average of 20% duties on the imported inputs, while Asian firms paid zero duties. These costs more than offset Africa's advantage of lower wages. Because of just these two differences, African firms could not compete in the European market. We have already discussed the importance of the Asian countries' proximity to Japan in reducing their shipping and production costs. We now turn our attention to the second element — low duties and free trade for exporters.

Manufactured Exports, Openness, and Industrial Policies

The recent experience of manufactured exports and economic growth in developing countries suggests that two elements are crucial for success: free trade (at least for exporters), and government institutions that help markets to work effectively. Many commentators have argued that one element or the other is the more important. However, the evidence from the most successful economies suggests that a combination of the two is required to achieve success. The growth of manufactured exports in East and Southeast Asia over the past three decades cannot be reasonably portrayed as the product of generalized free and open markets throughout the region. Only Hong Kong, with perhaps the most open market in the world, can truly be classified as a laissez-faire economy. Singapore is in many respects also a very open economy, but it still has significant state involvement and ownership. Without question, other Asian countries often strayed far from the neoclassical ideal of competitive free markets and limited government interventions. By some measures, price distortions in Taiwan and Korea (as well as Japan) were larger than the average for all developing countries, and larger than for Mexico, Brazil, and Pakistan (World Bank, 1993). Wade (1990) and others have shown that import tariffs and quotas were neither very low nor uniform in Korea and Taiwan. Some Asian countries intervened heavily, often brutally, in controlling labour markets. Most governments directed subsidized credit towards chosen industries. And all of the Asian countries (except Hong Kong and Singapore) pursued textbook-style (albeit limited) import substitution for some sectors. Whether these interventions were effective is an important issue to which we return later in this paper. The main point at this juncture is that free markets were not always at the core of Asia's success — *except when it came to exporters competing on world markets.* The common element between the open markets of Hong Kong and Singapore, the more interventionist states of Taiwan and Korea, and the natural resource abundant, more state centred economies of Malaysia, Indonesia, and Thailand was their orientation toward world markets and their overriding goal of expanding exports of manufacturers.

The competition in world markets for manufactured products is so intense that even moderate barriers to trade can spell the difference between profitability and loss for exporting firms. Exporters must be free to sell on world markets without cost-increasing restrictions to sell domestically. Even more important, exporters must have access to imported inputs unhindered by tariffs or quotas. Labour-intensive manufactured exports tend to have high import content, reaching as high as 85% of the export value for electronics components. Under these circumstances, even an import tariff as low as 18% (specifically, a tariff at the rate 15/85) can effectively wipe out the entire potential profitability such from exports.

Asian countries have understood this better than other developing countries, and have kept import tariffs relatively low, and especially low — often zero — for intermediate and capital goods used by exporters. They have also limited the use of quantitative restrictions on such imports. Average tariff rates on capital and intermediate goods as well as the share of imports of these goods covered by quantitative restrictions in 1985. The eight fastestgrowing economies charged an average tariff on these goods of 12.5 percent. Hong Kong's tariff was zero, and Singapore's was 1.6 percent. Only two of the fast growing economies — the PRC and Thailand — imposed tariffs of greater than 14 percent. It is very important to recognize that *even these figures overstate the actual tariffs charged to exporters*, since almost all of these countries provided facilities under which exporters could receive capital goods and imported inputs duty free. In contrast, the average tariff on imported capital and intermediate goods in South Asia was 50 percent. India's tariff of 132 percent more than doubled the price of imported capital goods for Indian firms. Nepal's average rate of 10.4 percent was the lowest in South Asia, but since almost all capital goods imported into Nepal had to be transported through India, the actual cost to Nepali importers was higher than the nominal tariff indicates. The pattern was similar for quantitative restrictions (QRs). Hong Kong, Korea, and Singapore imposed almost no restrictions on imports of capital goods and raw materials. The only East Asian countries to impose significant QRs was Taipei, China, at 38 percent of imports. But even there, exporters faced far fewer QRs than this figure suggests. The Southeast Asian countries imposed only moderate restrictions on these imports, with the exception of the Philippines. The extent of coverage of QRs was substantially higher in Bangladesh and India.

India's combination of 132 percent tariffs and QRs on almost 90 of imports essentially prohibited domestic firms from importing the most advanced machinery, cheapest raw materials, and newest technology. Other elements of open and flexible markets for exporters were just as important. For example, the successful Asian exporters allowed free entry and exit of firms into export manufacturing activities and imposed relatively low taxes. Hong Kong embraced these ideals most fully, with perhaps the most open markets in the world. Singapore also established open and flexible factor and output markets. Other Asian countries, by different means, established conditions resembling free and open international trade, at least for exporters.

Export Facilitation

The process of establishing these conditions for exporters, however, was far from automatic. Asian government played an active role in encouraging and supporting export firms. The average tariff on capital and intermediate goods was relatively high in Korea, as was the share of imports covered by QRs in Taipei, China. Moreover, these simple average disguise a wide range of tariffs and QRs, as pointed out by Wade (1990). Factor markets were often distorted, and many prices were administratively determined. In purely theoretical terms, the best solution to address these distortions would have been for governments to attack them directly by removing price and quantity controls and reducing tariff rates. Hong Kong and Singapore basically followed this prescription by implementing very open trade regimes. For a variety of reasons, however, most other Asian governments either could not or would not remove these distortions directly. In some countries, this reluctance came from initial apprehension about the wisdom of an export-led strategy; in others, it was driven by the desire to protect vested economic and political interests. As a second-best solution, governments in East and Southeast Asia created several innovative programs and institutions to provide the means by which firms could overcome these distortions and become competitive exporters.

These facilities included subsidized credit, tax breaks, export processing zones, bonded manufacturing warehouses, duty drawback programs, privatization of customs administration, and direct export subsidies. Korea, for example, supported exporters with a complex system of export subsidies, cheap credit, and access to controlled imports.

Taiwan used a similar range of interventions. A common element in each of the successful countries in East and Southeast Asia was at least one facility that provided exporters with access to reduced or zero duties on capital and intermediate goods exports. Three of these facilities were particularly important: export processing zones (EPZs), bonded manufacturing warehouses, and duty drawback systems.

EPZs are enclaves located physically or administratively outside a country's customs barrier in which foreign and domestic forms are given access to duty-free imports, tax holidays and other incentives, and physical resources such as buildings and electricity, on the condition that they export all or most of their goods. A typical incentive package offered to firms locating within a zone includes tax holidays of up to 20 years, 100% profit repatriation, free access to foreign exchange, efficient customs clearance, preferential access to financing, and capital grants in the form of subsidized factory space or worker training. Some countries also explicitly limit union activity within EPZs.

EPZs grew rapidly during the 1970s and 1980s. By 1990, EPZs employed about 530,000 people worldwide, the majority of whom were young women. EPZs accounted for more than $13 billion in exports in 1990, equivalent to about 5 percent of total manufacturing exports from developing countries. EPZ firms concentrate mainly in electronics (Korea, Malaysia, Taiwan, the Philippines) and garments (Bangladesh, Indonesia, Sri Lanka). Malaysia's success in electronics exports can be traced directly to the establishment of the Bayan Lepas EPZ in Penang between 1970 and 1972. The Kaohsiung EPZ in Taiwan began exporting in 1966; by 1973 it employed 57,000 people. Korea followed suit in 1970 with the creation of the Masan Free Export Zone. More recently, a major reason for the surge in electronics exports in the Philippines since 1992 was the government's success in attracting firms from the U.S., Japan, and Taiwan to locate electronics testing and assembly operations in export processing zones.

EPZs have been especially popular in East and Southeast Asia, where about one-third of all EPZs are located, *accounting for two-thirds of all employees in EPZs worldwide.* They accounted for an important share of exports in several countries, including Malaysia and the PRC, and to a lesser extent, Taipei, China and Korea.

In Malaysia, for example, exports from EPZs accounted for 74 percent of total exports of manufactured goods in 1980; in 1990, EPZ exports still accounted for 57 percent of the total. Oddly, despite their success in East and Southeast Asia, they were little used in other parts of the developing world until the last decade.

India operated six zones in 1990, and Bangladesh just one, and all of these were of very limited scale. There were only 4 EPZs operating in Africa in 1990. They have been much more numerous in Latin America and the Caribbean, but generally have been less successful there than in Asia, for reasons outlined below.

EPZs provide several attractions for developing countries. First and foremost, EPZs facilitate the creation of the administrative and physical infrastructure needed for export-led growth, even when important distortions remain in the rest of the economy. Second, and related, EPZs demonstrate the potential profitability of exports, both to other firms and to the host government.

The success of these firms encourages other firms to export, and can help convince the government to change policies that inhibit the export competitiveness of the rest of the economy. Third, EPZs provide jobs for low-skilled urban workers. Because firms are competing on world markets, the potential for job creation is not limited to the domestic market, and wages can increase over time as workers gain experience and increase productivity.

Experience in wellmanaged Asian EPZs has shown their effectiveness in creating export-related jobs, and in promoting rising real wages of industrial workers as experience and productivity rise. Of course, EPZs alone do not generally solve a country's unemployment problems, but they can make an important contribution both directly and through their demonstration effects to other exporting firms.

Fourth, EPZs have the potential to (eventually) create demand for locally produced intermediate inputs. The empirical record for creating backward linkages is mixed, however, and depends critically on the competitiveness of the domestic suppliers. Firms located in EPZs will not be interested in purchasing inputs from highly protected, high-cost domestic suppliers when cheaper and more reliable inputs are available on world markets. A major problem in creating linkages has been that domestic suppliers (which do not export directly) do not always have access to duty free imports for their *own* inputs, placing them at a competitive disadvantage with suppliers on the world market. These "indirect exporters" are usually ineligible for EPZs or duty drawback systems. Korea and Taiwan, and to a lesser extent Indonesia, have been successful in overcoming these problems and creating linkages to the rest of the economy.

Although many EPZs, especially those in Asia, have succeeded in creating jobs and spurring exports, others have failed. Some fail because of broader macroeconomic or political instability — EPZs, on their own, will not attract foreign investment in a highly unstable economy. Others have failed because of unrealistic expectations. Hill (1994) points out that when zones have been located in underdeveloped areas (e.g., rural remote areas or small cities) as a means of jump-starting local industry, they are rarely successful. In addition, the success or failure of EPZs depends critically on their ownership, and the rules governing their establishment and operation. EPZs that have imposed requirements that inhibit firms' ability to export, rather than providing firms' with the flexibility to compete on world markets, have not succeed in encouraging exported growth. For example, zones with high entry fees or strict regulations on hiring and firing workers are unlikely to attract investment and promote exports. In general, the effectiveness of EPZs stems precisely from their "enclave" nature — that is, their ability to allow firms to circumvent the distortions and related costs (e.g., import duties, high marginal tax rates, restrictions on exports) that so often are present in developing economies and that inhibit firms from competing on world markets. Firms typically point to seven critical elements for successful zones:

- unrestricted access to inputs and foreign exchange;
- minimal government interference on production decisions (e.g., the right to hire or fire workers);
- favourable location with respect to ports, airports, etc.;
- reliable communication links;
- efficient management and administration of the zone (e.g., rapid customs clearance);
- guaranteed profit repatriation; and
- majority foreign ownership guarantees with well defined property rights.

A second, and closely related export facilitation institution used in Asia is bonded manufacturing warehouses. These warehouses are essentially single-factory EPZs, designed for larger firms producing exclusively for export markets. Approved warehouses, with a customs officer stationed at the site, can receive duty free imports of capital and intermediate goods and bypass other customs procedures. Firms post a bond as a guarantee against any duties that might be applicable to imports that are diverted to the domestic market.

A third, more broad-based method of assisting exporters is duty drawback systems, in which firms pay duties on imported inputs and are then reimbursed upon export of the final product. In some cases, firms with a strong history of compliance are exempted from paying duties on imported inputs, as long as they continue to provide proof of exports.

In this way, duty drawback schemes provide exporters with access to inputs at world prices. The main advantage of a duty-drawback system is that a firm can choose its location, rather than being confined to a predetermined area such as an EPZ.

This provides the firm with more flexibility, helps encourage backward linkages to the rest of the economy, and saves the government the cost of establishing the special zone. However, duty drawback mechanisms can be difficult to administer, and have been subject to some abuse, since duty free imports leak to the domestic market. Despite these difficulties, well designed programs have been used successfully in Singapore, Korea, Malaysia, and Indonesia. None of these facilities, on their own, would have been enough to spur rapid export growth in Asia. The key point is that most of the successful countries in East and Southeast Asian used a *combination* of facilities to support exporters. Korea provides a good example.

Korea had high and uneven tariff rates on imports in the 1960s and 1970s, and continues to do so today, especially for agricultural products. But very early in its post war development process, the Korean government ensured that these distortions did not affect export competitiveness by establishing a complex system of export subsidies, cheap credit, and access to controlled imports. At the core were facilities for exporters that allowed duty free access of imported capital and intermediate goods. Hong Won-tack (1979) described the early genesis of these initiatives: "The tariff law has allowed duty free imports of basic plant facilities and equipment for important industries since 1949. On the basis of this law, imports of machinery for export production received a tariff exemption from 1964 until 1974 when the tariff exemption system was changed into a deferred payment system on an installment basis. Capital goods imported for foreign investment projects were also exempted from tariffs after 1960. After 1961, raw materials directly used for export production were imported duty free."

What is striking is that date that these facilities were introduced: as early as 1961, Korea was taking strong steps to ensure free trade for exporters. Later these facilities were complemented by two large export processing zones (which opened in the early 1970s) and over 200 bonded warehouses (by 1981). Exports from EPZs and bonded warehouses accounted for 15 percent of total Korean exports in 1981. Exporters located outside the zones used duty exemption and drawback facilities. Access to duty free imports was also provided to indirect exporters (domestic firms that do not export directly, but sell all of their output to exporting firms). In this way, indirect exporters could compete more readily with international suppliers, helping to deepen the backward linkages of exporting firms.

In Taipei, China, the shift toward export promotion began in earnest in July 1957, when the Bank of Taiwan began offering subsidized credit to firms that were attempting to penetrate export markets. In August 1959, the government unified the exchange rate, shifting incentives markedly away from import substitutes and towards exports. It also began to reduce tariffs and relax controls on imports of capital and intermediate goods used by exporters. In 1966, the government established the Kaoshing EPZ, the world's first EPZ for manufacturing. Two other zones were opened in the early 1970s. In addition, by 1981 there were well over 300 bonded manufacturing warehouses operating in Taipei, China. Together, exports from the EPZs and warehouses accounted for over 20 percent of the country's total exports in 1981.

Almost all other exporters took advantage of a well-functioning duty drawback/exemption system. Indonesia has used a four-pronged approach to support exporters since it began its deregulation program in the mid-1980s. First, broad-based tariff cuts reduced the cost of imported inputs for all domestic producers, including exporters. Second, the government introduced a successful duty drawback/exemption system, which was used widely by many manufactured exporters. Third, when weak customs administration threatened the export promotion strategy and undermined the government's revenue collection efforts, the government effectively privatized customs administration by hiring the Swiss surveying firm Societe General de Surveillance (SGS) in April, 1985.

SGS took over the investigation and clearance of import consignments worth more than $5,000, and customs control over exports and inter-island domestic shipping was abolished altogether. Although the SGS contract was expensive, government revenue collections rose sharply, and traders benefited from more transparent, predictable, and rapid customs clearance. Fourth, and more recently, Indonesia has had some success with its version of bonded warehouses. Indonesia had little success with its EPZs (outside of those on Batam Island) during most of the 1980s, largely because firms had to pay high entry fees and were forced to buy water, power, and security services from the owners of the zones at relatively high prices. Its newer bonded warehouses (*Entrepot Produksi Untuk Tujuan Ekspor*, or EPTEs) provide firms with much more flexibility in their location, employment policies, utility purchases, and other production decisions.

Asian exporters have also taken advantage of the facilities offered by industrialized markets to a greater extent than other developing countries. A good example is U.S. imports from developing countries under the Generalized System of Preferences (GSP), which are totally dominated by Southeast Asian countries. That of the $18 billion in U.S.

imports of GSP articles in 1995, the four Southeast Asian countries alone accounted for $10 billion, or 55% of the total. Malaysia by itself sent nearly $5 billion in GSP articles to the US, accounting for over one-fourth of the world total, more than any other entire *continent.* The only country that comes close to using the GSP facility as much as the Southeast Asian countries is Brazil, which exported $2 billion of goods under the system in 1995. The four East Asian NICs similarly dominated the U.S. GSP system until they became ineligible in the late 1980s.

Although EPZs, bonded manufacturing warehouses, duty drawback/ exemptions systems and other facilities are only second best solutions to removing trade distortions, they have played an important role in accelerating the process towards openness to free trade in Asia. In each of the countries where these facilities were most successful, governments have subsequently introduced more broad-based tariff and quota reform. Although the causality from successful EPZs and drawback facilities to trade reform is impossible to prove, there are at least three reasons to suspect that this pattern is more than a coincidence. First, successful EPZs and drawback systems demonstrated that exports can be profitable, reassuring those who doubted the potential for developing countries to successfully compete in global markets for manufacturers.

Second, these systems created a political interest group that supported exports. Third, some duty-free imports intended for use in EPZs and drawback systems inevitably leaked to the domestic market, undermining the high tariff walls protecting inward-oriented industries. It is tempting to speculate that as the "effective" levels of tariffs are eroded, it eventually becomes easier for the government to lower the actual tariff rates.

EPZs, bonded manufacturing warehouses, and duty drawback/ exemption systems have become less important over time in countries that have eventually undertaken more broad-based trade liberalization. In some sense, these facilities work themselves out of a job: when a country begins to be successful with manufactured exports, it tends to reduce tariffs and remove other impediments to trade, reducing the need for export facilitation. Similarly, these facilities are likely to play a less prominent role in the future in other Asian countries as these countries lower tariffs in accordance with the WTO accords. But in situations were distortions remain, these innovative institutions created by government policy can help markets to work better and to provide the means by which firms can become competitive on world markets.

Industrial Policies

Not all forms of government intervention in Asia should be understood as contributing to the success of manufactured exports. Though some scholars have argued that the promotion of heavy industry through industrial policies was critical to rapid growth, careful international comparison does not support this view. Without question, three of the most successful countries in East Asia — Korea, Taiwan, and Japan — intervened heavily to promote specific import-substituting industries. Effective rates of protection in Korea, while moderate on average, were highly dispersed. In addition, an elaborate web of trade associations had informal but effectively exclusive rights to import certain goods.

According to Wade (1990), Taiwan applied restrictions to over half of its imports as recently as 1984 (although, as we have seen, there were far fewer restrictions on imports for exports). In financial markets, Korea controlled both the allocation of credit and the interest rate through its state-owned banking system. The largest conglomerates, or *chaebol*, had access to subsidized credit, while smaller firms were forced to borrow in informal markets at much higher rates. The government leaned heavily on the *chaebol* to meet export targets, and, during the 1970s, to invest in infant heavy industries. Taiwan also directed credit towards favoured industries, although they used subsidized credit less extensively. Credits markets did not fully clear, and many small firms had to borrow in informal markets. The government supported this curb market by ruling that post-dated checks (which were the most popular credit instrument in the informal market) were recognizable by the courts as enforceable contracts.

Were these policies at the core of Korea and Taiwan's success? Did they simply correct for other distortions in the economy, or did they give these countries an extra push that would not have been possible otherwise? Some of the favoured industries were clear success stories, such as Korea's Pohang Iron and Steel Company and Hyundai Motor Company. But Korean industrial policy also had it failures, such as Korean Heavy Industries, and Okpo Shipbuilding, both of which avoided bankruptcy only with large state subsidies. The Hanbo steel and construction group went bankrupt in early 1997, with serious adverse repercussions for the Korean financial system. Hanbo borrowed around $6 billion from financial institutions to build a large steel works that proved uncompetitive in the end.

Of course, the correct method of evaluating these kinds of industrial policies in Northeast Asia is to measure the net impact of these success and failures, and whether the economy would have done better in the absence of these interventions. It is possible that industrial policy did provide such a fillip to development in Taiwan and Korea, as several analysts have concluded based documentation of government interventions and case studies of success stories. However, to our knowledge, there are not any truly rigorous studies calculating the full benefits of successes and complete costs of failures that demonstrate that this is the case. Hughes (1993) has criticized the industrial policy literature for giving too little attention to the costs imposed by these policies, and several recent studies that have examined both successes and failures have cast doubt on the overall effectiveness of the interventionist strategies. For example, Lee (1996) found no clear relationship between industrial policies (e.g., subsidized credit and tax incentives) and total factor productivity growth in Korea; and he found a significant *negative* relationship between trade restrictions and growth rates of labour productivity and total factor productivity.

Perhaps more importantly, import protection and directed credit in support of heavy industry clearly were *not* central to the success of Hong Kong, Singapore, Thailand, Malaysia, the PRC, and Indonesia. Hong Kong, of course, is probably the most open market in the world, and state intervention played little direct role in its industrial development (indirectly, the government's main role in industrial policy was probably the promotion of effective infrastructure facilities). Singapore intervened in favour of chosen industries, but in a very different way than the Northeast Asian economies. Singapore's industrial policy was always aimed at promoting export industries, at first in labour-intensive sectors and later in more skill-based manufactures and services, but always consistent with its comparative advantage. Around 90 percent of all of Singapore's manufactured exports are actually the products of multinational firms operating within Singapore. Its most important foray into promoting capital-intensive industries by artificially raising wages in the late 1970s and early 1980s was unsuccessful, and the policy had to be reversed when economic growth slowed. Singapore used tax incentives as its policy of choice, and stayed clear of using protectionist trade policies (except for a brief period of mild import substitution in the early 1960s) and never used subsidized credit. It also established several extremely well-run state enterprises to support its export industries.

In Thailand, Malaysia, and Indonesia, governments ruled the markets with a much heavier hand, and not always in support of export markets. Often, interventions were designed to provide economic favours for important individuals, families, and firms in return for political support, and have failed to support broader development objectives. Roemer (1994) described government interventions in Southeast Asia as follows:

> Treecrop exports are cartelized, ostensibly to stabilize domestic prices, but actually to protect processors by reducing prices paid to farmers. Log exports are banned or heavily taxed to promote cartelized plywood industries that use political influence to retain their protection. Steel mills and cement plants are constructed by clients of the regime, or by the regime itself, behind high protective barriers that remain in place long after the industry is mature, stifling export growth from downstream industries. Technological advances, such as the auto industry in Malaysia and the airplane industry in Indonesia, are disciplined neither by competition nor by ambitious export targets.

The major point is that while the promotion of heavy industry may have been beneficial in some identifiable cases, *it surely was not the common denominator that accounts for the rapid growth across East and Southeast Asia.* Instead, the common denominator was manufactured exports, supported by a regime best characterized as free trade for exporters.

The varied experiences of the countries of East and Southeast Asia indicate that both an open market and a more interventionist approach that offsets other distortions can be made to work, as long as manufacturers face the acid test of operating on world markets, both for imported inputs and exports. *East Asia's successful industrial policy strategy was to support labour-intensive* manufactured exports, not capital intensive heavy industries.

Despite the different views amongst analysts of the effectiveness of industrial interventions in East Asia, there appear to be several areas of consensus.

- First, to the extent that government's choose to use targeted industrial policies, they should be geared towards removing existing biases against exports and ensuring the competitiveness of exporters. Amsden (1989) argues that a critical aspect of Korean industrial policy was that export targets were "an objective, transparent criterion by which firm performance is easily judged."
- Second, government policies may be effective in pushing the pace of change in comparative advantage, but they will not be effective if they stray too far from the basic direction of market forces. Korea's Heavy and Chemical Industry drive and Singapore's attempt to move quickly into high-wage exports are two examples of the problems that can arise when governments try to force the pace of change too aggressively.
- Third, government interventions of the type employed in Taipei, China and Korea could only be successful in countries with an effective and disciplined civil service. The potential for replicability to other countries is limited, as indicated by the failure of these types of policies in the majority of countries where they have been attempted. Hill (1996) makes this point convincingly for Indonesia.
- Fourth, Korea and Taipei, China's example is probably not relevant in today's international trading environment. When these two countries employed interventionist strategies, few competitor countries paid close attention. But with the establishment of the World Trade Organization and the associated agreements reached in the Uruguay round of the GATT, developing country governments today would be prohibited to use policies such as subsidized and directed credit for exporters.

Explaining High Saving Rates in Asia

Savings lies at the heart of economic growth theory. The early workhorse growth model developed by Roy Harrod (1939) and Evsey Domar (1946, 1947) linked growth directly and nearly exclusively to the savings rate. Solow's neoclassical extension, while providing for substitution between capital and labour, continued to focus on savings as the primary determinant of growth. Savings rates in Asia were not unusually large thirty years ago, but they have grown substantially and are now among the highest in the world. As we saw earlier, savings rates were significantly larger in Asia than in other regions of the world in 1990, even after controlling for structural and geographical variables. We also saw the close association between government savings and economic growth. This section examines savings rates across Asia, and explores some of the factors that appear to determine private and national savings rates.

Savings Rates in Asia: The Historical Record

In the 1960s and early 1970s, national savings rates in Asia were only slightly higher, on average, than in other developing regions. Between 1965-69, national savings rates averaged 19.7 percent, 17 percent, and 9.5 percent in the Four Tigers, Southeast Asia, and South Asia, respectively, compared to 16.2 percent in Latin America. But these simple averages disguise substantial differences across countries. China, Hong Kong, Taiwan, Malaysia and Thailand all recorded national savings rates greater than 20 percent. Hong Kong led the way with an average of 25 percent, even during this early period. By contrast, Singapore saved only 13 percent of GNP in 1965, and averaged 16.9 percent over the five-year period 1965-69. South Korea saved just 9 percent in 1965, and 14 percent during 1965-69. Indonesia, in the midst of political and economic upheaval, recorded the lowest savings rate in East and Southeast Asia at 5 percent. India recorded the highest rate in South Asia at 14 percent, but Nepal's reached just 3 percent.

These patterns began change during the 1970s, when national savings rates rose in each country in East and Southeast Asia, as well as in China. Between 1970-79, national savings rates exceeded 20 percent in all of these countries, and surpassed 27 percent in Hong Kong, China, Malaysia, Taiwan, and Singapore. The spectacular rise in savings rates in Singapore is especially noteworthy, from 13 percent in 1965 to 30 percent in 1975 and over 40 percent in 1982 and each year thereafter. Similarly, Indonesia's savings rate jumped to 25 percent in 1976, up percentage points in less than a decade. In South Asia, India's savings rate climbed steadily to 19 percent during the 1970s, Sri Lanka's grew slightly to 13 percent, and Nepal's reached 8 percent. However, in all the other South Asian countries, savings rates stagnated or fell, and averaged just 10 percent across the region. Despite these lower rates in South Asia, by 1990 savings rates for all of developing Asia were about 8 percentage points higher than the average for the rest of the world, after controlling for differences in income, population, and other structural characteristics. The higher national savings rates in East and Southeast Asia are reflected by higher rates of both private and government savings in the region. Before examining these data, however, some caveats are in order. Public sector savings is properly defined as the current budget (or operating) surplus of all public sector institutions, including the central government, provincial and local governments, and state-owned corporations. Private sector savings is normally calculated as total national savings minus public sector savings, because more direct information on private savings usually is not available. However, that data on the basic components of public sector savings other than central government savings are generally very weak. (This, in turn, implies that private sector saving data are not always very reliable). For many countries, complete data on public sector savings are unavailable. Those countries that do report information on public saving generally limit it to the central government budget (the data on central government saving, when reported, generally are of higher quality than those on private saving, since they are derived from government budget data). We rely primarily on World Bank data for central government current budget balances as our basis for government savings rates, because it appears to be the most complete and comparable set of data available.

Central government savings rates have been especially high in Singapore and Indonesia, averaging 9-11 percent of GNP. Indonesia has long displayed strict fiscal discipline, enforced by a rule which prohibits the government from borrowing domestically to finance expenditures. Taiwan's government saved nearly as much, averaging 5-7 percent of GNP. Each of the other countries in East and Southeast Asia consistently maintained government surpluses of between 1-3 percent of GNP; in Thailand and Malaysia government savings reached 6-7 percent in the early 1990s. By contrast, government savings rates have been close to zero, or even negative, for all of the South Asian countries. Private saving rates did not differ by as much as government savings across regions. India's private savings rate, for example, has hovered around 20 percent of GNP since the 1970s, and averaged about 22 percent between 1990-93. This latter rate is higher than either

Indonesia or the Philippines recorded during the period, and only slightly lower than in Taiwan and Malaysia. Pakistan's private savings rate has been greater than 15 percent since 1983. On the whole, private savings rates across Asia have exceeded those in Latin America, and been more than double the average rate recorded in sub-Saharan Africa.

The Determinants of Savings

Why have national savings rates in Asia exceeded those of other developing countries, and why have they increased so rapidly since the 1960s? How are Asian savings rates likely to change during the next thirty years? These critical questions are not easy to answer completely. Despite the centrality of savings in growth theory, previous research has not reached a consensus on the determinants of savings, and the two-way linkages between savings and growth are not fully understood. Nevertheless, four broad groups of variables appear to play an important role in determining national saving rates: demographic factors (including dependency ratios and life expectancy), economic growth, government policies (broadly including central government saving, credit to the public sector, social security expenditures, and inflation), and financial sector development.

Demography

At the core of saving theory is the life-cycle hypothesis, which suggests that individuals pass through three broad phases of savings and consumption during their lifetimes. First, children who have not yet reached working age consume more than they earn, resulting in negative savings rates for this age group. Second, during their working years (aged 15-64), individuals earn more than they spend, generating the bulk of an economy's savings. Third, after retirement, individuals generally revert to negative saving rates. Accordingly, the larger the young-age dependency ratio (population younger than 15 years as a percentage of population aged 15-64) and the old-age dependency ratio (population 65 years or older as a percentage of population aged 15-64), the lower the saving rate. Although some analysts have found little connection between demographic composition and saving, others have found a strong relationship. The ten East Asian countries stand out among developing countries in their demographic composition, especially on the youngage dependency ratio. East Asia's young-age dependency ratio averaged about 64% between 1970-92 (the period over which we have complete data for a large set of countries world-wide), well below the averages for South Asia and Latin America, and substantially below sub-Saharan Africa's very high ratio of 86%. There was much less difference across regions in the old-age dependency ratio. East Asia and South Asia both recorded ratios of about 6%, and sub-Saharan Africa's ratio was actually slightly lower at 5.7%. Similarly, a population's life expectancy is likely to influence savings rates. Low life expectancies tend to indicate high rates of infant mortality, widespread disease, and short time horizons, so savings tend to be quite low. As disease becomes less pervasive and life expectancy increases, individuals are more likely to be able to save more of their earnings. It is also possible that the relationship is non-linear, with the impact of increases in life expectancy diminishing as it gets larger. In other words, each successive one year increase in life expectancy may be associated with smaller increases in savings. Even as early as 1965, East Asia's average life expectancy was already 55 years, already far higher than South Asia's 47 years and sub-Saharan Africa's 42 years. Over the full 1970-92 period, East Asia's life expectancy averaged 65 years, compared to 59 years and 50 years, respectively. However, Latin America's life expectancy was higher than East Asia's, at 66 years, so life expectancy clearly does not provide a full explanation for differences in savings rates.

Economic Growth

Although economic theory closely links economic growth with savings, the precise nature of the relationship is unclear. There are several reasons to believe that rapid growth is associated with higher savings. For example, individuals may find it easier to save when their incomes are growing very rapidly. As long as consumption grows more slowly than income, saving rates will increase. Moreover, the simple mechanics of aggregating income and savings across age cohorts could lead to a positive association. In a growing economy, higher savings from the working age population is likely to increasingly outweigh the dis-saving of the non-working population. However, economic growth could also lead to lower savings. If individuals expect their income to continue to grow during their lifetime, they may adjust their current consumption upward, reducing savings rates. Most studies have found a positive relationship between income growth and savings rates. The relationship between savings and growth is further complicated because the causality is likely to run in both directions. Not only does growth foster saving, but economic theory identifies savings as a primary determinant of growth. The World Bank (1993) referred to this two-way causality as the "virtuous circle" between growth and savings. In the empirical work that follows, we treat this simultaneity problem by estimating the relationship between savings and growth using instrumental variables for the economic growth rate. In an alternative specification, we estimate the relationship with the lagged (five-year average) rate of growth as a an explanatory variable in the saving equation, to test whether there is evidence that rapid growth precedes increases in savings.

Government Policy

Government policy can influence private saving, both through the rate of government savings and the size of the public sector social security program. Higher *government* saving is expected to be associated with lower *private* saving, as households partly compensate in their own saving behaviour for shifts in government saving. The strongest form of this hypothesis, known as Ricardian equivalence, posits that any increase in government saving will be offset one-for-one by a fall in private saving, leaving national saving unchanged. If governments choose to borrow, far-sighted individuals will plan on the government raising taxes in the future to repay the debt. These individuals will therefore increase their personal savings to offset the decline in government savings. Previous research has verified a strong negative relationship between government and private savings, but has found little support for the strict one-for-one relationship of Ricardian equivalence. Most studies have estimated offset coefficients of between 0.40 and 0.65. That is, a rise in government saving of one percent of GDP is associated with a fall in private saving of between 0.40 and 0.65 percent of GDP. Since the offset coefficient is less than 1.0, a rise in government saving increases total national saving, but by much less than one-for-one. If a 1.0 percent of GDP increase in government saving leads to a *reduction* of private saving of 0.40 percent of GDP (that is, an offset coefficient of 0.40), the effect on national saving, evidently, is 0.60 (= 1.0-0.40). Thus, the high government saving in most of East Asia is likely to be an important contributor to high domestic saving, but the effect is muted by the offset on private saving. Available information on government savings is limited to central governments only — few countries regular report data on provincial and local governments or state-owned enterprises.

Indicators of saving by provincial governments or state owned enterprises are hard to find, as are related measures, such as the profits and losses of state-owned enterprises. One widely available measure that provides some indication of the financial state of the public sector is the amount of outstanding credit from the banking system to the entire public sector, taken from the monetary survey. Large amounts of outstanding credit indicate a large public sector with large debts to the banking system, and presumably lower rates of public sector savings. We expect, therefore, that credit outstanding to the public sector would be negatively associated with saving. Credit outstanding to the public sector averaged just 1.5% of GDP in East Asia, compared with 25% in South Asia and 14% in both sub-Saharan Africa and Latin America.

Real interest rates may also affect savings rates, but there is little consensus on this issue in the literature. Data limitations present a major problem. The specific interest rates which governments report vary widely across countries, and many countries do not report interest rates at all. Perhaps more importantly, many countries have artificially fixed their official interest rates over long periods of time, so these data give little indication of the true time opportunity cost of money. Largely because of these problems, we were unable to find an interest rate series which we found sufficiently credible across a large number of countries through time to test this relationship. Instead, we estimate the relationship between savings and inflation. Inflation provides an indirect measure of real interest rates, since inflation erodes real returns on financial assets, undermining incentives to save. In addition, very high rates of inflation are indicative of wider macroeconomic instability, which can lead to capital flight, and lower national savings. In particular, very high rates of inflation — such as the average of 196% recorded in Latin America between 1970 and 1992 — may deter savings. In this view, East Asia's relative low inflation rates suggest a conducive environment for higher savings. One possibility is that at relatively low levels of inflation, the marginal impact of a change in inflation (say, from 8% to 10% may have little impact on aggregate saving. But once inflation reaches higher levels, people begin alter their saving behaviour. We test this proposition by examining the impact of inflation greater than 20% on national saving.

The size and nature of government pension systems can also influence saving. Feldstein (1980) and others have argued that pay-as-you -go pension systems are likely to lead to lower savings, as households rely on future government transfers rather than their own savings for retirement purposes. Gokhale, Kotlikoff, and Sabelhaus (1996) found strong empirical support for this hypothesis in the United States, as did Edwards (1995) for developing countries. We use current social security expenditures by the government (expressed as a portion of current income) as a proxy for expected payouts from the system after retirement. Between 1970 and 1992, social security expenditures in East and Southeast Asia were, on average, just one percent of GNP, compared to 2.1 percent in South Asia and 3.8 percent in Latin America. However, analysis of this relationship is complicated by the presence of different types of pension systems in the region, from non-existent in many countries, to large statutory self-funding systems in Malaysia and Singapore.

The development of financial systems is also likely to affect saving. In countries with rudimentary banking systems, or artificially controlled interest rates, the incentive to save is lower. In contrast, countries with well-functioning and profitable banking systems, active and efficient stock and bond markets, and well-developed insurance systems offer individuals and businesses a wider array of remunerative mechanisms by which to save. In practice, the relationship between saving and financial market development is difficult to capture, not only because it is hard to find a good measure of financial market depth for many countries, but also because it could be that higher savings themselves promote deeper financial markets. We use a crude measure of financial depth, the ratio of broad money (M) to GDP. This ratio was far higher in East Asia (57%) than 2 in either South Asia (33%) or Latin America (31%), in part indicating the more sophisticated financial systems of Singapore, Hong Kong, and other economies in the region.

Estimation Results

We estimated the impact of these variables on national saving rates for a sample of 72 countries for which the complete set of data were available. The data are organized in panel form, with each observation an average value for a five-year interval between 1970 and 1992 (1970-74, 1975-79, 1980-84, 1985-89, and 1990-92). We use a random effects generalized least squares estimation procedure.

The estimated coefficient for the young-age dependency ratio is negative and highly significant, as suggested by the life cycle hypothesis. A one percentage point increase in this ratio is associated with a decrease in the savings rates of 0.19 percentage points. This negative association is consistent with Coale and Hoover's (1958) prediction that populations with a large portion of young people would divert savings towards care and maintenance of children. Higgins and Williamson (1996) and Harrigan (1996) obtain similar results with different methodologies. Thus, one reason for East Asia's high saving rates was that they were further ahead in the demographic transition than other developing regions, with fewer young-age dependents supported by each worker.

By contrast, the estimated coefficient on the old-age dependency ratio is statistically insignificant, suggesting that the relative size of the population over age 65 is not a major determinant of difference in saving rates across countries. Given the small amount of variation in this variable across developing countries, this outcome is not completely surprising. Life expectancy is another powerful determinant of savings. As expected, we find evidence for a non-linear relationship between life expectancy at birth and savings. At low levels of life expectancy, increases in life expectancy are associated with higher savings rates. The effect is large at first, with an additional year of life expectancy matched by a substantial jump in savings. For example, an increase in life expectancy from 40 to 41 years is associated with a 0.8 percentage point increase in the savings rate. Each successive one year increase in life expectancy is associated with smaller increases in savings, such that, for example, the increase from 60 to 61 years is matched by a 0.2 percentage point increase in savings. Moreover, once life expectancy reaches 68 years, further increases are associated with *lower* savings, as indicated by the negative coefficient on the life expectancy squared term. A plausible explanation is that at this stage, higher life expectancy is indicative of a larger retired-age population, and that retirees are living longer. Since retirees tend to consume out of their lifelong savings, national savings declines. This finding is consistent with the fact that savings rates in the United States and Europe have declined in recent decades, and are lower than in the upper middle income countries of Asia.

We find a strong relationship between lagged per capita GDP growth and national savings. Each one percent increase in the lagged growth rate is associated with about a one-third percentage point increase in national savings. Similar, but somewhat statistically weaker results are obtained using the contemporaneous growth rate. Because of the strong simultaneity between growth and savings, we also estimated the relationship using instrumental variables for per capita GDP growth. The instruments are the variables from our basic growth equation. These findings provide some support for the idea of a "virtuous circle" between saving and growth, in which faster growth leads to higher savings, which in turn support more rapid growth.

However, the strongest results are in column 1 using the lagged growth rate, suggesting that the most important channel leads from faster growth to higher saving. This is consistent with Carroll and Weil (1993), who used causality tests to conclude that growth positively affects savings. The relationship between central government savings and national savings is very strong. Our results suggest that a one percentage point increase in the rate of government savings is associated with a 0.59 percentage point increase in national savings, with a t-statistic of 6.51. Government savings adds to national savings, but the effect is less than one-for-one, suggesting some offset through a decline in private savings. More specifically, our results indicate that a one percentage point increase in government savings is offset by a 0.41 percentage point decline in private savings, yielding an overall increase of 0.59 percentage points in national savings.

Thus, our results reject the theoretical outcome suggested by Ricardian equivalence, which posits that increases in government savings would yield zero change in national savings, and instead point to a strong positive association between fiscal policy and national savings. Similarly, the public sector's credit position with the banking system has a strong negative association with national savings. Each percentage point increase in credit outstanding (measured as a share of GDP) is matched by a 0.8 percentage point decline in national savings. A larger public sector credit position would tend to indicate less profitable state owned enterprises, creating a net drain on national savings. We also find a strong negative link between high rates of inflation (greater than 20%) and national savings. Countries with average rates of inflation greater than 20% have recorded national saving rates about 2 percentage points less than countries with more moderate inflation.

Government pension policies also powerfully affect national savings. Each one percentage point increase in central government pension payouts is associated with a 0.42 percent decline in national savings. This result supports Feldstein's (1980) hypothesis that with pay-as-you-go pension systems, individuals are likely to decrease their own savings as they expect to receive transfers from the government upon retirement. Finally, we find evidence in support of a relationship between financial development and savings.

Increases in our rough measure of financial development (broad money/GDP) are associated with higher rates of savings. Specifically, each ten percentage point increase in the ratio of M to GDP is associated with an increase in the national savings rate of about 0.5 percentage points. This results suggests that households save more with more sophisticated financial systems that may offer more flexibility, choice, and security in savings instruments. Column 2 shows the results with three other variables that might affect savings: the old age dependency ratio, degree of urbanization, and political instability. In each case, the estimated coefficients are not statistically significant. Column 3 adds regional dummy variables for the countries in East/Southeast Asia, South Asia, Latin America, and sub-Saharan Africa. These dummies add little to the explanatory power of the regressions. Each of the estimated coefficients is insignificant, indicating that the other independent variables explain the broad differences in savings rates across regions. Still, the estimated coefficients for South Asia and sub-Saharan Africa are large. Moreover, the adjusted R2 for these regressions, while very good compared to other statistical analyses of saving, indicate that we have explained less than two-thirds of the variation in saving rates across countries.

One way to gauge these results is to compare actual saving rates for Asian countries with the saving rates predicted by the regressions. In some countries, the fit is very good. For example,.... In other countries, there is a larger unexplained difference between the actual and predicted rates. While part of this may be due to data weaknesses, there is clearly much about the determinants of national saving rates that we do not yet fully understand.

Accounting for Differences Across Regions

Although the regression results provide some broad ideas of the most influential factors affecting saving rates, they tell us little about the relative importance of each independent variable. We can, however, use these results to determine the most important factors contributing to the differences in saving rates across regions. For example, average saving rates in South Asia were 12.7 percentage points lower than those in East and Southeast Asia, and the regression results can account for 9.9 percentage points of the difference. The higher young age dependency ratio and shorter life expectancy in South Asia combined to reduce saving rates by about 2.9 percentage points. Government polices had a large impact on saving rates, especially central government saving and bank credit extended to the public sector. These two variables, combined with differences in social security expenditure and inflation rates, accounted by 4.4 percentage points lower saving in South Asia compared to East Asia. South Asia's lower economic growth rate reduced its saving rate by 0.7 percentage points relative to East Asia, and it lower level of financial sector development reduced savings rates by another 1.7 percentage points. In the case of sub-Saharan Africa, the regression results account for 15.0 percentage points of the actual difference of 15.8 percentage points relative to East Asia. In this case, the demographic variables are the most important factor, accounting for an enormous 9.5 percentage points of sub-Saharan Africa's lower saving rate. Policy variables and differences in financial sector development are also large contributors. In the case of Latin America, the combined affect of the policy variables account for 4.9 percentage points of the 9.6 percentage point difference in saving rates.

These results suggest that demography and government policy are the main determinants of saving rates across countries. Government policies can influence saving rates through higher rates of government saving, less bank credit to public sector institutions, lower levels of spending on pension systems, and greater financial sector development. More prudent government policies and smaller public sectors clearly had a positive impact on national saving rates in East Asia. East Asia's rapid demographic transition also supported saving rates, especially compared to sub Saharan Africa, where the transition lags. According to our results, differences in economic growth rates are one factor in accounting for saving rates, but its direct impact appears to be smaller than the impacts of policies choices and demography.

Governance, Leadership And Economic Management

There is little question that policy makers in East and Southeast Asia have been so much more successful than their counterparts in other regions of the world in managing their economies. Through the course of several turbulent decades, Asian governments maintained stable economies, even when economies in other regions spiraled out of control. As we have mentioned, Asian governments kept fiscal deficits under control. Rates of inflation have rarely exceeded 15-20 percent, and in most countries remain at 10 percent or lower, compared to rates well over 50 percent or higher commonly recorded across Latin America during the late 1970s and 1980s. Hyperinflation was nearly non-existent in Asia, with Indonesia's hyperinflation following the political and economic crisis of the mid-1960s the only case during the last thirty years among the fast-growing economies in East and Southeast Asia. More recently, both Cambodia and Mongolia have suffered through bouts of hyperinflation; in both cases, the government appears to have brought the situation under control. In addition, Asian policy makers deftly managed exchange rates, by-and-large avoiding major overvaluations and moving quickly to restore stability when foreign payments imbalances arose. With the exceptions of Indonesia, Korea, and the Philippines, governments did not rely heavily on foreign borrowing, and only in the Philippines did foreign debt evolve into a crisis. Macroeconomic management was especially challenging for the resource rich countries of Southeast Asia, which had to maintain stability through several commodity boom and bust cycles. As we have pointed out, nearly all other resource-rich developing countries (except Botswana) experienced intense macroeconomic instability and slow growth.

Less obvious, however, is *how* these governments have managed their economies so well. What set these governments apart? Why have they been better able than other governments to promote macroeconomic stability and long term-development? The reasons are far from fully understood, but several factors appear to have made a difference.

Sustained political stability in most of these countries enabled governments to be consistent in their approach and to implement longer-term economic strategies.

Almost all of the successful Asian economies had stable political leadership, with few changes in heads of state and little shift in underlying economic direction. President Park led Korea for 18 years, President Suharto has ruled Indonesia for nearly three decades, and Lee Kuan Yew presided over Singapore's development for over a quarter of a century. Thailand's frequent changes in prime ministers make it an exception, but even there, economic policy-makers remained in their positions even when prime ministers changed, providing constancy to economic policy. Of course, stable political leadership is far from sufficient to engender sustained economic development. Look only at North Korea, Myanmar, and several other countries in Asia, as well as many countries in Sub-Saharan Africa with long-lived governments and poor economic performance. Asia's successful governments can be differentiated from other long-standing governments *by their ideas about and strategies for sustained economic development.*

Governments must have an approach for economic management and development than can be implemented and that will ultimately succeed in achieving long-term economic growth. During the past several decades, many perhaps well-meaning governments followed misguided development paradigms: extensive central planning with non-market allocation (in East Europe and the former Soviet Union for instance), long-term and widespread import substitution (throughout Latin America), or the extraction of resources from the agricultural sector to support urban industry (in many countries in sub-Saharan Africa). Numerous countries withdrew at least partially, if not wholly, from the world trading system in an attempt to develop more self-sufficient production systems. In Asia, these kinds of ideas were manifested in their most extreme form in the communist regimes of the PRC (until 1978), the central Asian republics, North Korea, and later in Viet Nam, Cambodia and Lao PDR.

In South Asia, although ideas about the role of the state in the development process were far less extreme, they had a profound impact on government strategy and policy choices. India, after its independence in 1947, followed the Fabian socialist ideals of its leaders (reinforced, no doubt, by the interventionist tendencies of the British colonial regime) to a planned and regulated economy. Other countries in the sub-region broadly followed India's lead. Market pessimism was influential in East Asia as well in the 1950s. Witness Taipei, China's and Korea's early import substitution strategy.

By the early 1960s, however, Japan's success with a more outward oriented strategy based on labour intensive exports began to strongly influence East Asian ideas on development strategy. Governments in Hong Kong, Taipei, China, Korea, and later Singapore, all were constrained by small domestic markets and were wary of the centrally planned, non-market approach advocated by the PRC. They could not help but notice Japan's success based on manufactured exports. Japan's influence was reinforced by the shared institutions that had developed in several countries following decades of Japanese colonial rule, and by the growing presence of Japanese firms throughout the region. Exports became even more appealing when U.S. foreign aid began to dry up in Korea and Taipei, China in the early 1960s. U.S. advice to Korea and Taipei, China amplified the case for export-led growth. Moreover, for strategic reasons, the U.S. took special measures to ensure market access to East Asian exporters. East Asia's leaders were strongly committed to their strategy of stimulating exports and supporting rapid economic growth.

In one famous example, President Park personally presided over monthly export meetings attended by senior government officials and business leaders, and continuously put a high priority on achieving annual export targets. Lee Kuan Yew was in many ways Singapore's chief salesman, never tiring of expounding on the attractiveness of Singapore as a destination for foreign investment. Perkins and Roemer (1994) and others have argued that economic policy-makers and government leaders in some East Asian countries may have put an unusually high premium on rapid economic growth because they saw it as essential to the survival of their regimes. In the 1950s and early 1960s, many observers questioned whether such small and unstable countries as Korea, Taipei, China and Singapore could survive in the face of external threats. Failure to grow rapidly and distribute the gains relatively equitably might have doomed these governments, or even the existence of these nations. In Southeast Asia, national survival was less of an issue, but leaders nevertheless seemed to understand that political legitimacy and stability depended in part on a well-managed and growing economy, and in some cases, on improving the welfare of the rural poor.

To implement their development strategies, the successful Asian economies consistently placed well-trained, able economic technicians in charge of macroeconomic management. These technicians were given wide latitude in setting economic policy. For example, in most East and Southeast Asian countries, authority for establishing the budget rests primarily with the Ministry of Finance or a related board, and not with the parliament or cabinet. Perhaps even more importantly, government leaders consistently insulated economic policy-makers from political pressures, and supported them when they made tough decisions that placed long-term development ahead of short-term political expediency. Thailand's popular and revered monarchy protected senior economic policy-makers, despite frequent military coups and changes in the prime minister. President Park of Korea invariably shielded the Economic Planning Board from political pressures and kept the military from having undue influence on economic policy, as did President Suharto in Indonesia.

Finally, in at least some of the more successful countries, policy implementation was aided a competent civil service. Singapore separated the civil service from the political party, and based promotions on competence rather than longevity. Similarly, Korea bases hiring and promotion decisions on examinations and on performance. Korea upgraded the quality of economic analysis available to its policy-makers by establishing the Korea Development Institute in 1971, which could attract well-qualified technicians without directly hiring them into the civil service. Civil servants are generally well paid, especially in Singapore, both to enable the government to attract top talent and to diminish the incentives for corruption. However, civil service performance lags in the larger Southeast Asian countries, especially Thailand, Indonesia, and the Philippines.

The Total Factor Productivity Debate

The "conditional convergence" framework that we elaborated earlier can be cast in terms of an aggregate production function. Suppose that GDP is a function of capital, K, labour, L, and a general efficiency parameter A, so that GDP = A * F(K,L). The efficiency parameter, in turn, will be a function of policies (for example, open trade will increase the division of labour, and therefore, efficiency), economic structure (for example, geography), and the level of technology. As a shorthand, we might write A = A(Policy, Structure, Technology). In this case, technology represents improvements in productive techniques, as well as the introduction of products with improved quality.

The parameter A is typically called total factor productivity (TFP). One of the debates about Asian growth involves the relative contributions of A, K, and L to overall GDP growth. Through standard techniques introduced by Solow (1956), it is possible to decompose the contributions of capital, labour, and the "rest" (designated by A) to overall changes in GDP. Note that even if we can get a meaningful measure of changes in A, we still have the problem of interpreting such changes as due to policy reforms or technological improvements. (Presumably the third determinant of A, the geographic and resource structure of the economy, while importantly affecting the *level* of A, may not necessarily contribute much to *changes* in A).

However, even getting a meaningful estimate of changes in A can be problematic. Since it is calculated as the residual of the growth accounting exercise, what is labelled as TFP is actually a combination of errors in the data, omissions of other factors that should be included in the growth equation, as well as efficiency gains. As a result, there is a danger of reading too much into these data. Indeed, the residual has been referred to as a measure of our ignorance about growth. One of the surprises of recent analytical studies is that changes in K rather than changes in A have apparently been the main engine of growth in Asia. That is, the rapid growth has been proximately caused by rapid capital accumulation rather than rapid advances in TFP growth.

In his most surprising and widely quoted result, Young found average annual TFP growth in Singapore of -0.003 percent for 1966-90. Such results do not, in any way, invalidate our earlier findings about the importance of economic policies or structure. It simply requires that we interpret such findings carefully, in the following manner. *Good economic* policies and a favourable economic structure raise the returns to capital and thereby stimulate rapid investments in capital. Without the good policies and the favourable structural conditions, the returns to capital would be much less, so that capital accumulation would be much lower, *and overall growth would be much slower as a result.* At a minimum, Asia's policy stance and structural conditions allowed the countries of the region to accumulate capital more quickly than other regions, and thus grow faster. Moreover, while changes in A are not the *prime* mover of Asian growth, in most countries changes in A nonetheless have made an important contribution to rapid East Asian growth.

The debate over TFP is not an all-or-nothing proposition. Both growth in TFP and growth in capital have contributed to rapid output growth. In fact, TFP growth in the Four Tigers has been the highest among any region in the world, averaging 1.4 percent per year during the period 1970-92, according to recent calculations by Bosworth, Collins, and Chen (1996). By comparison, the industrialized countries in their sample averaged TFP growth of 0.6 percent annually during the same time period. In addition, TFP growth rates have been rising over time in the Four Tigers, from an annual average of 0.7 percent in the 1960s and 1970s to 1.2 percent between 1980-86 and 2.8 percent between 1986-92. Bosworth, et al, found zero aggregate TFP growth in Singapore between 1970 and 1986 (similar to Young's numbers); the figure jumped to 4 percent annually between 1986-92. A separate, more detailed study on Singapore reaches a similar conclusion. Rao and Lee (1996) found annual TFP growth in manufacturing of -0.4 percent in Singapore between 1976-84; and 3.2 percent for the period 1987-94.

The debate over TFP growth is important. If most of East Asia's rapid growth were in fact the result of rapid increases in A, there would be less reason to believe in conditional convergence. It would be more likely that East Asia could continue to grow at current rates without a slowdown in the future. The fact that most of per capita growth is the result of capital accumulation, however, suggests that growth will slow down as capital deepening takes place (that is, as the capital-labour ratio rises sharply in the economy), since capital deepening will be associated with a declining rate of return to new investments. This is in fact the case in East Asia: as capital accumulation has progressed, rates of return on capital have declined, suggesting that indeed both capital accumulation and growth will taper off in the future. Paul Krugman (1994) has provocatively compared the pattern of large capital accumulation and relatively small TFP growth in East Asia to that of the former Soviet Union, implying that East Asia might face a collapse in growth similar to that experienced by the Soviet Union.

Although Krugman is correct that much of East Asia's growth was due to a rising share of capital to labour in the economy, and that growth rates are likely to fall in the future, his comparison of East Asia to the Soviet Union is mistaken. As the capital-labour ratio rises, returns to new investment will tend to decline. This decline in profit rates is mitigated by two factors: (1) improvements in TFP (which thereby raise the marginal productivity of capital), and (2) a high substitutability of capital for labour in the basic production function. The second condition means that capital deepening (rising K/L) can take place *without* sharply reducing the profitability of new investments. Thus, in thinking about the prospects for future profitable investment, TFP growth is not the only measure of the production function that should be examined. As important, perhaps, is the elasticity of substitution between capital and labour. A high substitution elasticity signifies good prospects for continued profitable investments in future years.

The aggregate production function GDP = AF(K,L) is of course merely a fable, not a real production process. A real economy is based on millions of interacting productive units, and the technical mathematical conditions for aggregating those millions of separate activities into a single function are generally not fulfilled. Therefore, when we speak of *the* elasticity of substitution between K and L, we are speaking in parables as well. What is probably true, however, is that flexible economies, with a high degree of intersectoral mobility of capital and labour, will act as if there is a high elasticity of substitution between aggregate capital and aggregate labour. The Soviet growth strategy was based on the non-market allocation of capital under conditions of virtual autarky. As a result, the Soviet economy was inflexible and inefficient. Capital was administratively allocated to areas of the economy that had low or even negative productivities of capital. Empirical estimates of the aggregate elasticity of substitution between K and L in the Soviet Union have been very low. The conditions for investment in Asia are completely different. To a very large degree, investment is allocated under competition and — especially in industry — with an eye towards market conditions. The East Asian economies are far more flexible, and most investment is subject to a market test.

Although there are no internationally comparable statistics on rates of return on capital for a large number of countries, partial information exists for Hong Kong, Singapore, Taipei, China and Korea. According to data collected by the OECD, the rate of return on capital in Korea declined gradually from around 22 percent in the mid 1980s to about 14 percent in 1994. In Singapore, a comparable indicator-the rates of return on US foreign direct investment-fell from 27 percent in the late 1980s to 19 percent in the mid-1990s. In Hong Kong and Taipei, China rates of return fell from around 21 percent to 15 percent. While these declines do confirm the neoclassical prediction of declining returns to investment, and are consistent with the rapid accumulation of capital documented by Young and interpreted by Krugman, the important point is that they are still well above the worldwide average return on US foreign direct investment of 11 percent. *In contrast,* the Soviet rates of return on investment fell from 26 percent in the 1950s to just 5 percent a *decade later and to zero by the mid-1970s.* Hence the flawed nature of the Soviet analogy. East Asian growth will not go the way of Soviet growth, because it is sustained by flexible markets, open economies, and high profitability rather than bureaucratic fiat. A more likely pattern is that growth will gradually decline, rather than collapse, as the income gap between East Asia and the advanced economies narrows.

Growth Projections for Asia

The cross-country growth regressions estimated in section one of this paper can be used to construct long-term forecasts of economic growth for individual countries. We use the basic regression results from column 1 to project growth rates of real income per capita for 14 Asian countries for the period 1995-2025. The projected growth rates for the fourteen Asian countries in the sample are estimated by multiplying 1995 values (or the closest year possible) for each of the "Z" variables by the estimated coefficients, and adding the resulting terms, including the originally estimated constant term. (In effect, for the baseline projections, we begin with the assumption that every country will maintain its current policy stance for the next 30 years). The values for the geographical and structural variables remain the same as in the base projections, except the natural resource abundance variable (natural resource exports as a share of GDP) is updated to its 1995 value. For the demographic variables, we use the projections for the 1995-2025 period from the United Nations population database. For Malaysia, which was the largest outlier of the Asian countries in the estimated growth relationship, we added the difference between the "fitted" and actual growth rates for the 1965-90 period (about one percentage point) to the projected growth rate. This change reflects the subjective judgement that the model's relatively large under-prediction of Malaysia's past growth suggests the strong possibility of an important under-prediction of the future. A likely reason for Malaysia's strong performance in the past (relative to the model's prediction) is its ability to manage the challenges arising from natural resource abundance better than most other resource abundant countries. Assuming that this strong management continues, it seems reasonable to add the error term to the projected growth rate. This adjustment was not made for any other country. Of course, these projections are meant to be indicative, rather than precise. Many factors will influence income levels and growth rates in ways that cannot possibly be foreseen or predicted accurately. No allowance is made for the possibility of major wars, breakdowns of open trade, substantial changes in world commodity prices (such as the oil price shocks of the 1970s), financial crises, or significant technological breakthroughs that could fundamentally alter the global division of labour. Nor can important changes in individual countries be foreseen. The estimates are simply an attempt at highlighting broad current trends that have an important bearing on growth. The precise estimates of each country's growth rates are less important in this exercise than the broad direction of change over time. These estimates are much better, however, than naive extrapolations of recent growth, in that they explicitly take into account the implications of conditional convergence — therefore building in the proposition that countries tend to grow more slowly as they rise in income levels relative to the technological leader (assumed to be the United States).

In comparing these projected growth rates to actual growth during 1965-95, three forces are at work. First, for most countries, higher levels of education and life expectancy and improved policies (relative to the earlier period) lead to increased growth rates. Second, operating in the opposite direction, as incomes rise, growth rates fall in accordance with the convergence condition. Third, demographic shifts will slow growth in aging societies and spur growth where fertility rates have fallen more recently and the workers make up larger share of the population.

It is no surprise, then, that the Four Tigers are forecasted to grow much more slowly in the future. Although these countries start with somewhat more favourable education and life expectancy indicators, their dramatically higher initial income levels suggest that the rates of return on new investment will steadily decline during the next thirty years, leading to slower income growth. In addition, a larger share of their populations will reach retirement age, further slowing growth. Our rough projections suggest that per capita income growth in the Four Tigers will slow to an average of about 2.8 percent per year on average, down from the 6.6 percent recorded between 1965-95. The projected slowdown in growth is similar to the pattern displayed by Japan in recent decades, when its per capita growth rate declined from an annual average of 9 percent during the 1960s to 3.5 percent in the 1980s. The convergence effect is most visible for Hong Kong and Singapore, which have the highest per capita incomes in 1995. The growth rates are projected to decline less in Korea and Taiwan, both because of the dramatic improvements in their education, life expectancy and policy variables since 1965, and because they still have lower income (and thus more room for economic catch-up) than Singapore and Hong Kong. In Indonesia, Malaysia, and Thailand, growth rates are projected to remain roughly the same as they were in the recent past. In this case, the positive impact of improved initial conditions and better policies are basically offset by the convergence impact of higher income, with little change in aggregate growth rates.

In the PRC, the Philippines and much of South Asia, however, improved initial conditions and better economic policies dominate the convergence effect. South Asian countries should receive an additional boost from demographic trends which are leading to a rising proportion of the working-aged in the overall population. Of course, more rapid growth will not come automatically in South Asia and other countries that currently lag. In South Asia, and in other places where the reform process is relatively new, sustained growth will require further progress on trade liberalization, market opening, and institutional upgrading. In the absence of continued reform, future growth is likely to be slower than these projections suggest.

These projections imply that Asian countries are likely to continue, and in some cases accelerate, the process of catching up with the world's economic leaders. To illustrate, we compare the projected levels of GDP per capita in 2025 for each of the Asian countries (derived from our baseline projections) with a projected level of per capita income in the United States in 2025. Based on our model, we estimate that the United Sates is likely to grow at around 1.55 percent, slightly slower than the 1.76 annual rate achieved between 1965-95 (the main reason for the slowdown is the continued aging of society in the United States, which implies a larger (and longer living) retired population, which is likely to reduce saving rates and slow growth slightly).

The results suggest that the Four Tigers will largely complete the catch-up phase of development, and join the ranks of the world's economic leaders. Our projections imply that GDP per capita in the city states of Hong Kong and Singapore will be the equivalent of about 117% and 107% of U.S. GDP per capita in 2025, slightly surpassing the U.S. average. This level of income would be consistent with many large modern cities in industrialized countries. Taiwan and Korea will be much closer to, but still slightly below, parity with average U.S. income.

Malaysia's expected rapid growth, albeit perhaps slightly slower than in the past, will bring its income from its current level of 37% of U.S. income to about 70% in 2025. This is approximately equal to the 1995 average for the Four Tigers. China, Thailand, Indonesia, and the Philippines are likely to reach the equivalent of between one-fourth and one-half of average U.S. income. India and Sri Lanka are likely to jump from about 10% to 25% of U.S. income, while Pakistan and Bangladesh should be able to grow to around 18% of the U.S. level. With these forecasts, Asia's share of world GDP is likely to grow substantially to 57% from its current level of about 35%. Thus, Asia will continue a remarkable economic transformation that has stretched over the last 200 years or more, since the dawn of the industrial revolution. In 1820, at the beginning of the industrial age, Asia made up about 58% of world GDP, according to estimates compiled by Angus Maddison (1995). This share fell sharply during the next century to only 27% in 1920, and plunged further to a mere 19% in 1950, following the world depression and the ravages of World War II. This was a very small share, considering that Asians accounted for 60% of world population at the time. Thus, if our forecasts are reasonably correct, Asia's share of world GDP will have increased from 19% in 1950 to 57% by 2025, an astounding 38 percentage point increase in just 75 years, returning the region back almost exactly to its share in 1820.

These baseline projections assume no further improvements in policies after 1995. With additional policy reforms, the South and Southeast Asian countries can achieve even higher growth rates. The penultimate column of the table provides a set of growth projections which assume an *improved* policy stance. For illustrative purposes, we assume that all Asian countries adopt the 1995 policies of the Four Tigers, including a higher government savings rate, improved institutional quality, and increased openness. In each country, the projected growth rates accelerate markedly. This scenario is obviously very optimistic, and can be thought of as a "best case" situation, but it illustrates the upside potential from continuing the process of economic reform. Of course, such an optimistic forecast is not the only possibility. Asia's rapid growth could be derailed by a turn toward protectionist policies around the world and a reduction in the growth of world trade. Similarly, if Asia follows the path of much of Europe and the United States towards higher government spending and social welfare programs, growth would slow. Alternatively, reforms could be derailed in China or India by political upheaval or tensions from growing divergences in incomes in some regions. A pessimistic scenario for the future would therefore include a reduction in economic openness and a fall in government saving. If, for instance, the average level of openness in Asia halved and the average rate of government saving fell by 5 percentage points of GDP, future growth rates in almost all Asian countries would be lower than those recorded during the last quarter century. The only exception might be in South Asia, where the effects of the continuing demographic transition are likely to provide a boost to growth per person. But even here, as we have pointed out, future growth will depend on the continuation of current reform programs.

Such an inward turn with slower growth is not only feasible, but has several precedents in world history. Latin America's growth, for instance, was long interrupted by fiscal mismanagement and inward-looking industrial policies. Economic growth around the world stagnated with the collapse in world trade during the Great Depression in the 1930s. Clearly, continued rapid growth in Asia is no certainty, especially if there is a serious deterioration in the conditions of the world trading system.

Conclusions

Asia's episode of rapid economic growth since the 1960s, as remarkable as it was by historical standards, can be explained in an international comparative context. Special theories of Asian growth are not necessary. East Asian countries grew faster than the rest of the world for four key reasons: they had substantial potential for catching up (since the entered the 1960s with relatively low incomes), their geography and structural characteristics were by-and-large favourable, demographic changes following World War II worked in favour of more rapid growth, and their economic policies and strategy were conducive to sustained growth. Most importantly, the high performing East Asian countries recognized the imperative of joining the world economy through the promotion of labour-intensive manufactured exports. These economies promoted exports through a combination of policies — relatively free trade, convertible currencies, macroeconomic stability — and through a set of innovative institutions — such as export processing zones, duty exemption schemes, and incentive packages for foreign direct investment.

In essence, East Asia took advantage of key opportunities that other countries either neglected or rejected. Developing countries in South Asia, Africa, and Latin America could have followed the same basic strategy as East Asia in the early 1960s, but instead they chose to turn away from international trade, protect domestic industries from international competition, and follow more profligate fiscal policies. The results were little or no growth, stagnant wages, and continued widespread poverty. Of course, export-led growth is only part of the story. Rapid growth in East Asia was also supported by key demographic developments, favourable trends in literacy and education, public health policies which raised life expectancy, government attention to the agricultural sector, high levels of budgetary saving, and the protection of private property rights. Even salutary geographic considerations, such as favourable natural harbours and proximity to major sea lanes have played a role. Quantitatively, however, it seems clear that economic institutions and policies have been the most important factors differentiating the performance of fast-growing and slowgrowing nations.

These findings have profound implications for the next thirty years. For the fast-growing countries of East Asia, there is a continuing opportunity for rapid growth, though at rates that are likely to be somewhat slower than in the past, precisely because the process of catching up has been so successful to date. Yet future growth will require successful institutional adaptations to new challenges, including: an aging population; increasing urbanization and political participation; and pressures related to increasing integration of the world economy. As a result, these countries will face increased stresses on public-sector budgets, pressures for continued reforms of the legal system, and the need for flexibility and adjustment of political institutions, including the allocation of powers between central and local governments. For countries that grew more slowly during the past thirty years, the main message is that faster growth is possible, and indeed likely, as these countries adopt market-based strategies and increased openness to world markets. South Asia has the opportunity for the kind of dynamism displayed previously in East Asia. However, such good performance will depend on continued institutional and policy reforms in trade, the budget, health and education.

Bibliography

Anindya Bakrie & Morendy Octora.: *Schooling, Experience, and Earnings*, New York, Singapore National University, Columbia University Press 2002.

Baran, Paul A.: *The Political Economy of Growth*, New York, Modern Reader Paperbacks, 1975.

Bardsley, N., Cubitt: *Assessing Experimental Economics*, Princeton, Princeton University Press, 2009.

Basu, Kaushik. *Analytical Development Economics, The Less Developed Economy Revisited*, Cambridge, Mass.: MIT Press, 1997.

Bazilevskii, Y. Y.: *The Theory of Mathematical Machines*, Pergamon Press, Macmillan Co., New York, 1963.

Benería, Lourdes. *Gender, Development, and Globalization, Economics as if All People Mattered*, New York and London, Routledge, 2003.

Borcherding, K., : *Contemporary Issues in Decision Making*, Amsterdam, North-Holland, 1990.

Burke, Frank M., *Valuation and Valuation Planning for Closely Held Businesses*, Englewood Cliffs, NJ, Prentice Hall, 1981.

Caplin, A. and Schotter, A.: *The Foundations of Positive and Normative Economics*, New York, Oxford University Press, 2008.

Caviglioni O. : *Mapwise: Accelerated Learning Through Visible Thinking*, Network Educational Press, 2000.

Cohen, Lizabeth, *Making a New Deal, Industrial Workers in Chicago, 1919-1939* Cambridge University Press, 1991.

Commons, J. R., *Institutional Economics-Its Place in Political Economy*, The University of Wisconsin Press, Madison, Wisconsin, 1934.

Cootner, Paul : *The Random Character of Stock Market Prices*, MIT Press, 1964.

Copeland, Tom, Tim Koller, and Jack Murrin, *Valuation: Measuring and Managing the Value of Companies*, New York, Wiley, 1994.

Damasio, AR.: *Descarte's Error: Emotion, Reason and the Human Brain,* New York, 1994.

Daniel Kahneman, Amos Tversky.: *Choice, Values, Frames,* The Cambridge University Press, 2000.

Desmond, Glenn, and John A, Marcell, *Handbook of Small Business Valuation Formulas and Rules of Thumb,* Valuation Press, 1993.

Dimson, Elroy: *Stock Market Anomalies*, Cambridge University Press, 1988.

Fraser, Steven, *Labor Will Rule, Sidney Hillman and the Rise of American Labor,* Reprint ed. Ithaca, N.Y.: Cornell University Press, 1993.

Fruhan, W. E.: *Financial Strategy, Studies in the Creation, Transfer and Destruction of Shareholder Value.* Homewood, 1979.

Goleman D.: *Emotional Intelligence,* New York: Bantam, 1995.

Gowdy, J., *Coevolution Economics: The Economy, Society and the Environment,* Kluwer, Boston, 1994.

Granger, Clive W. J.: *Empirical Modeling in Economics, Specification and Evaluation,* London, Cambridge University Press, 1999.

Guala, F.: *The Methodology of Experimental Economics,* New York, Cambridge University Press, 2005.

Guarti, Luigi, *The Valuation of Firms,* Blackwell Publishing, 1994.

Gul, F. and Pesendorfer, W.: *The Foundations of Positive and Normative Economics,* New York, Oxford University Press 2008.

Harrigan, K. R.: *Strategies for Declining Businesses.* Lexington, MA: Heath, 1980

Hausman, D. M.: *The Inexact and Separate Science of Economics*, Cambridge, Cambridge University Press, 1992.

Hayek, F. A. *Individualism and Economic Order,* The University of Chicago Press, Chicago, 1948.

Hunt, E. K. *History of Economic Thought, A Critical Perspective,* New York, HarperCollins, 1992.

Janis, I. L., & Mann, L.: *Decision Making, A Psychological Analysis of Conflict, Choice and Commitment.* New York, Free Press, 1977.

Kasper, Larry J.: *Business Valuations, Advanced Topics,* Westport, CT, Quorum Books, 1997.

Knapp, C. L.: *Commercial Damages, A Guide to Remedies in Business Litigation,* Matthew Bender, 1993.

Lindblom, C. E.: *A Strategy of Decision: Policy Evaluation as a Social Process*, New York, The Free Press, 1970.

Link, Albert N.: *Evaluating Economic Damages, A Handbook for Attorneys*, Westport, CT, Quorum Books, 1992.

Lipsitz, George. *Rainbow at Midnight, Labor and Culture in the 1940s*, Urbana, Ill.: University of Illinois Press, 1994.

Loomes, G.: *Current Issues in Microeconomics*, New York: St. Martin's Press, 1989.

Magnussen, L., *Evolutionary and Neo-Schumpeterian Approaches to Economics*, Kluwer, Boston, 1994.

March, J. G.: *A Behavioural Theory of the Firm*, Englewood-Cliffs, Prentice Hall, 1963.

Marris, R. L., and Wood, A.: *The Corporate Economy*, London: Macmillan, 1971.

Martin, Gerald D.: *Determining Economic Damages,* Santa Ana, CA: James Publishing, 1995.

Meyer, M. W.: *Theory of Organizational Structure*, Indianapolis, 1977.

Mooney, J. D., and Reiley, A. C.: *Onward Industry*, New York, 1931.

Nelson, Judy A.: *Feminism, Objectivity and Economics,* London and New York, Routledge, 1996.

Peirson, G., Bird, R., Brown, R., & Howard, P.: *Business Finance*, Roseville, 1990

Pennings, J. M.: *Decision Making, An Organizational Behaviour Approach*, New York, Markus Wiener Publishing, 1983.

Pfeffer, J., and Salancik, G. R.: *The External Control of Organizations, A Resource Dependence Perspective*, New York, 1978.

Plous, S.: *The Psychology of Judgement and Decision Making,* New York, McGraw-Hill, 1993

Rappaport, A.: *Creating Shareholder Value, The New Standard for Business Performance*, New York, Free Press, 1986.

Ross, D.: *Economic Theory and Cognitive Science*, Cambridge, Mass., MIT Press, 2006.

Roth, A. E.: *The Handbook of Experimental Economics*, Princeton, Princeton University Press, 1995.

Santos, A.C.: *The Social Epistemology of Experimental Economics,* London, Routledge 2009.

Schumpeter, J. A., *The Theory of Economic Development*, Harvard University Press,Cambridge, Massachusetts, 1934.

Scott, W. R.: *Organizations: Rational, Natural, and Open Systems*, Englewood Cliffs, 1981.

Selznick, P.: *Leadership in Administration, A Sociological Interpretation*, New York, Harper & Row, 1957.

Smith, Gordon V., and Russell Parr, *Valuation of Intellectual Property and Intangible Assets,* New York: Wiley, 1994.

Smith, V. L.: *Papers in Experimental Economics*, Cambridge, Cambridge University Press, 1991.

Taylor, F. W.: *The Principles of Scientific Management*, New York, 1917.

Throsby, David, *Economics and Culture*, Cambridge University Press, 2001.

Tietenberg, Tom, *Environmental Economics and Policy,* New York, HarperCollins, 1994

Tinbergen, Jan.: *On the Theory of Economic Policy*; Amsterdam, North-Holland 1952.

Towse, Ruth ed.: *A Handbook of Cultural Economics*, Edward Elgar, 2003.

Trugman, Gary R., *Guide to Conducting a Valuation of a Closely Held Business*, New York, American Institute of Certified Public Accountants, 1993.

Ullman, D. G.: *Making Robust Decisions,* Trafford, 2006.

Warwick, D. P.: *A Theory of Public Bureaucracy*, Cambridge, MA: Harvard University Press, 1975.

Weber, M.: *The Theory of Social and Economic Organizations*, New York, Oxford University Press, 1947.

Weibull, J. W.: *Advances in Understanding Strategic Behaviour*, New York, Palgrave, 2004.

West, Thomas L.: and Jeffrey D. Jones: *Handbook of Business Valuation*, New York: Wiley, 1992.

Woodward, J.: *The Oxford Handbook of Philosophy of Economics*, New York, Oxford University Press, 2009.

Yegge, Wilbur M., *A Basic Guide for Valuing a Company*, New York, Wiley, 1996.

Zipp, Alan S., *Business Valuation Methods* New York, American Institute of Certified Public Accountants, 1990.

Index

A

Agreement, 37, 120, 138, 173, 174, 175, 176, 177, 188.

Agricultural Sector, 10, 193, 276, 287.

B

Biodiversity Convention, 174, 178, 179.

Bonus, 195.

Business Environment, 125, 128.

C

Capital Mobility, 116.

Central Banks, 117.

Climate Change, 33, 52, 84, 87.

Commission, 25, 33, 37, 38, 39, 140, 141, 175, 180.

Commodity Prices, 218, 283.

Communications, 12, 23, 111, 145.

Compound Rates, 57.

Conditions, 8, 22, 32, 36, 43, 49, 83, 102, 106, 108, 123, 125, 126, 127, 128, 132, 133, 136, 137, 142, 146, 186, 187, 196, 209, 210, 211, 212, 214, 215, 218, 223, 224, 233, 244, 252, 279, 280, 281, 284, 287.

Consumers, 32, 51, 52, 62, 63, 66, 84, 127, 163, 166, 169.

Corporate Governance, 106, 122, 129, 131, 137.

Crops, 181, 182, 183, 184, 185, 186, 187, 188.

D

Dependency Theory, 8, 9, 11.

Developments, 100, 110, 117, 119, 136, 164, 198, 287.

E

Economic Growth, 1, 2, 3, 8, 11, 21, 22, 23, 26, 35, 42, 43, 44, 45, 46, 47, 48, 49, 50, 51, 52, 53, 54, 55, 56, 57, 59, 65, 66, 67, 68, 69, 70, 71, 72, 73, 74, 75, 76, 77, 78, 93, 94, 98, 111, 119, 136, 137, 160, 189, 190, 191, 192, 193, 195, 198, 199, 203, 204, 205, 207, 209, 210, 211, 212, 214, 215, 216, 221, 222, 226, 227, 228, 229, 230, 231, 233, 237, 238, 239, 240, 250, 262, 263, 264, 266, 267, 268, 274, 275, 276, 277, 282, 286, 287.

Economic Independence, 121, 133, 134, 135, 139.

Economic Management, 91, 124, 133, 149, 225, 276.

Ecosystems, 34, 35, 51, 84, 86, 181, 182, 183, 188, 190.
Employment, 6, 23, 30, 41, 83, 121, 131, 162, 258.
Environmental Degradation, 28, 29, 33, 40, 189, 190.
Environmental Impacts, 50.
Environmental Protection, 26, 38, 78.
Environmental Sustainability, 26, 27, 28.
Evidence, 34, 47, 70, 74, 75, 77, 106, 109, 180, 183, 187, 200, 210, 211, 215, 218, 224, 226, 228, 231, 234, 238, 250, 268, 271, 273.
Exchange Rate Stability, 191.
Export Facilitation, 256, 259.
Exports, 23, 133, 134, 135, 136, 139, 149, 151, 152, 153, 160, 162, 163, 164, 193, 196, 198, 207, 208, 209, 210, 216, 217, 229, 235, 236, 237, 238, 239, 240, 241, 242, 243, 244, 245, 246, 247, 248, 250, 251, 253, 254, 255, 256, 257, 258, 259, 260, 261, 262, 263, 277, 283, 287.

F

Foreign Investment, 62, 159, 242, 247, 248, 255, 257, 277.
Forestry, 52.
Foundations, 6, 188.
Free Markets, 79, 80, 100, 203, 250.
Free Trade, 45, 126, 138, 249, 250, 257, 259, 262, 287.
Freedom, 1, 32, 64, 65, 67, 110, 124, 126, 127, 128, 138, 159, 160, 161, 162, 188.

G

Global Integration, 239.
Governance, 41, 42, 80, 106, 109, 115, 122, 129, 131, 137, 275.
Governments, 6, 43, 49, 61, 63, 65, 66, 67, 68, 73, 77, 81, 84, 96, 99, 106, 120, 121, 123, 125, 127, 135, 139, 149, 175, 179, 194, 212, 217, 221, 227, 237, 250, 252, 253, 259, 262, 263, 265, 268, 269, 275, 276, 277, 288.
Guidance, 24.

I

Industrial Cooperation, 38.
Industrial Policies, 237, 260, 261, 263, 286.
Industrial Pollution, 182.
Industry, 3, 6, 7, 23, 24, 38, 41, 42, 44, 45, 94, 127, 139, 140, 141, 147, 152, 163, 164, 175, 176, 178, 180, 181, 183, 205, 219, 235, 236, 247, 248, 255, 260, 261, 262, 263, 276, 281.
Information Society, 40.
Insurance, 141, 161, 187, 219, 250, 270.
Interest Rate, 64, 81, 166, 170, 260, 269.
International Trade, 11, 70, 163, 214, 219, 220, 226, 252, 287.
Investment, 7, 11, 24, 37, 38, 39, 44, 46, 47, 48, 49, 52, 56, 57, 58, 61, 62, 66, 69, 70, 71, 72, 73, 74, 75, 76, 77, 86, 93, 94,

95, 98, 105, 106, 113, 114, 115, 116, 118, 119, 122, 126, 127, 130, 134, 136, 137, 140, 141, 149, 150, 151, 153, 159, 161, 164, 165, 192, 193, 199, 200, 205, 207, 208, 209, 210, 218, 221, 222, 227, 230, 235, 236, 237, 238, 240, 241, 242, 244, 246, 247, 248, 255, 257, 277, 281, 282, 284, 287.

Investment Freedom, 161.

L

Labour Freedom, 162.

Laws, 35, 116, 128, 132, 149.

Leadership, 6, 17, 24, 234, 275, 276.

Legal System, 49, 66, 68, 132, 237, 249, 288.

M

Macroeconomic Policy, 132, 133, 136, 137, 138.

Maintenance, 15, 27, 125, 214, 233, 241, 271.

Manufactures, 219, 238, 239, 240, 246, 261.

Market Economy, 32, 51, 65, 67, 73, 79, 81, 82, 93, 95, 99, 106, 110, 111, 115, 117, 120, 121, 122, 123, 124, 125, 126, 128, 129, 133, 134, 136, 137, 138, 139, 141, 142, 147, 159.

Market Failure, 30.

Market Structure, 139.

Measurement, 3, 7, 43, 225.

N

National Security, 77.

O

Opportunity, 40, 86, 90, 96, 104, 150, 173, 194, 218, 269, 288.

Organizations, 2, 4, 6, 7, 28, 84, 86, 120, 121, 123, 125, 127, 133, 138, 139, 141.

Ownership, 19, 79, 80, 83, 100, 104, 105, 106, 113, 121, 124, 129, 130, 131, 132, 133, 137, 150, 159, 161, 211, 238, 250, 255, 256.

P

Partnership, 6, 37, 38, 40, 41, 85, 86, 188.

Performance, 24, 42, 50, 66, 98, 105, 107, 113, 114, 119, 136, 137, 142, 163, 164, 186, 187, 192, 193, 194, 195, 196, 208, 212, 217, 224, 226, 228, 229, 232, 234, 263, 276, 278, 283, 288.

Private Equity, 38.

Private Sector, 63, 64, 66, 77, 78, 81, 103, 104, 105, 109, 115, 119, 128, 130, 143, 144, 159, 194, 265.

Production, 1, 2, 22, 41, 44, 46, 47, 48, 50, 52, 54, 55, 57, 59, 61, 63, 64, 67, 71, 77, 83, 84, 93, 97, 98, 102, 103, 113, 114, 115, 121, 123, 124, 126, 132, 136, 147, 148, 149, 152, 153, 161, 163, 174, 182, 196, 197, 204, 217, 222, 235, 236, 237, 238, 240, 243, 248, 250, 256, 257, 258, 276, 278, 281.

Production Decisions, 256, 258.

Production Process, 240, 281.
Project Information, 12.
Projects, 6, 7, 13, 23, 24, 38, 39, 40, 44, 87, 89, 90, 95, 98, 144, 205, 240, 257.
Promotion, 38, 39, 40, 79, 129, 134, 135, 139, 141, 257, 258, 260, 261, 262, 278, 287.
Property Rights, 32, 49, 61, 63, 65, 66, 71, 72, 73, 74, 77, 79, 80, 106, 109, 160, 161, 176, 177, 188, 204, 211, 214, 245, 256, 287.
Protection, 26, 29, 36, 38, 40, 65, 66, 68, 74, 77, 78, 188, 204, 205, 237, 240, 241, 243, 260, 261, 262, 287.
Public Finance, 151.
Public Policy, 116, 117, 203, 204, 206, 207.

R

Relationships, 17, 41, 212, 228, 234, 235, 242.
Return on Investment, 282.

S

Security, 12, 37, 38, 39, 40, 71, 73, 77, 124, 169, 184, 185, 222, 230, 235, 236, 258, 266, 268, 270, 273, 274.
Social Impacts, 30.
Social Welfare, 286.
Society, 7, 10, 13, 30, 34, 36, 40, 51, 57, 63, 109, 124, 125, 135, 143, 145, 154, 156, 181, 285.
Sustainable Development, 25, 26, 27, 28, 29, 31, 32, 33, 34, 35, 36, 37, 38, 40, 113, 114, 189.
Sustainable Economic Development, 36, 37, 41, 42, 172, 189.
System Development, 132.
Systems Theory, 9.

T

Technological Development, 139, 144.
Technology, 3, 4, 6, 7, 8, 16, 27, 38, 53, 54, 56, 59, 61, 63, 93, 119, 121, 149, 150, 154, 157, 160, 185, 193, 194, 195, 213, 217, 218, 219, 221, 222, 223, 224, 225, 228, 233, 237, 262, 264, 268, 269, 271, 274.
Transition Economy, 79, 82, 93, 116.
Treatment, 18, 27.

V

Venture Capital, 116.

W

Welfare, 22, 28, 33, 194, 217, 278, 286.
World Systems Theory, 9.
World Trade Organization, 70, 138, 263.